HAUNTED FAMILY HISTORY

Haunted Family History

A Mixed Methods Approach to Paranormal Research

By Jed Silva

Table of Contents

DEDICATION

Dedicated to my family, who have always supported my unending curiosity.

PREFACE

I've had an interest in cryptids and the paranormal for as long as I can remember, although I was likely more interested in beasts like the Loch Ness monster and other cryptids seemingly related to dinosaurs than I was ghosts, aliens, or Bigfoot.

As I grew older, however, I was surrounded by stories of a faceless man with a plaid shirt, of people behaving oddly and walking into closets only to disappear. I was told of what were apparently my own experiences that I couldn't remember. And I grew curious. Why? How?

I have a degree in Psychology with a Sociology minor, and I was a practicum away from becoming a Licensed Professional Counselor. As part of my undergraduate and graduate degree coursework I've been trained to think critically, compassionately, and I was forced into a basic understanding of statistics.

Eventually, my background turned my continuing interest in the paranormal into frustration as on the one hand the academic world willfully continued to turn a blind eye on one of the most prevalent experiences known to man, and the incredibly popular ghost investigators on television appeared content to abandon the scientific method in return for being entertaining.

So, I had to decide. Did I want to continue to complain, or could I bring some actual value to the space? I would like to think the latter, but ultimately that's up to the reader.

I think it's natural to be entertained by stories of the paranormal. I certainly enjoy reading them, and there are in fact several paranormal podcasts I'm subscribed to. This book is as much a research project as anything, but it's not necessary to be read as such, or to even read the final discussion section to be enjoyed. The book consists of two parts: true ghost stories collected via interviews (simple conversations really), and an analysis of those interviews conducted using qualitative research methods.

The analysis is my attempt to use qualitative research methods to quantify and conduct analysis that adds value to these experiences beyond titillation. The analysis is basic, far from the statistical analysis you would find in a peer-reviewed journal. However, I honestly don't know that something like this has been attempted before. Ultimately, I decided a sincere and simple effort, even flawed, would be a valuable step forward.

The experiences related in the interviews range from odd to outright frightening. As I read and reread the transcripts, I found myself checking corners and closing doors behind me to eliminate the unease that grew as I worked into the night.

The interviews are with family members who trusted me. Trusted me to believe them, to treat their stories with respect, and like anyone who opens themselves up, trusted me not to exploit them. I've done my best to preserve that trust. I question their experiences and try to find some context when I have the wherewithal, but there are things they share that are so far beyond anything I expected that I'm too surprised to do so adequately. The interviews have been edited to aid in reading comprehension. Beyond their interviews and my analysis, I look for alternative explanations in psychology and biology, not necessarily because of disbelief, but because I believe it's irresponsible not to consider more mundane causes. To paraphrase, when you eliminate reasonable explanations, you are left to consider the unreasonable.

Should evidence and research indicate that there are physical manifestations (sight, sound, touch) to these experiences, so be it. Let the research dictate where further inquiries venture. This project is not a psychological study, but uses similar methods, and I think begins to describe how we can use scientifically accepted methods to understand paranormal experiences and study them further. Hopefully, one of the takeaways from this project will be recognition that there are individuals behind the ghost stories. Real people who have had their lives impacted, often negatively, by experiences that the world repeatedly and forcefully denies.

I suggest you read while the sun is still out, and perhaps not when you're alone. Enjoy.

INTRODUCING THE METHODS

There's a lot to get into: types of experiences or places that seemed to be related, how the interviews were turned into data, how this can then be further turned into research, and especially how the method could be adopted by the paranormal community in general. We begin with the research methods used, then transition to the interviews with general observations about the families. The interviews are organized by family, allowing me to conduct analysis separately, and finally both families together. The families interviewed consist of the brothers and sisters of my father and mother respectively, and so they are all of the same generation and organized in the text by their family names (Santiago, Cortez). I am not present in the family trees depicted, and the given names are all pseudonyms. I discuss the challenges as if this were a peer reviewed research study, attempt to question the findings and possible causes objectively, and see if the reported events can be narrowed to eliminate some of those challenges.

We begin by assuming all those interviewed are recalling details correctly, while acknowledging that memory is imperfect. A good portion of the following may appear dry as I attempt to turn these many experiences into meaningful data, so I do not begrudge anyone treating the interviews as a book of ghost stories and choosing not to read the analysis at all. While I took these stories at face value growing up, I do my best to question and provide alternative explanations. Frankly, this may come off as nothing more than stream of consciousness questioning as I try to organize the data, but I hope it helps you consider these experiences as more than entertainment.

I invite you the reader to look at both the interviews and the analysis with a critical eye, as I undoubtedly had and have blind spots as I approached the questions in the interviews and ultimately the analysis as well.

METHODS

I believe that using qualitative analysis allowed me to make some interesting generalizations and comparisons in categories of experiences, between individuals, and between families. It further allowed me to organize the experiences into comparable data, rather than relying on simple memory. To this end I'd like to briefly describe the population interviewed, how the data was acquired, and the limitations.

The participants consisted of eight members of the Santiago family (three brothers, four sisters and one of their sons), and seven members of the Cortez family (six sisters and one of their daughters). I have anonymized everyone's names to protect their privacy, although they were all aware that I intended to compile their experiences into a book, and they are all welcome to retell their stories to anyone they wish to.

The data was acquired over a series of formal and informal interviews with family members over the course of three years. Those interviewed were willing to share and answer questions regarding past events they believed were paranormal experiences. The data was aggregated and compiled based on paternal and maternal familial background. The cloud-based organizing and data management software NVivo was used to categorize experience types and frequency to produce usable qualitative data. At this point, one might do statistical analysis to find significance. However, the limited sample set, inconsistencies in how the data was gathered, and my admitted lack of knowledge regarding formal statistics prevented deeper analysis. So, analysis was focused on more accessible comparisons using percentages and ratios. However, I believe there are still valid observations that can be made without the use of formal statistics.

The data collected, or variables, will be broken down into the following categorical subsets: people, places, time of day, and event type. People are noted as individuals and further broken down into subsets of families. Events are noted as occurring as a child (birth to age 21) or adult. The main reason the "child" category is so broad is that it was often difficult for those I interviewed to ascribe specific ages to events experienced 50 years before. Likewise, the "adult" category spans decades. Each of these events was also noted as occurring during the day, night, or unknown if the time of day was not stated explicitly or discernable through context. The events themselves can be generally described as those seen, heard, or in some way related to touch. These were then expanded to subcategories such as shadows, voices, pushed, etc. An example of an event with an experience in the auditory category might be an interviewee reporting hearing a voice, which then might be further described as mimicry, a whisper, or laughter.

Multiple types of experiences were coded to form a single event. For example, a person's experience of a knock, a voice, and a door slamming concurrently would be coded individually as categories of experiences. The cumulative experiences were treated as a single event and were categorized as occurring as a child or adult, and during the day or night. Finally, that event was coded to a location. Shared experiences were coded individually for the appropriate categories for all those who explicitly remembered the experience, and only for those categories they explicitly remembered and mentioned.

It's important to keep in mind how many types of categories of experiences a single event can encompass, especially when considering the total number of events with the total numbers of categories of events as they are coded, counted, and analyzed. It is not a comparison between events and experiences, but rather a way to organize the information. Additionally, while individuals reported seeing things often, they would infrequently report an auditory experience alongside it. For example, someone might say, "I saw a man walk into the room while I was alone in the house," without mentioning hearing footsteps, etc. This may not necessarily mean that that person only saw and did not hear anything. It may be the case they heard something at the time, but the only enduring memory is visual.

The review and analysis of experiences are organized much like the categories themselves, beginning at a high level such as auditory, then broken down into more detail where the data allows and suggests. For instance, smell wasn't very frequently cited as a paranormal experience by the Cortez Family. Three times individuals referenced the smell of sulfur. Contextually, they would say that they smelled it frequently, in and out of homes, but there are common environmental factors that could serve as an explanation.

The locations with the most frequent reports of experiences were identified by their street name; these were homes occupied during childhood and in two cases are still occupied by each respective family. The remaining locations where events occurred were separated into the following categories: other residences owned by the individuals as adults, events experienced while visiting someone else's residence, and publicly accessible places.

Time of day wasn't explicitly asked in the interviews, and where it couldn't be determined by context was left as "unknown". I did my best to code only specific events, but the matter was made complicated by statements such as "You'd always (hear/see)". I code such statements once to represent the sum of the experiences, but then disregard that statement when repeated unless it was another specific event. It can be argued that I should have either not coded such instances at all or coded every instance mentioned.

I immediately saw the power of quantifying these experiences when discussing whether events tended to occur during the day or night. Based on memory alone, I believed events occurred about evenly between day and night. However, transcribing and coding indicated roughly 64 percent of the Cortez events were at night, with the remainder split between "day" and "unknown" at 18 percent apiece. It may be that because daytime events stood out, they stayed fresher in my memory and made me overestimate their prevalence. Being able to look at everything as a number allowed me to reduce my reliance on belief and expectation and improve analysis.

While the approach likely has its share of flaws, I believe it is a valid example of the application of scientific analysis to the paranormal.

INTERVIEWS

SANTIAGO FAMILY

The paternal and maternal lines of the Santiago family can be traced from Mexico, with reports of Native American lineage on both sides as well. Their grandfather worked the railroads, and while I don't know the economics of the society of the time in general, I was told a story of their father finding a dollar bill on the side of the road as a child that paid for the whole family to see a film.

Their father in turn worked the railroads until he met their mother and eventually joined the Air Force. He must have seen a massive change in technology from when he was a child to when he began his career in the Air Force. Their father was stationed in Greece, where the two oldest boys Noah and James spoke Greek as children, Libya, the Philippines, and several states in the U.S. until they settled in Texas. Several of the Santiago family would eventually join and retire from the Armed Forces like their father. Their mother stayed at home to raise the family while their father worked.

The Santiago family eventually moved into the Sheffield house, where several of the events described as paranormal occur. While the oldest children had already moved away from home, others like Carl grew up in the Sheffield house. Noah, Grace, and Rene are not interviewed.

The house itself isn't particularly remarkable, but might be considered large as it's a single story with 4 bedrooms and 2 baths, with large front and backyards. There is a small room when you enter with 2 small bedrooms facing the street to the South, the large main bedroom in the back, and another bedroom on the East wall. The main hallway follows East to West between the bathroom and the bedrooms in front. Past the living room in front, you walk into the kitchen and the open den, both from which you could see the backyard through the glass sliding door.

As you read, look out for recurring items. For instance, events described near sleep, images of persons, what they're wearing. There are items that I felt were repeating, or at the very least were frequently described, and I would like you to look for items that appear to be associated. Conversely, there may be themes or items that I focus on, that might be readily explained or could be shown not to be associated. I undoubtedly have blinders, and so welcome additional critical reviews.

The interviews are arranged in order for the most part, as the family members began discussing what was brought up between themselves and would bring items up in response. However, Tina's is moved forward in order to keep the interviews that reference the Flannel Man together.

The family tree is below.

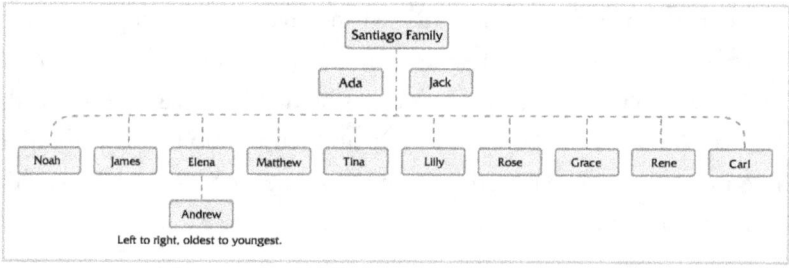

MATTHEW

[Matthew was the first person I interviewed from the Santiago family, and the second interview overall. I met him at his home and conducted the interview at his kitchen table, the living room behind me.]

Matthew: I was 16, and that was in '70. No, I was 15. That was in '72. I remember we were living on base in a Japanese barracks that they converted into a house. There were several of these barracks they converted into homes. It was like a seven, eight-bedroom house with a wraparound porch. I mean, it was really nice. Get up at night, you couldn't see. You'd walk around your house because you had a wraparound porch. Screened, I mean. Nothing was gonna get in, the way it was made. I guess one night I had my window open and the fan blowing, and I was just lying in bed. I wasn't asleep, because I couldn't sleep. I was lying there, and all of a sudden there was a bright light. It didn't light up the whole room, it's just that bright light right by me. I couldn't move, but that bright light was going back and forth next to me. I just laid there, and I tried to turn my head, but it's just like something held me from moving. You know? I just kept trying to move, and all of a sudden... I don't know, it just happened so fast, it just went away. You could see the light just moving away, then I was able to move again. And then I got up and started walking around. I never told my parents that. I never said a word. But yeah, that's the only thing that ever happened to me when I was in the Philippines, right then and there, nothing else. Never happened again. But I was awake. I do remember getting up, walking around several times after that happened. It scared me. It really did.

Jed: When you said it was a light, was the light reflecting off the walls?

Matthew: No, no. It was just reflecting off of me. You're lying on your back and your head is straight, you know, you want to move, but you can't. And the only thing I could do was just turn my eyes, make my eyes go to the left. That's the way it was, the way I was laying. I tried to see if I could see it, but that light was real bright. You know what I mean? And like I said, that light went back and forth, up and down *[motions with his hand]*, and then it finally looked at me for a while, and then it just slowly moved away. As it got out of sight, I was able to move. But that's the only thing that ever happened to me in the Philippines. Nothing else happened 'til we moved back here to Texas, here in San Antonio. I guess I was 17, and that's when we first moved into that house.

Jed: The one on Sheffield?

Matthew: Yeah. The one on Sheffield. We moved into that house, and I remember that that was in uh... I was 16, that was in '74. Yeah, '74. Since I worked at the commissary bagging groceries, I stayed at home, because I had to make sure the dog was taken care. Our German Shepherd we had, Lady. She was a female German Shepherd, Lady was. I went to work, came home, the parents left on vacation. Like I say, once I was at that age, I never went anywhere with my parents. They kind of just left me at home to take care of the house. That was the thing. Well, there was a couple of nights pass, nothing. Just same old house routine, watching TV. And then, a few nights later, I could hear a baby crying. You know, I could hear that baby crying.

Jed: You were there by yourself?

Matthew: I was there by myself; everybody was gone. I got up, and even Lady's ears stood up, you know? She was just looking down the hall, and we could hear that baby crying. I went checking the rooms. I said, nah, there's no baby here. I'm even getting goosebumps thinking about that thing.

[He stops to show me his arm, covered in goosebumps. He rubs them away and continues.]

Matthew: But we walked down the hall, and all of a sudden Lady was beside me. We could hear the baby crying up in that corner room that's closest to the street. I open that room up and I could hear the baby crying. It wasn't loud, but I could hear the baby crying. All of a sudden, Lady, she got behind me. It's like she was scared. And the crying went away. I closed the door and went back to the couch. I just stared down the hall and Lady was laying on the floor next to me, but she wasn't asleep neither.

So, we didn't hear any more that night at all. No more. Finally, I went to sleep. Who knows what time of the morning, but I had to get up tired as hell to go to work. I hated to leave her at home, but I put her outside and went to work. And she stayed in that backyard, but you know what? When I got home and I tried to get her in the house, she kind of hesitated a little bit, to come in. But I brought her in anyway, because she slept in the house at night with us. And she kind of walked around, back and forth for a while, and then finally she settled down. But we never heard anything, any more of that.

Jed: People always say that cats sound like babies crying.

Matthew: That's true. That's very true. And you know what, usually if there's a cat around, Lady would not back off. You know? She'd want that cat, because every time we saw a cat in the yard, I'd always say "cat, cat", and she chased it out of the yard. Yeah. No, no. This scared her. I know it did, because it scared the hell out of me. And like I said, nothing like that ever happened again in that house. I told my mom, you know my mom said she's heard stuff before like that, but she never paid any mind to it because she never saw anything. But, yeah, that's what happened there. I got older and grew up and I moved from the house, and I moved to the next street over on Derrickson. I bought a house over there on Derrickson, not too far from Dad's house, just a block away.

Well, in that house, I was getting up to go to work. CPS called me to come to work. It had to be about three in the morning. I came outside, warmed up and started the truck. And you know, once I started the truck, I got out and walked around my yard a little bit while the truck warmed up. It was wintertime, and I guess I was, lemme see, 22 years old. No, I take it back. I was older. About 25 I believe. Yeah, 25. So I backed the truck up, slowly. I looked to the right as I was coming to the street, and I saw a figure coming towards me. And you know I thought it was a girl, because the Winter coat that they had on had like the ruffles on the front? You know, like an Eskimo would have coverin' her face?

Jed: That's when it was Winter?

Matthew: Yeah, it was Winter. And you know it wasn't really cold, but I saw that figure coming, and as I was backing up, I looked. And there's a streetlight right there, in front of the house. I could see the figure, but I couldn't see the face. Not at all. Normally, I could see a face for that light shining down in the middle of the street, but it was dark. And I waited for the figure to go by, and then as that figure—I looked out my rearview mirror and I could see that person just moving, you know? I looked the other way when I was backing up, I looked in front, it was gone. That quick. And I said, where'd it go? And it was in the street not too far, it couldn't have been no more from me to the wall as it passed me up, but I didn't see it anymore. You know, and I just kept looking. I know I would've seen it go into somebody's yard, but the lights would always light up their porches. And I said, golly, where'd it go? It just disappeared that quick. Then I just went on to work like it was, you know... And don't get me wrong, it scared me. Because I looked in the back of my truck, the seat, but yeah, I just went on to work.

Then after being in the house for a few years, another time getting up early in the morning I heard something fall in the house, like something broke. But it didn't. I didn't see anything broken. I got up, walked down the hall by the front door. I was looking at the front door, and looking right there by the window, and you could just see waves. Like, like nothing moving, but like a clear wave, you know what I mean? Like you could see the, you look at it, at the heat, a heat wave? And you could see it moving? That's what I saw. Two waves, right there, just... They were maybe about three feet from the floor. And the waves, they're just moving.

Jed: This was outside?

Matthew: No, this was in the house. In my house where I lived on Derrickson. I saw two waves right there. And you know, the waves went away. I walked over to see, golly, the window can't be open, current can't be blowin'. I walked over there, and believe it or not, Jed, it was cold. I was cold right there. That was summertime, but it was cold right there. I opened the front door, and it's not cool outside. It's summertime morning, you know, humid and all, but it was just cold right there for that instant. And I said, our AC's off because we had the fans on. I turn it off at a certain time at night, except the backroom AC, but we had the one in the living room turned off. I do remember that it was cold right there, and then the coldness went away.

Jed: You said it sounded like something broke?

Matthew: Yeah, something broke. But it didn't, there was nothing broke. I thought it was the glass window, but it wasn't. But that's what it sounded like, someone's breaking in, the glass broken. Now it wasn't at all, but that's what I remember in that house. As the kids were getting older, we needed a bigger home, so we moved here, to this one. Mara was a little girl. Well, she was in high school. At night, certain nights I'd stay up and watch TV late. Well, she watched a show late, but she never told me until she got older. One day she says, "Daddy, I see a little girl in our house." Because she was sitting right there on the love seat, where it's at?

[He gestures to the love seat and recliner behind me that face the TV.]

Matthew: And I would sit there, too, and I even noticed that. Because we had the love seat and then we had the recliner over there toward the fireplace. And I always sat on the recliner.

She didn't describe her, but I could. *[The little girl]* used to peek around the corner right there, the corner right here of the wall? Peek around the corner, 'cause you're watching TV at night. And I told Mara, I said, "You did, you saw her? Did she have curly hair, kind of long curly hair, and peeking around corner?" She goes, "Yes." And I said, "Yeah, she kind of looked kind of transparent in a way, right?" And she goes, "Yeah." And I told her, "Well, you know what, Mara? I've been seeing her, too, off and on."

Not all the time. Until one day while I was watching TV, I saw the little girl walk from the hall this way, go into our kitchen. The TV was on bright, the show I was watching? I looked at her, and she had on a dress. It had kind of like little ruffles the little girls wear, and she just looked at me and walked into the kitchen. I got up and followed, I said, "Where in the hell did she go?" It kind of leaves goosebumps on me thinking about her.

Jed: The little girl actually looked at you as she walked by?

Matthew: Yeah. She looked at me. She couldn't have been more'n maybe like six, maybe. Six years old, maybe seven, somewhere in there. A little girl. But I do remember her, I even got up. Gosh damn I got a lot of goosebumps on me.

Jed: Did you see her disappear, or did you lose sight of her?

Matthew: I saw her walk around the corner. As I got up to walk around the corner, I saw her just fade away, because it's dark over here.

Jed: What's that, 10 feet away?

Matthew: Probably about a good 13 feet away, because I was right there where the chair is now, coming toward her, and she was already up, and I couldn't see her no more. You know, but that's what's happened in this house. Angie's never seen nothin', and never heard nothin' *[his wife]*. And, you know, even the dishes at night. I've even heard them shuffle a little bit. Maybe they're settling, I don't know. But I've heard that, too. But, yeah, I've always felt like there's always somebody around, you know, at night? Especially if I'm outside, I'd be doing something. I always felt there was some presence there, but I don't see it outside.

Jed: How old were you when you were seeing the little girl?

Matthew: I guess about 42 years old, somewhere in there? Yeah, somewhere around there.

Jed: When's the last time that happened?

Matthew: Mara's already been out of the house probably about 10 years now. I haven't seen her anymore. Not gonna say she ain't gonna come back, but that was when I saw her. Like I said, it really surprised me. And there's been other times I was sitting on the love seat, watching TV? I was just laying back and all of a sudden something just hit the back of my love seat, in my back, real hard. It didn't hurt me; I could just feel the cushion come up where it moved me a little bit. It surprised me, and I said, "Will you please stop?" That's all I said, "Please stop and go away". I did get up a little after that, maybe a couple of minutes later. I decided to look behind and walk around the house. I knew everything was locked, you know? I knew it wasn't none of my kids.

Jed: How many times do you think saw the little girl?

Matthew: I'd say maybe about five times.

Jed: That's a bunch.

Matthew: Yeah. Five times. Well, Mara was seeing her I don't know how many times, too. But Mara only saw her face, she never saw the whole little girl, she said.

Jed: Was it a Hispanic girl, white girl?

Matthew: I couldn't tell. I couldn't tell. You know, but that's what I saw. But I have had somebody where they, where I'm sitting on this recliner, somebody doing this to my hand *[he runs the fingertips of one hand across the back of his other hand and up his arm]*.

Jed: You actually feel someone's fingertips up your arm?

Matthew: Yeah.

Jed: When was that?

Matthew: Oh hell, that's happened several times. That's happened in the last, golly, probably in the last three or four years. It's happened to me a few times here and there. I've always felt somebody doing this to me.

Jed: Like the fingertips up the back of your arm?

Matthew: Yeah, yeah. Yeah, because look at the goosebumps *[points to goosebumps on his arm]*. I still think about that when it happens to me, every time. But it's happened to me I don't know how many times. Or, I'll have my arm right there at the end of the deal, and I've had it do that to my hand.

Jed: You had your arm at the edge of the table *[in kitchen]*.

Matthew: Yes, yes. And I've had it at the edge of the arm rest, you know, of the recliner? And I've had it do this. Knocks it off *[mimics pushing his arm off the arm rest]*.

Jed: You actually feel somebody push you on one side of your arm, and off the other side of the arm rest.

Matthew: Yes, yes, yes. Yes. Oh yeah. And I look at myself, I say, I know I'm not asleep. I wasn't asleep, I was watching a Western. I like watching Westerns late at night. And you know, I don't, I didn't let that bother me at all. But that happened only once. Yeah, Elena says that happens to her all the time, too. But, but yeah, I've had that happen.

Jed: Do you remember being with Gerald *[my brother]* at the house on Sheffield, and all the doors slammed shut?

Matthew: You know what...

Jed: I think he said something about Beaver, I think it was with Beaver, like peed or something. Does that sound familiar?

Matthew: You know what, Beaver at the time was there, but shoot I really don't remember the doors slamming shut. Maybe Mom and all of them know that. And, but yeah, I would believe Gerald would probably see something like that, young kid he was.

Jed: That was something he remembered, so I was seeing if that was something you remembered.

Matthew: No, no, they told me about that, but you know I never even thought about that until now. You know it happened so long ago. No, no. But I do remember Beaver. Yeah, but you know, things like that, that's the only thing I remember happening to me. Like I said, I don't know if it's my body nerves or what's causing this to move or what *[mimics his arm being pushed off the armrest]*, but I've had that, just that feeling all the time. Angie says, "I've never had anything like that happen." And I said, "Because you're a non-believer."

[Laughter]

Matthew: You know? I said... I said, maybe it's just certain people, you know, this happens to.

Jed: I wondered if it could be in families.

Matthew: Yeah.

Jed: Because I think there was a survey, and it was like one in five people say they've seen, heard, or experienced something that they think might be paranormal. I was thinking about it, and it's not 1 in 5 people in our family, most everybody has seen or heard something at some point.

Matthew: Yeah.

Jed: I think that Dad said his mom never really liked to talk about it, or, my mom said the same thing about her parents, but did your mom or dad ever tell you about anything they saw or heard?

Matthew: No... Well, you know what? Dad told me a long time ago when he was, uh, this was when he was still married to Mom, Mom was still alive. He was lying in bed, and he told me it was like some big ol' figure over him. And he said he was swinging at it. He said his eyes opened up, and he saw a figure looking at him. But he couldn't see it. And he just started swinging at it, and you know, it just, it was gone. I said, "You sure you didn't dream that, or you were asleep?" He says, "I was asleep, but I opened my eyes and I laid there, and I looked," and he said, "I saw a figure over me, and I was swinging at it." And, Dad... You'd have to talk to Dad, but, but I was young then when he was swinging at that figure, because I was still a little kid living at the house, you know. The other thing he says he felt something grab his feet.

[He stops to take a break and serve us homemade tea.]

Matthew: Probably this year I've had this happen already, you know, the finger rubbing.

Jed: The finger on the arm?

Matthew: Yeah, yeah. This only happened to me one time *[mimicking his arm knocked off the table edge],* and I said what the hell? And I got to thinking, was I on the edge? And I said, nah, because I felt something. I know I felt it.

Jed: Have you seen anything recently?

Matthew: No, not at all. But like I said, on my hands, and wrists. I've always... This always comes on a little bit, you know? But I never pay no attention to it anymore. Only thing I can think, I said, well, maybe that's Mom trying to say hello. I don't know. Or Noah *[the eldest brother who has passed away].* You know, something like that. But no. And you know what? As many times as I've been to the cemetery, and I've been out there you know putting flowers for Mom, like I always go birthday, Mother's Day, like that? I put flowers out. Well, you know there's many times that I've gone by myself and nobody's out there and I don't see a single soul, and I'm always just looking around and looking around. Nothing. But it doesn't bother me to go there. There's times I've left the cemetery when Mom had first passed away where the sun's going down and I'm just leaving, nothing. You'd think you'd see something out there, and no *[laughing].* No, it's always happened, you know, here. Right here in my house. But I haven't seen anything in a long time. It's been a while since I seen anything.

Jed: You and your brothers and sisters, is it something you ever talked to each other about? Things that you saw?

Matthew: You know, your dad James used to tell me, he's had something like that happen to him, where he felt like somebody is touching him, or rubbing his neck. Or you know, a little rub across the back or something like that. But no, not really. I talked to Elena more about it than James. Tina and Elena have talked about it. Tina's got encounters with something. You know, I don't know if Rose, but, yeah. I guess Elena is the main one.

Jed: Especially since she's lived there so long.

Matthew: Yeah. And her- You know what? Talk to her son, Andrew. He's seen a lot of shit, too.

Jed: Does Andrew still stay in that back room?

Matthew: Yeah, he's in that back room, where I heard that before. But you know what, I've slept back there too before, and I've never heard anything in there in that back room of that house.

Jed: I was never really supposed to go in that back room anyway, so I didn't really. That house in general is just uncomfortable to be in. Like the hallway, or looking into the room it faces *[on the East wall]*, it just felt better when the door to the bedroom was closed.

Matthew: Yeah, yeah, that—You know what? That door is always closed to that bedroom, because that's Andrew's room. But it's always closed. I noticed that, too. That room's always been closed that I can remember. Yeah. But I haven't seen anything in a long time.

JAMES

[James is my father. He and my mother are divorced, so I met him at his home where he lives with his wife. They had not reported any paranormal experiences in this home at the time of this interview.]

Jed: You and Matthew are similar ages, so were you in the Philippines with him?

James: No, no. Not the whole family was in the Philippines, the five girls and Matthew, Rene, and Carl.

Jed: You were already out then?

James: I wasn't there.

Jed: So, when you were younger, you never had any experiences, saw anything...

James: Not out of the ordinary, no. Even if I saw something weird back then, I probably wouldn't have recognized it, you know?

Jed: Yeah. So, when was the first time?

James: I guess it would be across from Mom's house when we used to live there. You were real little at the time. For some reason or the other, I always felt like there was something in that room.

Jed: Which room, the one on Sheffield, that house?

James: On Sheffield. Yeah. Here's Mom's house, and then right across where we used to live right there. I never could really sleep comfortably because I'd wake up and I'd see, you know, shadows around me and stuff. And I used to get real scared. I get out to Fort Stockton and I'd be able to go to bed, but I'd leave a light on. I'd leave just a little light on in the restroom, because I guess there was something that was just scaring me in the dark. And I didn't know what it was, but I never experienced anything out there. It was just always in that room.

Jed: How old are you when you're seeing the shadows?

James: God, you weren't even two years old. You hadn't even started talking. Your first words at that time were water to me. And as a dad, Dada or Daddy, so "wahr" *[laughing]*. But anyway, you were born in what year?

Jed: '79.

James: So '79, that would be in about '80.

Jed: The room you're talking about would be the one in the—

James: Bedroom.

Jed: Front of the house in the far corner?

James: Yes. To the left. And I just never could, there's just something there that I…

Jed: Was it in the night or during the daytime that you'd see the shadows?

James: At night. Mostly at night, and I'd try to ignore 'em. That was the gist of it there.

Jed: So, seeing a shadow in the dark like what is- How would you describe that? Is it just something darker…?

James: Something blacker than black. It's hard to describe it. I wasn't…

Jed: Your eyes adjust.

James: Your eyes adjust. I could just see, it's just like, uh…

Jed: Is there—I remember there were windows with curtains, would it—

James: It was just like seeing stars, and just seeing somethin' black, you know?

Jed: So, something crossing in front.

James: Right. Yeah. And I couldn't move.

Jed: Yeah.

James: I could never move. It was like I was always paralyzed. It happened a lot. It happened a lot.

Jed: Could you move your eyes, or-?

James: Yeah. And I could make sounds. I was trying to move, you know, I was gruntin', trying to move and I couldn't move. It's like somebody held me down.

Jed: Yeah.

James: But that never happened to me anywhere else.

Jed: Only—

James: Only in that room.

Jed: So not even anywhere else in the house, it was just in that room?

James: In that room. Yeah, yeah. I just always felt uncomfortable. Yeah.

Jed: You said mostly at night, but sometimes it happened in the day too?

James: Sometimes in the day. If I was taking a nap or something, you know? It's just like there might have been something there that I felt. It's just hard to describe. Never could see a face, never see a real shape. I mean, just flashes, you know? But to me it was just uncomfortable. I've always felt like I was a little bit sensitive to things, because you know me and Mom were always real close. Even now I can think of things and people will think of them. It's kind of weird, but other than that, that's about it with that house. So, what else?

Jed: I guess the easiest way is to organize some of the stuff that you saw. You haven't had anything like that happen here, in other places you've lived, any hotels, motels while you were driving?

James: I may have had things to where I've heard things or felt things in hotels. Sometimes I'll get a sense that something is going to happen, and I'll get up and I'll check the whole house. It's just like maybe somebody's near, or something's near, and I'll get up because, uh... I remember this one incident when we lived out there in Somerset when I got up in the middle of the night and I just felt something, and I went and stood at the windows and just looked and looked and looked, and actually somebody was walking by. Then after that happened, I was okay. But that was in the dark through the yard. You know, somebody was walking through the yard.

Jed: Oh, they were walking through the yard?

James: Yeah, yeah, but I, I'd gotten up and I'd sensed something, and I stood at that window for about 10 minutes and then I, I had my gun. I had my gun in my hand.

Jed: How old were you?

James: This was about three years ago. I just stood at the window and watched them go through. And I just had my gun in my hand. But I had felt it and, you know, afterwards I was okay.

Jed: Basically, you woke up looking for something outside.

James: I felt somebody, I felt something. Yeah. And then every now and then I'll feel that, you know? It's kind of hard to describe.

Jed: What was the time you told me that you saw the farmer while riding your bike?

James: Oh, that would be in 2001 and 2002, and that was with my buddy Mac. Mac passed away last year. He was a driver. He was sick, he had diabetes and he didn't take care of himself. He pretty much died in a rest home. He was one of my friends at Kerrville. I was the first and only person to actually go up and introduce myself, and he said because I had done that, he had this idea that I was an okay guy or something. But anyway, we became real good friends and he moved out there right across the street from me in Somerset, where we used to go riding. We rode from where I lived in Savannah Heights to Somerset, seven miles up and seven miles back. That was a lot of miles for us, 14 miles.

And as we were coming up Smith Road, I see a guy, I see an old man with a hat. An old Mexican man, just leaning on a post on the fence. And

I said, "Mac," I said, "I wonder what that guy's doing over there?" And he goes, "What guy?" I said, "The guy on the fence." He goes, "What guy? You're seeing things." I said, "There's an old man over there, looked like he was working on the fence." And he says, "Wasn't anybody there, James." I said, "Okay, I'm just telling you what I saw. There was a guy there." He goes, "What're you smoking?" He was joking around. But as I was ridin' by, *[the old man]*'s just sittin' there, and *[the man]* just stared at me as I rode by. Just like that. And I said I guess he's taking a break or something. I'd say he was about 75, 75 or 80.

Jed: Was it on your side of the road?

James: Right side.

Jed: Or on Mac's side?

James: Oh, I was right behind Mac.

Jed: Oh, so it's not like you were in the way.

James: No, no, I was right behind Mac. He was in front of me, and I said wonder what that guy up ahead on the right is doing on the fence.

Jed: You asked him before you passed him.

James: Yeah. Yeah, I said what's that guy on the right doing. Fixing the fence or something. But you know, it's really weird. I'll tell you one time what happened—

Jed: Was that during the day?

James: During the day.

Jed: Yeah.

James: It was during the day, it was like right now, just bright. You know, with sunshine and everything.

Jed: Yeah, it was noon.

James: I should've look for a shadow or something. That would have tipped me off, you know?

Jed: What were you about to say? That there was this one time?

James: No, this is a totally different story.

Jed: That's fine, yeah.

James: It was when I first started with Kerrville and we were doing a lot of military stuff. We were on our way to a military base in Killeen, and we were taking a back road from the side of Georgetown off of 35, there was a back road to go to Killeen. It was about six or seven of us in a convoy. It was wintertime and it was dark, and we were just driving along. It was pitch dark out there. Over there on the right side, as I'm driving I'm looking out for deer, and you're looking out for stuff, and I just happen to see something kind of reddish in the dark. Kind of looked like a light pole with two red lights on it. You know, I thought maybe somebody had some kind of electric or something up there.

And as we're driving I just kind of glanced, and then we get to Killeen, and we're dropping off at the base, and Frank the lead driver—He passed away. He says, "Did you see that?" And I said, "See what?" He says, "Did you see that thing with eyes on it?" I said, "I saw something red, but I thought it was just a telephone pole or somethin' with some electronic lights on it or something." He goes, "No. That son of a bitch turned," he says, "As I was driving, that thing turned and looked right at me." And I said, "What do you mean a telephone pole looked at you?" He says, "No. That damn thing was moving." And I said, "I don't know what to tell you. I just saw some red lights, like little red lights." And I said, "Are you crazy?" He says, "No, that son of a bitch moved." We just blew it off, but you never know.

Jed: How high off the ground was this, and how far away from the buses? I mean, you said you just assumed it was a—

James: From here to the house. We're from here to the house. That's about what, about 20 yards? About 15 yards.

Jed: Yeah.

James: Yeah, and 'bout seven foot, eight foot. That's why I said I thought there were some lights on a telephone pole, or a post or something.

Jed: And it was like the main light wasn't on, but there's two red lights is what you're saying—

James: Just two little lights, yeah. It was just two little red lights. He swore up and down that it was moving and then it turned, and he said it looked like something moving in the dark. And I said okay, and nobody else saw it.

Jed: Were you in front of him or behind?

James: I was, uh, third bus.

Jed: Gotcha, was he—

James: He was the lead bus. Frank was always the lead guy; he was the senior driver. I didn't want to lead out there anyway, I didn't know how to get out there. And that was a time that we saw that even Frank would tell you... His thing, his thing, what would he always say? He says if I'm lying, I'm dying. That's what he would always say. He always had some kind of remark, you know, other things that I wouldn't even mention. But that was one time that I remembered, because it was cold. It was wintertime. It was cold. Yeah. It's just like coming down from Wichita Falls. When I was coming back to Brady, Texas. You have that one there *[referring to notes he'd sent]*.

Jed: Which one?

James: I was driving, and I had gone through that burial ground area.

Jed: Yeah. Tell me that.

James: Well, that area was basically ruled by the Comanches back then in the early 1800's and 1700's. That was their territory. And we had dropped off troops at Sheppard Air Force Base in Wichita Falls, and we had to go and fuel the buses for a return trip. Because back then, the buses didn't have the distance that they can go now with the bigger tanks and fuel. So we'd have to add fuel, and then we'd have to go to a hotel there off of, gosh, 280, 281 in Stephenville. We had to park the buses on a hill. There was a little grading on the hill in the hotel, because during the wintertime buses wouldn't start. They'd get cold or somethin' and they wouldn't start. So, we just turned the power on, put it in gear, let them roll, we'd pop the clutch and we'd get going. And out of the two buses, one of us would have to drive to Brady, Texas, to central Texas more so, many of them would head back to San Antonio.

Jed: And you'd be by yourself.

James: Yeah, we'd be dead-heading back and I was driving, and it was cold. It was after midnight. I was listening to a Walkman, remember Walkmans? It was when they came out, and I was just real comfortable. The bus wasn't toasty, but it was warm. All of a sudden, it was like I went through this cloud of sheer fright. I mean goose bumps, the hair stood up on my head. I've never felt this scared ever in my life. I flicked on the lights, because I thought there was somebody on the bus, and I looked in the mirror and I looked around and I was like this *[looking over both shoulders]. And* I said, what the hell happened, you know? After a while I started to calm down and I'm driving down the highway, and I pass a trooper. He turns around, turns on his lights, and he pulls me over. And I'm thinking, I wasn't speeding. I mean, I knew better than to be speeding in that area.

So anyway, he pulls me over and I get off the bus, and he comes walking up. I said to the trooper, "I know I wasn't speeding, and everything on here is working. What's the reason for stopping me?" You know? And he says, "Well, son, I was bored." He said, "I just want to talk to somebody there." He said, "There ain't been nobody come through here for a while, and I just wanted to see how you were doing. If you're doing okay." And we sat there, we were talking and stuff, and I said, "I experienced the weirdest feeling coming down the highway. I came through an area, and I got scared." I explained to him what had happened, and he says "Well, you probably went through an Indian burial ground. They say there's

Indian burial grounds all over the place in that area." And he says, "Maybe you went through one, maybe that's what you experienced. You're not the first one to tell me that. There's been other folks that have had the same experiences." And I said, "Well, it happened to me, and it scared the crap out of me." And all the way to Brady I had the reading lights on in the back.

Jed: How old were you at the time?

James: At the time? I was probably... What was it, the early '80s? I would be about 20, I wasn't even 30 yet.

Jed: How long had you been driving at that point?

James: Started in '79 and I was 25.

Jed: So, six years you'd been driving buses in middle of the night, by yourself. And no problems. You never had any problems.

James: No problems, never had any problems like that. That was the first time I ever experienced that. I've had weird stuff happen on Greyhounds, but nothing supernatural. Just kind of weird stuff. You know, like a guy with a snake that you don't want to hear about.

Jed: How about the... I think you said you and a passenger saw somebody off of, uh...

James: I-10.

Jed: You were with Greyhound.

James: Yeah. I was on the 1 a.m. out of Fort Stockton, and we used to call it the champagne run because they'd always be drunk after they've been in San Antonio for a couple hours. They'd get on the bus and people'd—I'd always have to tell everybody that I wanted a nice quiet ride or that they wouldn't be riding with me. I wasn't like a policeman, I just kind of talked to 'em like I'm talking now. I said I do not want to talk to anybody in the middle of the night about noise, or laughing, or this and that. I said keep it quiet, people are going to sleep.

So, this one guy up front, we're sitting there. We had just left Junction at about 2-something in the morning, and out there it's just wide open. I mean, there's trees out there, and there's brush and everything out there, but we get to this point North of the LLano river and you start seeing the big cuts of the rock that they had blasted to run the highways through back then. And as you cross the Llano river it goes uphill. And up in the distance, I thought I saw a deer up there, and I'm thinking, oh great, I hope it doesn't run in front of me. So, you know, I'm talking to him, and I'm telling the passenger, "There's probably a deer up here in the distance." And then we saw—

Jed: Was it—You could see because of the light reflecting...?

James: I had my brights. Yeah, I had my brights on and everything. And then I saw it moving on the highway, and I started thinking, oh crap, it's moving across. But then I saw, I saw that it was a person. And then to the guy, the person right next to me, the passenger, I said, "That's somebody walking across the highway." And from the distance, we could see where it looked like there was this woman wearing this long, San Francisco type of gown, you know the kind that had this big old ribbon or thing on the back and a parasol, walking across the highway. I get chills thinking about it, and the guy passenger says, "What the hell's a person doing out here?" And I said, "I don't know."

So, we see them walking across real fast. When we get over there, we're thinking we're going to see someone standing there and there's nobody there. And I said, "You did see somebody walking over there, you know, like a woman with a long dress and an umbrella?" And he goes, "A parasol." And I said, "Yeah, parasol." And there was nobody there. And we kind of talked about it, and he says, "Do you see stuff like that out here?" I said, "No, not really, not like that." That wasn't a deer, that was actually the figure of something walking across the highway.

Jed: How far do you think you were away from the woman that you saw, when both of you saw it?

James: 'Bout a hundred yards. Yeah, it was about a hundred yards that we saw.

Jed: It's like, remembering West Texas when you're going through those big rocky areas, there's not any, there's not like any homes or anything out there.

James: No, there's nothing out there. Not there. It's just a cut. You always kind of, when we'd come through the cut, you'd always want to be careful to make sure there wasn't any deer that had gotten into the cuts. 'Cause they'll just run right in front of you. But you know, only time I ever saw anybody in that area was somebody sleeping on the side of the road in a sleeping bag. I almost ran over them, because their feet were in the lane, and I honked, and they moved their feet out of the way.

Jed: Yeah. Can tell me about when you and the driver saw the insects?

James: Gosh, Bill. Bill was the kind of driver, he's one of those Billy Gruff drivers, always real serious, always had a look on his face. Nobody really would talk to him that much, because they thought he was, you know, a gruffy jerk. But he always liked it when I was on the one o'clock as a second driver, double. We called them doubles. Any time he knew that I was going to double him, he enjoyed it. Because a lot of the drivers didn't like doing the one o'clock, they got sleepy. I didn't get sleepy. 99 percent of the time, I was wide awake on the one o'clock.

Jed: You never had to take coffee?

James: No. Uh-uh, coffee didn't keep me awake unless I spilled it on me, which I did one time accidentally and it kept me awake. But we left that night and we're, uh, we're on our way to Fort Stockton, and we're on the one o'clock and we're coming into Junction. And believe it or not, where we're at it was raining. It was misting and raining. And as we're coming down the hill, I look at my mirror and he's right on my ass. And it's raining, right? Up ahead is a herd of deer, a herd of deer walking across the highway. And I can't put my breaks on. You know, it's raining, you put your brakes on and you're going to start sliding. I hit so many deer.

So anyway, we went on and as we went further West, it was clearing up. It wasn't raining, and the stars were coming out. The clouds are disappearing, and we get to the 200 mile point of the trip over there near Sheffield, Texas. And as we go through Sheffield and get on the highway, we're going up there and then up ahead I just see kind of like a greenish fog. Up in the air towards my right, just movin' like this, you know? And as I get closer, I see that it's just a bunch of insects, like a bunch of locusts or insects just flying by in a giant greenish fog.

Jed: Just so many it looks like it's fog.

James: Just so many, yeah. They're going across in a greenish fog. And mind you, this is at night. There are no other lights out there except our headlights, right? So, I'm seeing this and then as it passes by, I'm looking ahead and in the median I see trees. You know, I see trees. Just like... Only they don't have leaves on them. It's like it's wintertime, they don't have leaves and there's trees in the median. The thing about it is that there are no trees out there in the median. The only thing out there is brush. And that green haze I'm seein'; these trees. I'm driving and I'm like this *[shaking his head in bewilderment]* and I'm thinking, how do you see insects at night? You know, in the dark?

Jed: And you're going through them?

James: Yeah. And I'm like there's no trees out here. So anyway, I'm driving and about 15 miles down the road there's a rest area they ended up building, because truckers and people would fall asleep. There were always accidents in that area, so they built a rest area on both sides. And it was this side of Bakersfield, Texas which is 35 miles from Fort Stockton.

But anyway, I see Bill start to pull in over there. And I said, the heck's he doing? He never stops at the rest area. He just goes straight, you know? So, we pull in there and I pull up behind him, and then he gets out and lights up a cigarette. He comes walking towards me smoking a cigarette and he goes, "Did you see something funny back there?" And I said, "Like what? What do you mean, funny?" I said, "What did you see?" And he says, "What did YOU see?" I said, "I saw a bunch of insects flying in front of me up there. I know it's not possible 'cause you can't see them at night. They were off the ground bout as high as a tree up there you know just a cloud going across. And I saw trees where there shouldn't be trees."

And he looked at me. He looked at me smoking a cigarette, and he goes, "Damn. It's what I thought I saw." He says, "That's why I pulled in here. I thought I was seeing things, but you saw it too?" And I said, "Yeah, I saw something." And he says, "I wonder if we went through some kind of a cloud, some hallucinogenic cloud. You know the military is always doing stupid stuff." I said, "I don't know what to tell you, but I'm not going to tell anybody what I saw." And so, we kept it to ourselves.

Jed: Yeah, because you were drivers.

James: We were drivers, we don't want people to think we're taking...

Jed: Yeah, if they question if you're drinking or doing drugs…

James: Well, back then, none of that was really regulated like it is now. I couldn't tell you how many times people were either drinking, or hung over, or taking amphetamines.

Jed: To stay awake?

James: To stay awake. Back then, nothing was regulated everybody would, could take anything. Even the old senior drivers were taking diet pills if they had trouble staying awake. And I always wondered, so that's how they're staying awake at night. And somebody even smoked cigarettes out the window while they were driving. I even knew one that would nip whiskey on the way to Big Springs. An old timer, you know. Can you believe it?

Jed: What about when you saw, I think you said, you saw the ball of fire in the sky? When was that?

James: That was probably in the late '80s. I was coming back out of Fort Stockton and I'd left out of there at about nine o'clock at night. And, uh, and I always met a bus in Ozona. He was the one that got in there at two-something in the morning. So, I would say it was about 11:30 at night, 11:30, 11:45. And as I was coming up the hill from, uh, we used to call it Sheffield Hill. We'd come up, and it was at the top of the hill and I was only about maybe seven miles from Ozona. It was like 200 miles from San Antonio. As I was coming East, I looked up and I saw a light coming from the right side. At first, I thought that maybe a plane was on fire or something, you know, and was burning because it was moving that slow. And it just looked like a ball of slow-moving fire, going from South to North. Like it was just moving slowly across. And I couldn't see what it was. I didn't see anything; I just saw a ball of fire.

And a passenger on the right side of me saw it, too. And I said, "Do you see that?" He says, "Yeah, I do. What is it?" I said, "I don't know." And it just, it just moved on to the north, you know? It was at a low altitude; I'd say it was probably at a thousand feet or more. It wasn't high, it was low. And it just kept on moving. It wasn't moving fast; it was just moving slow. It wasn't until a week later I ran into a driver. We were on our days off or at the shop or something, and he goes, "James, did you happen to see anything strange the other night?" And I said, "Like?" And he says, "You know…" I said, "You mean like a ball of fire?" He goes, "Yeah, I saw that." I said, "Anybody else see it on your bus?" He goes, "No, they were all asleep. I saw it movin' across real slow, just fire, burning." I said I didn't know what it was.

Jed: It wasn't a light, there were flames.

James: It was flames. It was like a ball of fire. It was like a low, moving ball of fire.

Jed: And, I think most people would assume, maybe there's a meteor or something like that, but…

James: Yeah. No, this was burning. This was going way too slow, like a little Cessna. You know a Cessna speed, like a small engine Cessna, you know what I'm talking about right?

Jed: Yeah.

James: That slow. Yes, you know or—

Jed: Not slow like a jet or something flying at a high altitude.

James: Yeah, if it would have been a jet, we would've known, we woulda heard it.

Jed: That it was noticeably lower. Like, you could get a sense of size and distance from it?

James: Yeah, about a thousand feet up, yeah, in altitude. Because we both met each other like that, and it was goin'.

Jed: The directions you and the other driver were coming from were almost perpendicular.

James: Exactly. It was in the middle. It was in front of him and it was in front of me. And it was just going across real slow. Slower. It wasn't a jet. And I've seen Cessna's fly faster than that, you know, prop jobs. But nobody ever, never heard anything about it. So, even if the military had it on radar, they wouldn't say anything about it.

Jed: Yeah. Tell me about when you were driving and heard your mom's voice.

James: I was in that same area. That's that weird area where I saw that ball of fire. Let's see, Junction is 200, let's see, Sonora about 230 miles west of San Antonio, just West of Ozona. About the same place I was when I saw that ball of fire. Anyway, about that time I was sitting there driving and tired, and I was actually drinking coffee and chewing gum, everything. I was tired, and I was actually to that point to where I was getting' real drowsy. Just as I was hitting that real drowsy point, I heard a yell, "Tito!" real loud, "You're going to sleep!" She called me Tito. That was my nickname, Tito. And she says, "You're falling asleep!" It was so loud that I snapped awake and looked around to see who had yelled at me in the bus. I was looking in the mirror and everybody's asleep. And I hadn't gone off the road or anything.

I was wide awake, and I heard her voice. She had yelled at me. I stayed awake the whole time. So, I came back that morning, I guess it was morning. Let me see. It had to be in the afternoon, because that's when I was picking you guys up to go back home. We lived out in the country, out in Converse. We were talking and she was telling me, "You were falling asleep the other night." I said, "No, I wasn't," and she's, "Yes, you were." I said, "I tell you Mom, I must've been dreaming about it as I was falling asleep, and I heard you screaming at me to stay awake." She said, "You were falling asleep, that's why I told you to stay awake."

And that was the weirdest thing, you know, because the last time that that happened, I was in Montréal, Canada, and that was in the early '90s. I was below ground at Murrayhill Bus Company in Montreal. It's like a catacomb because a lot of things were built underground there because of their harsh winters, and their whole facility is like underground. And it's like a catacomb, you just hear it. You can sing down there and get some good feedback on sound.

So anyway, I'm waiting for this guy to finish fueling my bus and cleaning it, and I'm walking around, and I heard this real loud shout. A real loud voice, you know, Mom's voice. And it was like, "Tito, hablame!" In Spanish it means call me. I'm looking around to see who the hell yelled at me. So, I go over there, and ask the guy where's there a pay phone. I used my calling card; we had calling cards back then that you dialed for long distance calls. I called her up and I said, "Is everything okay?" And she said, "It's about time you called, I've been trying to call you for the last two or three hours." And I said, "Really, you've been trying to call me for the last two hours? No wonder I heard you screaming for me to call you."

And I used to always ask her, how do you hear? How do, you know, when you want to get a message to me? She goes, "I just do like My Favorite Martian." It's a show we used to watch years ago when we were little. But she says, "If I want you to call me, I'll send out a message and you'll call me." She said she was wantin' me to call her when I heard something. Did you want me to tell you about the phone call in the middle of the night after she passed away?

Jed: Sure.

James: I was, uh, I was asleep, and this phone kept ringing and ringing and ringing. I finally say, "Somebody answer the phone," and nobody would answer the phone. I got up and walked down these stairs, and there was an old black phone on a table stand. I picked it up, and it was Mom. We got to talking and the whole time that I was talking to her, I could hear her doing dishes over the phone. And I said, "What are you doing?" She goes, "I'm just washing some dishes." And then she went on to ask me how everybody was doing now that she was gone. And I said, "Well, everybody's adjusting, and we're trying to get on with our lives." And I said that everybody misses you and everything. Finally, I remember saying, "Can I come over and see you?" And she goes, "Not yet," she says, "I'll let you know. I've got to go now. I'll talk to you again." So, I hung up and the next morning I went to Elena's house right across from Mom's house, Dad's house, but on the corner.

When Elena lived on the corner, I would always meet Matthew there before he went to work at CPS, and we'd always have toast and coffee. And I was sitting there telling Matthew about it. But the whole story Matthew is like "Really? Wow. That's one heck of a dream." Then Elena turned around, she was looking at us kind of pale, and she says, "You need to call your sister and ask her about her dream." So, I called up Rose, I said, "Rose, Elena wants me to ask you about the dream you had last night."

And she says, "Well, you know James, it was really weird." She says, "I was sitting there laying down asleep, and the phone kept ringing and ringing. I picked it up and it was Mom. We started talking and she started asking me how everybody was, how I was," and this and that. She says, "We talked for a little while, and then she says I have to go now, and I'll talk to you again." And Rose says, "I said bye, and I hung up and went back to sleep. Why?" And I said, "I had the same dream last night." And that actually happened.

[Rose is interviewed and confirms the experience of a phone call from her mother in a dream that night.]

Jed: Since I can't ask her, what are some of the things that she told you happened to her—

James: Elena?

Jed: No, I'm going to talk to Elena. Your mom.

James: Mom? Mom would be in the kitchen, and she would always see somebody going by in the hall.

[This will be a recurring topic in the Sheffield house.]

Jed: This is the house on Sheffield?

James: In the house on Sheffield. She would be doing something, and she would see somebody walking, a shadow, walking past her. And she always felt a little cold, a little cold air in certain rooms. Like if she went into that corner room. Like if you're looking at the house in the front, it's the room in the corner. And she said she would feel things, but she wasn't afraid. She just felt the presence. Just like the time when you guys were little and making a lot of noise in one room, and she goes and tells you guys to keep it down, because you're going to wake up your grandpa, 'cause he's trying to sleep, 'cause he had to work at night. And she said, "Why are you guys making so much noise?" There was about five of you. You guys were all little. And you guys were laughing, and said, "'Cause he's making us laugh!" And you guys are pointing at the bed, and she looks over there and she goes, "Who is making you laugh?" And all you guys say, "The man with farmer pants, and red checkered shirt, lotta hair.

He's making us laugh." She looked over there and she said her hair stood up. She felt a chill. She says, "Okay everybody out, go outside and play with Beaver." You know, you guys go outside, go outside and play.

And her and her China cabinet. Every time she would arrange her stuff, somebody would rearrange everything. Every time she did it, it was rearranged. It's like, that's not the way they wanted it. The kitchen light would come on all the time at night. Dad would come home at night, or at night after midnight and get mad because somebody left on the light and the light bulb was using a lot of electricity. You know how my dad was at that time. So, they were always trying to let 'im know we didn't leave anything on. I changed out the light switch. Nothing, lights still would come on at night. In the morning my mom would get in trouble, the kids would get in trouble. I changed out the breaker. Still. It wasn't until Mom for some reason bought this poor little crystal lamp, miniature crystal lamp with a little lampshade like something you'd see in a little dollhouse. You'd plug it in an' it had a real faint little light on it. As long as that light stayed on in the kitchen, the kitchen light wouldn't come on.

And, uh, one day I went over there, and I turned off the light, you know during the day, and Mom goes, "Turn that back on!" And I said, "Why?" She says, "He doesn't like it when you turn it off. Leave it." So I turned it back on. I said, "Who?" And she says, "The ghost, the guy with all the hair." The same guy that told her the night before she passed away that everything was going to be okay. And then she, you know, she passed away.

[From a follow up conversation with James.]

James: Right before my dad took Mom to the hospital, to Lackland, she was having a hard time breathing. She said, "I talked to the man." I said, "What man?" "The guy with all the hair. He told me I was going to be at peace, I was going to be okay." "Are you talking about the guy you seen before?" And she said yes. And that was right before she went into the hospital.

[We return to the original interview.]

James: That same ghost, that guy with the overalls, the checkered shirt, curly hair and beard. You know, the same guy that Gerald saw going into the room, go into the closet. Same guy that probably looked like Carl when Gerald was on the couch. Carl goes into the bedroom and looks around, looks at Gerald with a smile on his face motioning him to follow him into the room. And Gerald told me that he told Carl, no, I don't want to go in there. 'Cause you know mom kept jars of pickles and goodies for the kids. Do you remember that she always kept snacks in there for you guys?

Jed: Vaguely.

James: Yeah, she always kept stuff in there just so that older people wouldn't get into it. She always had it for the kids. And so, after a while Gerald got up to go see what the hell Carl was doin' and he went in there, nobody was in there. He looked in the closet, bathroom everywhere. And there's no way Carl fit through that little window that's in Mom's bedroom.

Jed: Did your grandparents, your parents, ever tell you anything about things that they saw or heard in any places that they lived or...?

James: Just my dad. My dad told me—My dad's always been skeptical. If he actually saw something, he never really talked about it. He actually did tell me the time that a year before I was born in Uvalde that he, uh, they were sleeping... The house, at the time we were little, the house was big to us. But I saw it the other day. It's just little, and wooden floors and everything. Mom and Dad are sleeping in one bedroom, and he heard the door open up, he heard that screen door open up. He heard footsteps on the creaking wood. The door to the bedroom opened, and the footsteps came up to him and grabbed his boot or something. He could hear the footsteps as that person ran from the room and went out the front door, closed the front door, and the screen door slammed. And that's when he got up lookin' and found that the front door was locked.

Found that the screen door was locked. He had heard the door and the screen door, because they make a lot of noise. If you open up an old-fashioned screen door, you're going to hear that spring.

Jed: You hear the hinges.

James: You hear everything, yeah. You can hear somebody walk through that whole house.

Jed: You said it was pier and beam, so the floor gave in the old houses.

[At its simplest, pier and beam foundations can be described as wooden girders standing on concrete pads. These girders in turn hold up floor joists that your flooring will sit on. Over time, and without upkeep, the flooring and joists can warp and move.]

James: Oh yeah, yeah. Just wooden floor. You could hear *[makes creaking sounds]* and stuff. And it's just like, it's just like my grandpa. This happened with Matthew, for some reason or the other he opened up the car door. Matthew was little and was playing with matches. He started a little fire in the back on the floorboard and it started burning. My grandpa happened to see smoke coming from there and he grabbed, uh—There was always a bucket near the water faucets.

So anyway, my grandpa grabbed the bucket of water and he went over there, and he put the fire out. And he was chastising Matthew for lighting a fire and this and that. You know, yelling at him. And he says, "Who told you to do something stupid like that?!" Just tellin' him, trying to talk English. Spanglish I guess? And Matthew was just sitting there looking at him. And Matthew pointed behind him, he goes, "He did. He told me to do it." And my grandfather's lookin' at him, he goes, "Who?" Matthew goes, "He kinda looks like the devil?" And my grandfather said that the hair stood up on the back of his neck. He didn't want to turn around, but he turned around to see if there was anybody there. But he said that at the time, he told my mom that he felt a chill. That's when he told Mom what Matthew had done, and Mom spanked Matthew. But, I don't know, I thought that was kind of funny.

Jed: Your grandfather told you about that?

James: Mom told me about that. That grandpa told her word for word what happened. Oh, my aunt, my aunt Yessica who's still alive in Uvalde. She was sleeping in the bedroom in the front corner bedroom, spent the night there. There was a rocking chair in that room. She was woken up in the middle of the night by the creakin' of the rocking chair, and she looked and it was my grandfather who had passed away. She just sat there looking, didn't say anything. Covered up, you know? 'Til finally the creaking stopped, and she looked and there was nobody there. And I was askin', "Why didn't you talk to him?" She goes, "I was scared!" And I said, "Should've talked to him, maybe he woulda talked to you back." She goes, "I should've, but he was probably there to see if I was okay." But she actually saw him rocking in the rocking chair. And that, isn't that crazy? And she'll tell you that to this day.

TINA

[I met Tina at her home, where she lives with several pets. She is a Navy veteran and subsequently retired from the Navy Reserve. We sat down at her kitchen table over coffee where I asked her to share her stories of the paranormal.]

Tina: Like here?

Jed: I want to hear all of it.

Tina: I don't know. Honestly, as a kid I can't remember. I'm sure maybe things happened, but I think there's really just more incidents, like a couple, at Mom's house and here.

Jed: Okay. So, what happened at…?

Tina: At Mom's? When I used to live there with Jimmy a long time ago with the kids, and I was going to school at the time—Well, I finally finished. And I was lying in that room where, the front room? The front bedroom, like when you go into the living room, and you turn, its your first right.

Jed: The first right, not the corner.

Tina: I was lying there studying my book. And it was during the day. I was, what, maybe like 34 or something like that. I'm lying there reading my book for school, and I'm facing the hallway, because the bed was facing that way. Then I heard somebody, I heard a voice, calling my name. And I'm sure that's happened to a lot of my family members here, because they've all said that, too. And it was a low voice like, "Tina" *[whispers]*.

Jed: Male or female?

Tina: Like a male. "Tina" *[whispers]*. And I look up from my book, you know, and I'm like—And I'm the type of person that I really have to see something to really get scared or anything. And even scared is not the word, because I don't, I just feel like, okay, there's got to be something. And then I look back down in my book, and then again, couple of times more calling my name. I looked up, and I'm like… I'm there by myself, but it's during the day, the house is lit up and everything. You know, sunny and stuff. I think to myself, okay, I don't know what it is. I don't know who it is, but I'm not going to let it bother me. And I didn't. My other incident—

Jed: When you said you heard the voice, did it sound like it was coming from the hallway, another part of the house?

Tina: To me it sounded like it was coming from the hallway. From out that way. It didn't sound like it was in the room. It sounded more like…

Jed: There was a direction to it.

Tina: Yeah, yeah, like right there, you know, in that hallway right there. It gives me chills just thinking about it. So that was kind of weird, but I'm like, okay, well, I shrug it off. Even here, I just always feel like, okay…

Jed: If there's something threatening…

Tina: But I've never had that yet. Except, God, it's probably been about maybe five years ago. I used to go to Elena's house at night because I was living here by myself. I would call Elena, "Hey, Elena, can I come over and spend the night? I'm going to bring a couple of my dogs." At the time, I only had like three dogs, now I have all these. And she's like, "Yeah." She'd always wait up for me, or we'd stay up talking at midnight or one o'clock.

So anyway, I would sleep in Mom's room, Mom and Dad's room. It didn't—I just didn't want it to bother me, you know? So anyway, one night, I did the same thing. I said, "Hey, I'm coming over. I'm bringing my bag. I'm bringing my couple of Chihuahuas." And she said, "Okay, I'll fix the bed," and stuff. So, after we talked and stuff, I went to Mom's room, and I got ready for bed, and I had probably fallen asleep. It was about one o'clock, I remember getting up to go to the bathroom. And I always slept with the light on in the bathroom. I never turned it off. When I slept in Mom's room? I always had the door cracked and the light on. So I got up to go to the bathroom, and I came back to bed, and I looked at my phone and it was about 1:13, something like that.

I'm like, oh, I got to go to sleep, I'm tired. So, I lay down, and you know how Mom's room is when you go in? The wall is that way, the window's there, the other window's facing the back of the patio, the yard? Well, the bed was pushed against that way, it's not the way it is now. It was pushed against the wall long ways. So okay, I get back into bed and I start getting all comfy and getting ready to go back to sleep. All of a sudden, the bed is like—This is the wall, the backyard and the side of the house facing, you know the neighbor's house *[using her hands to describe the orientation]*.

Jed: So, the two sides of the bed were touching...

Tina: Yeah, the wall.

Jed: The corner of the bed was fit into the corner of the wall.

Tina: Right, like that. Way in the corner. So, I get in bed and all of a sudden, the bed is jerked from the wall like this *[spreads the palms of her hands apart violently]*. And I'm lying in it, and it's like somebody just jerked the bed from the wall.

Jed: How far did it move?

Tina: It probably moved about like this *[holds her hands apart at a slight angle, wrists together and fingers spread]*, maybe. It wasn't like all the way; it was like a jerk. And it was away from the wall.

Jed: Like a foot away from the wall at the far end?

Tina: Maybe, I'm saying that probably...

Jed: These tiles are a foot *[pointing to the floor]*.

Tina: Yeah, yeah. Okay, yeah, something like that. Because I'm like lying on the bed and all of a sudden, it's like a jerk, like that. And I'm like, lying in bed...

Jed: Was it just the mattress, or the entire—

Tina: The entire bed.

Jed: The frame, too.

Tina: The frame. And it was a jerk, Jed, it was a jerk. And I'm lying in bed, and I got my Chihuahuas, and I'm like, okay, what was that? So then, and I said that to myself, and then all of a sudden, it jerks back against the wall. It's like somebody just pushed it back. And, uh, so I laid there.

Jed: When it pushed it back, you were still in the bed.

Tina: Yeah, I didn't even get up. I just like, because I'm trying to figure out what's going on. So then I laid there for a minute, less than a minute, it was seconds. I sat up, and I'm like, okay. So, I got my two Chihuahuas, and I got out of the bed, and I walked slowly out of the room. Because the door was open. I just had a partition so the dogs wouldn't jump over. And I walked over, and I walked all the way around to where Elena and them were. And I told her, "Hey, Elena," I knocked on the door, and she was awake, and I said, "Hey, Elena, something just happened in Mom's room." And she said, "What?" And I said, "The bed just moved away from the wall, and pushed back, and I was lying in bed." I said, "I don't know what happened. I don't know what it was, but it just happened." And she said, "Okay, well, let's go get your stuff and you can come by and lay with me." And then that was it. And after that Jed, I never went back to go and spend the night anymore at Elena's. And if I did, maybe a couple of times, I would lay on the couch. Even on the couch, I felt eerie. I felt like I just was never comfortable, even laying in the living room right there on the couch. And I just stopped.

Jed: Was that mostly after that happened, or you didn't really have any problems before that?

Tina: No.

Jed: Before the bed moved, when you got up, went to the bathroom... Nothing felt off? You just got up.

Tina: Nothing felt off, but I always had a, you know, cautious feeling in that room all the time. You know, anyone who goes in there is feeling something. And even now when I go to the restroom if I'm at Elena's house, if Andrew's in one restroom, she'll say go in the other one. I'll go and I'll leave the door open, you know, 'cause I know nobody's home and stuff. So, I always had that feeling there, you know? There was always something eerie about it. But I wasn't going to let it get to me.

And then that day, it got me. After that, a couple of times when I spent the night at her house on the couch, I just stopped doing it. And, I just don't, you know—But when I go over, of course, we're there and we're talking, and she'll tell me about certain things that are going on. There are noises and stuff like that. But I'll never forget that. Never forget that because that was so real. And I wasn't asleep. Somebody said, "Well, maybe you were like half asleep, and you thought it, you were dreaming it." And I'm like, no, I wasn't asleep. I was getting ready, getting all comfy with my Chihuahuas, and what could have done that?

Jed: How did the dogs react?

Tina: They didn't react like nothing. It was my little Chihuahuas, my two older Chihuahuas. They didn't bark. They didn't do anything. Which was weird, but they didn't do anything.

Jed: That's real weird for Chihuahuas.

Tina: Yeah, yeah, but it's weird because they were quiet. And I think I was just getting all ready to get all cozy with them, and they didn't react to nothing. You know, but then when I sat up, of course they sat up with me. And then I just grabbed them, and we just walked out. Even walking out I just felt like, I'm walking out slowly. You know? Like I felt like there was something, there had to have been something in there. What could make the bed move from the wall? Does the ground shift underneath? What makes a bed move from the wall? Why does the—? What—? How could—? What pushed my bed?

Jed: And then pushed it back.

Tina: Yeah, and then pushed it back. And like you said, it was probably like the size of the tile. It just pushed it away from the wall. It was like letting me know, hey, I'm here. You're not alone, or I'm here. But, that's—Wouldn't that be like a threatening type of force or something, or someone is using force? That's like becoming more physical.

Jed: It's definitely how we take it, I think. But, I mean, it's also like you said, I'm here. But I guess there's no way of knowing, to ascribe intent to something that you can't relate towards.

Tina: It didn't hurt me. It didn't boo, it didn't whisper in my ear, it didn't do anything. It was just physical, moving the bed and moving it back. And I'm like, holy crap, what just happened? Let me go and get Elena. We talked about it then. And I'll never forget that. So really, I don't feel anything else when I've been alone in that house, when I've been there. But Elena and I talk about noises and stuff like that. Yeah.

Jed: So, you said there's also some stuff here *[in her home]?*

Tina: Yeah.

Jed: Basically, here and at that house is where things have happened.

Tina: Yeah. Yeah. Well, okay. When I was overseas doing my deployments, Lilly used to live here. And one time she told me that, I think one New Year's Eve, they had a party here. And her and Kara and all of them were here partying and playing with the tarot cards. And I don't like that, and I'm not into that. But Lilly used to do a lot of tarot cards. And then she says, yeah, we had a party, we were playing this and that. Well, anyway, after that I remember I was here by myself, and I was lying in that room.

I was sitting in there one morning, because I like to get up early and drink my coffee. I didn't have as many dogs, so it was nice and quiet, and I like to just get my coffee and just sit down and watch TV. That's what I like to do. So, I went and sat in the room over there, on the bed. And the bed is right here. And like, here's the wall, and the bed is at the wall and next to it is the closet. And then I have a window right there, facing outside to the patio. So, I was sitting at the edge of the bed, just watching TV, drinking my coffee, and all of a sudden, my hair on this arm starts going up. I'm there and I look at my arm, I look around, but I could feel my hair just going up. And after that happened, I felt like something touching me, up my arm like this. I felt that. I'm sitting there, and I'm like—

Jed: Like a finger or something?

Tina: Yeah.

Jed: Where did it start from?

Tina: Like here. It was just right here.

[Tina touches her forearm with her other hand and slowly draws it up, much like Matthew described.]

Jed: Mid-forearm, up your arm.

Tina: Yeah. But first my hair goes up, and then the touch. And I don't know if that has happened before, been written before, about people feeling their hairs go up and then they feel something. I just sat there and I'm trying to think of the logical things of what is going on, that's how I am. I don't get up, and I don't run out of the room. I just like to figure out, okay, well, I wonder who was touching me, or what was touching me. So that was one incident. And I shrugged it off, because like, I'm the type of person, I don't, you know, there has to be—

Jed: There are other possible reasons.

Tina: Yeah, there are other possible reasons, but I think it has to do, to me, like maybe there was a spirit in there? Because I always felt like maybe there was just bad in there, you know? My girlfriend would tell me I need to get sage and go around and do this, or you need to go and get holy water. Which I would go and put holy water all over the house, because I've done that. And I'm not religious, religious, but I do like my crosses and stuff like that.

Then another incident was in my room. I was lying in my bed late at night, and I was here all by myself. I like to put a partition in my doorway, so my little dogs don't come out. This was a plastic, Plexiglas partition. I was watching TV, late at night, and I had probably accumulated some dogs by then. I was just lying down; it was probably about 11 o'clock at night. And this was probably about, I don't know, maybe three, four years ago. Because that incident happened, what, maybe almost 10 years ago with the room. I had just come back from deployment. So that was in 2007. Well, this thing happened maybe four or five years ago.

I was lying in my bed and watching TV, and I'm by myself, and all my pets are with me on my bed. I didn't have as many pets. I always had Sweetness, and I don't know if I had another cat. My bed faces—For instance, this is my bed, faces the wall, my window's right there, and then my closet, and then the door coming out of my bedroom is right there. And the partitions right there. So, all of a sudden, I heard my partition— You know, like if something had hit it. And it starts, you know, like "doi-yoi-yoing" like that. You know like bouncing, like something had just hit it, and it starts—What do they call it? Vibrating.

Jed: Yeah.

Tina: I heard it, and it was a pretty good sound that hit it, and it's vibrating. And I look, and I get up and I turn on my light, and I'm looking around. I'm like, okay, what was that? What hit it? None of my dogs were there. They couldn't have done that. Sweetness was with me, she doesn't do that, she hardly ever comes out of the room only if someone comes over. So, I can't explain what hit that partition, because it was Plexiglas. It's Plexi, so, it's gonna move. It's vibrating like something hit it, and it's just bouncing back and forth. But it made that noise.

Jed: How did they react when that happened?

Tina: I think we all looked that way. But that was it, but nobody—

Jed: Just looked with surprise.

Tina: Yeah, but they don't, they didn't start howling or barking or anything like that. But right away, you're looking that way, trying to figure out—And my TV was right there next to the door, and so the light from the TV's illuminating towards me, and I could see, but I couldn't—

Jed: There was ambient light over there.

Tina: Yeah. And I'm like, something hit it. I don't know what it was, but something hit it. And I could never figure out what it was or anything. But there have been times here, also, that I hear like… Like I'll tell the dogs, "Stop it!" or stop, or something. And sometimes when the dogs are barking, I don't even say anything, but I could hear someone else say "Stop!" or "Be quiet!" I have heard that.

Most recently, now that I'm home—I don't know what it is, because sometimes when I get home, the dogs look up. I'm sure that I don't know they can see, what I don't see. It's weird, because I've even heard if I'm lying down, I've heard someone say, "Tina!", and it startles me. One time in my room, I remember I was lying in bed and I saw this light illuminating, and it went from one side of the corner, all the way to my ceiling over by my door, bedroom door, and it just disappeared. But it was a light. It was like—And it wasn't a streetlight. It wasn't a headlight. It was like a straight light going like that *[motions across wall]*.

Jed: Like a line of light?

Tina: A line of light. And I don't know what it was. And I'm watching it, you know, and I watched and I'm like… And I always try to find some kind of logic to what's going on. And I look around and I'm thinking, where did that come from? How did—It's not from the outside, because I—You know, the window's here, and it's like a straight thing, you know, like that, and then it disappeared *[uses hands to describe how the light doesn't match the orientation of the window]*. So, those are some things that have happened here. I think more now that I'm home I hear…

Jed: 'Cause you're here more.

Tina: Yeah. I hear more. You know, or I sense things. There is one more thing that happened. I was lying in bed, and all the lights were off. This probably happened a couple of months ago. I woke up all of a sudden and I'm looking towards my hall. Because from my bedroom door, you could look into my little hall right there where my bedroom is at? I felt like I had seen the shadow of somebody, like standing there. And it was small, like this.

[She motions beside her, but it's difficult to gauge the height as she's sitting.]

Jed: Like maybe waist high?

Tina: Yeah, something small. And it's like, they were standing right there on this side of the partition, like looking that way. And when I woke up to look, I don't know what possessed me to wake up and look that way because I'm a very light sleeper. It just kind of like turned around, and went *[inaudible on tape]* and walked out, walked away. And I'm thinking, okay, was that one of the dogs? But my dogs aren't that tall. Even her mommy *[points to medium sized dog]* is not that high, and she was a big dog. It looked more like a slender, slender form.

Jed: Like it was a shadow, but there was depth to it?

Tina: Yeah, it was like a slender—It was dark. It was like a dark... dark image, but it was small.

Jed: And it had the appearance of like, turning around.

Tina: Yeah. The appearance like it, it looked at—Once I looked at it, it turned around and went out. And I'm like, okay, what was that? But I'm like, it couldn't have been the dogs because it was slender, didn't look like a long body like my dogs. I just don't know.

Jed: Tell me again about the pictures you were showing me?

Tina: Oh, yeah. Well, it's so weird, because when that morning—Like I said, I get up every morning, either to take Jacob or whatever to school. Hailey was taking them that morning, so I'm sitting on my bed drinking my coffee already. And I like to take pictures of the cat, of the animals.

So, I started taking a picture of Tom, one of my cats, and I see this light. And I'm like, what's that? It's got to be my phone. So, I did it again and I started to see a form of something. I did it again, and it was coming out more like a cream color type, you know? And I'm like, what is that? I would look at my arm, and it can't be me because it's not my finger. I don't have it in front of me or anything. It looks like it's coming out more and more, and it's like a cream color. It's like a light color, you know. And then I did it again, and it's right there again. And then it forms more, and I'm like, is that a leg or is that an arm? Because you can see it, you know?

Jed: Yeah. When you first showed me the first picture, I didn't know what I was looking at, because I thought I was just—

Tina: It's like a cream-colored form right there.

Jed: Yeah, I thought it was the flash from your phone at first, because it was just so much brighter than what was around it. And I just assumed the blanket was closer to it.

Tina: No.

Jed: Then the next picture I actually thought it was the cat, just the angle changed. And it wasn't till you started showing me the progression, that you can kind of see that...

Tina: Then once I stopped. The last picture of Candy in the crate and it's there too, and then I said, well, let me take another picture of Loki, you know, the yellow cat, and then it was gone. So, it was, uh… I don't know what it was. To me, I think someone was in there.

Jed: And this was all in the same room?

Tina: Yeah, it was that morning. I was sitting on my bed still; I hadn't even moved. I sat there and I'm taking pictures and pictures and pictures to see if it's going to go away. And it finally did when I took a picture of my yellow cat. I'm like, okay, it was somebody in here.

Jed: And my first thought was, okay, when was the next picture taken? How long ago? The first thing you think of, was there something wrong with the camera?

Tina: No, I'm just like—

Jed: And the very next picture—

Tina: I'm even cleaning the lens as I'm doing that.

Jed: Yeah, I like how iPhones tell you the time.

Tina: Yeah.

Jed: So, it was a little more than 15 minutes later, and it just looks like a regular iPhone picture.

Tina: Yeah.

Jed: Did they *[her siblings]* tell you about anything they saw or heard while they were there?

Tina: Where, at the house?

Jed: Sheffield, or in general. Like, for me, I was always interested in that stuff. So, I'd ask my mom every now and then. But I was talking to Carl, and it doesn't seem like he remembered your mom saying anything to him about the house. He said he'd come home and see her blessing the house on occasion. We kind of got the feeling that if anything happened while she was there and everybody was gone, she wasn't bringing it up with you guys.

Tina: I think she would probably say that the spoons would drop, or something. Or a spoon or something would rattle. I remember her talking about utensils. So that was really the only thing I ever heard her talk about. Maybe that's why she liked us sleeping with her when dad was working nights, because she didn't want to sleep in the room by herself. Because we did sleep with her, you know.

Jed: So, when your dad was gone, she would have you sleep with her in the back room?

Tina: Yeah. Yeah, because Carl was still sleeping with her, and then us sisters would take turns sleeping with her. Because we wanted to sleep with Mom, too. But maybe she liked the comfort of us sleeping there, because maybe there were things going on that she'd never really talked about. Like in the room, because I don't remember anything really going on there except, you know, I mean…

When we moved into that house, I was a sophomore. I remember I used to sleepwalk. I did sleepwalk during my teen years. And I remember one night I got up, and Elena was on one bed and I was on the other, and it was in the bedroom where—Not the front one, but the next one in the back? And I remember getting up, and Elena said that I woke her up and she says, "Where are you going?" And I said, "Shut up, or I'll kill you with a knife." So, she said she just covered herself up. So, I got up and I remember, because I sleepwalked, going to the living room door, touching the knob, and then coming back and laying down. And I did sleepwalk several times, but I remember saying that to her, and it was weird, but she said she got scared and she covered herself.

Jed: Do you normally remember when you sleepwalk?

Tina: Well, yeah, because even when I was—I don't do it anymore, but even when I was in elementary, like 10 years old, I would end up being in my brothers' room lying down with them. And I'm like, what am I doing here? Let me go back. I remember sometimes where I would wake myself up, and I wouldn't be where I was supposed to be. Thank God I didn't ever go out of the house, but I did sleepwalk. I don't know why, that was weird.

There was one incident when I was younger, we lived on Rigsby. And I guess that's when your dad and mom met each other, too. Because we were living there, and dad was stationed I think at Kelly, and that was before we went overseas to the Philippines. We were all in that house, and I remember one night we woke up with the sound of like, utensils falling and stuff, and—

Jed: Almost like, as in the drawer?

Tina: In the kitchen. Yes, in the kitchen.

Jed: Like how loud, I mean.

Tina: Like, pull it out, and you drop it, like the rattling.

Jed: Like the silverware drawer.

Tina: Yeah. Yeah. And I remember Mom and Walter, because Walter was there still, and I think your dad and stuff. They all went to the kitchen to see what happened, and nothing. Nothing had happened. So, I think on Sheffield, I think there would be incidents like that. I remember that as a teenager. I think Mom would mention that sometimes.

Jed: She probably wouldn't mention some things because, I kind of realized talking to Carl, my parents might tell me because they know I'm interested. But, if they thought it would scare me, and I was living there, then there would probably be things that they wouldn't tell me so they wouldn't make me feel uncomfortable in my own house.

Tina: Yeah. But everyone's got a story in that house. You know, all of them have a story.

Jed: So, my mom told me about interviews [she had] with your mom, because they both saw me in that first room when you take a right when you come in—

Tina: Oh, when you were a baby, or what?

Jed: Uh, old enough to talk. Because apparently, I had an imaginary friend I talked to. And Mom said she'd even see me looking up and talking to somebody, and writing, and stuff like that.

Tina: Do you remember that?

Jed: I asked my mom if I had an imaginary friend anywhere else. She said, no, just that house.

Tina: Yeah.

Jed: Mainly in that room. Did Grandma ever say anything about the kids, about us doing anything weird, or…?

Tina: Mom never said anything. I remember having problems sleeping, and if I did go to sleep, I remember trying to wake up. And that's when I would feel like these figures would be around me. I don't know what that meant. I don't know why I would have that. And it would scare me, they'd be like hovering over me, and around and stuff. And I remember one time, it was in the evening. I think Charles worked nights and I was by myself and I remember, you know, getting ready to go to sleep and stuff and all of a sudden, I felt like my—I'm lying on my bed, but I felt like I had come out of my body. And I was hovering over the door, you know, the top of the door? In a corner, and I could see myself. It's like my bod—Something just came out and I could see myself lying on the bed.

And I'm like hovering in the corner, and I'm looking down, and I'm thinking to myself, what am I doing up here? Why am I up here? I don't want to be up here; I want to be back in my body. Once I said that, it was like a suction pulled me back into my body. I've read that people have had the same experiences, and the same, the same... You know, description of it. And I'm thinking, it had to have happened to me. I know it did.

Jed: Can you describe specifically what you saw, because you were looking at the room from a different perspective.

Tina: I could see the whole room. But, um, I'm high up. And it's just, it's weird, because... You're not physical, you're just... Something, you know, you're there. Where's your body? It's not here, it's down there. So, what's up here hovering? Mist or what? I don't know, but I just remember that it was like I had just come out, like I had come out of my body and was looking at myself, and it was so weird. But it was like a suction, and it feels like a suction that you're sucked back into your body.

I've read stuff like that, where people can train themselves to do out of body experiences and travel around, and then come back. But that was scary as hell. I was scared. I was like, I don't want to be up here, I want to be back in my body. Once I said that, I was back in my body. I'll never forget that. And I'm thinking, why do things happen to me like this? Why do things happen to certain people? Are they perceptive to— Intuitive? Yeah, so I don't know. It's weird.

CARL

[I interviewed Carl at the home he shares with his wife, Kara. She had heard some of the family stories, and so sat in out of curiosity. I did not code her experiences, but made it clear she was welcome to share any experiences of her own or thoughts on what was shared.

We sit facing each other on the living room couches, on one side the kitchen, on the other the front yard. From the front door the door to the game room is on the right, and the stairs directly ahead.

In this interview are the first mentions of the Flannel Man and individuals whose faces can't be seen.]

Carl: I would say probably what I can remember was back in elementary school. Maybe as young as five years old even. I would hear footsteps in the hallway. But before I start, you know, the neighborhood was a great place to live, because there were so many kids everywhere. We had so many friends in that neighborhood, and it was awesome, so much to do, but it just seemed that when nighttime came, it just turned into something else. You know? And I can remember, even as a kid, starting to get anxiety about it being nighttime because I was going to have to go to bed. And I would hear footsteps and I would have this, just this overwhelming sense of just being watched while I'm lying in bed. I can sometimes feel, uh, something touching me. You know? Poking me? While I'm just lying in bed. And I would start crying or screaming because something would, I would hear something or... Just that sense like I said of being watched or being poked to where I would scream or run to my mother's room and lay in bed with her. And...

Jed: How old were you?

Carl: I was just in elementary school. I mean this happened, stuff like that I can remember. Like I—

Jed: It wasn't a one-time thing?

Carl: No. It was often. It happened so often that when I would just be lying in the room, me and my brother shared a room together, I would hear footsteps down the hallway. Or something just standing in the doorway. And I would get up and I would go lay down with my brother. I would get out of my bed and go lay with my brother, but I actually saw the bed, like somebody was lying on top of the bed after I got up.

This was all as a child. I can remember being so scared one time, you know. My dad worked at night and I went to go to sleep with my mom, like I did a lot, because it just seemed like I was so scared at night, almost every night. And when we're lying in bed, we both could hear... Like there was a group of people in the next room. Like they were just talking, but you couldn't understand what they were saying.

And she even whispered to me, "Mijo, can you hear them?" And I said, "Yes. Mom, what are they saying?" She said, "I don't know." And it just sounded like there was a group of people in the den, just having a conversation. It was just the weirdest thing, and I could just remember going to sleep.

Another time as a kid, again in elementary school, I was going to bed and I put my hand under the pillow, you know, just to get comfortable. While my hand was being grazed under the pillow, I felt another hand underneath the pillow. I jumped out of bed, and I was just trying to— Even as a kid, I was just like rationalizing with myself, what the hell was that and...

Jed: Trying to tell yourself you grabbed your own hand.

Carl: Yes. So, I just went back to bed. But, again, to this day I don't know... It felt like just a cold hand. And I just went to sleep. But the scariest thing when I was maybe five or six years old is seeing the hag in the doorway. And waking me up and just screaming after I saw it. And it just disappearing. You know, telling me to come to it, but it wouldn't cross the threshold of the door because of the cross. It was pointing at me and then it would point at the cross, and telling me to come to it, and you know it was, uh—

Jed: What woke you up?

Carl: Just the sense of being watched. I could remember just waking up and looking down the hallway. And seeing a silhouette of who I thought was my sister Rose, because my sister Rose had really frizzy hair at the time. It seemed just not combed or anything, and it was just like standing there, motionless. And I asked it, "Rose?" Because I thought it was my sister, I said, "Rose, what are you doing?" And still no answer. All of a sudden, it just kind of crouched down a little bit and it started pointing at me, to tell me to come to it, and just kept doing that motion at me. It would point up at the cross that was over the threshold of the door, and then it would tell me to come towards it, and... For some reason, I just started screaming. You know, because it kept doing that. Then it seemed to get startled from my scream and just disappeared.

Jed: You said it seemed to get startled, how could you tell?

Carl: Because the way it turned, and the way it like kind of looked or something. It was just weird. That was one of the things, too, is that when I started to scream, it just kind of like—Even though I only saw a silhouette, I could see some sort of reaction from my screaming and then it just faded away. Because then I heard Beaver barking, and he was outside.

When I was in elementary school, I could remember the whole family watching TV in the living room. We were all in there watching TV, and all of a sudden, we just hear running across the roof of the house. Boom, boom, boom, boom, boom, boom, boom! My dad got up real fast and my brother got up real fast, and they went searching around the house. They couldn't hear, they couldn't see anything. But that happened at night, too, late at night. A couple of times we heard footsteps running across the roof, and then waking up and my dad even going outside. I could see the flashlight outside, and him with Beaver. Or it could have been lady at the time.

But this was all when I was in middle school. It seemed that when I got older, as I got older, it seemed like I kinda wasn't afraid anymore. I would see stuff in the corner of my eye. One time I saw a man in red, like a red plaid shirt. I couldn't see his face. He was in the hallway, just walking across the hallway. And it was real quick, but I knew, I remember the red.

Another time I had stayed home from school and was lying in bed. So, I was about 17 maybe, and I just didn't go to school one day. It wasn't because I was sick, I remember I just played hooky. I was petting my cat and she was just, he was just lying on top of me. I was watching TV and all of a sudden, my cat just went *[motions like cat shooting off and away from him]* like, you know, freaked out, and it hissed and scratched me, and it ran off and out of the room. I looked up to see what it was, what it was afraid of. And I saw that same man that I had seen before. Couldn't see his face. Red and black plaid shirt. And it was just the top of his body. And I turned around again, and I ran, and he was gone, and I ran outside, just to see, and there was no one there. 'Cause it was right there in the corner room of the house. The corner front room. And I ran outside real quick and there was nothing there. Because I knew what it was, because I couldn't see his face. If you see somebody, you're going to see some traits of their face. But it was just a blur. So...

Jed: Was that always your room?

Carl: Yeah. Pretty much.

Jed: The front corner, looking at it?

Carl: Well, as a kid it was like the one where Elena's in right now. That front corner room used to be Grace's. The one next to it was Lilly's. The one where Elena and Ray stay right now next to the bathroom used to be mine and my brothers'. But as I got older it didn't bother me anymore being in the house. I could be in the house. Every once in a while, I'd be in the other room and you'd hear like a door slam. And, like when you're home alone and you just look over there and—I just wasn't afraid anymore. I came back and I actually lived in the house. I feel like I was maybe 21? Off and on until I got my first apartment.

Nah, I was probably like 20 when I got my first apartment. But when I was in my late teens after Mom passed away and stuff, I lived there for about a good year by myself. And during that year, thank God, I didn't see nothing really. Nothing ever happened, I didn't see anything. Yeah, I got this sense when I was living there by myself that I was just being watched. And what I would do is, I would go get Andrew *[Elena's son]*, 'cause Andrew lived across the street, and Lucas *[my and Andrew's cousin]*, who lived like two streets away, and they would come stay the night. Or they would even stay a week. And I had a thing with them that you can do whatever you want, just clean up, and they cleaned up after that. So, I didn't have to worry about them. So basically, they stayed with me a lot of the times.

Jed: Did they know why you were having them over?

Carl: Oh yeah, oh yeah. Because even Andrew will tell you, and Lucas will tell you that—You know, that's their story, but one of 'em was washing dishes, and the other one, while he was washing dishes got tapped and they both met in the hallway. Nothing ever happened, except every once a while I would spook myself or, like I said, Andrew and Lucas would come and stay with me for a little bit. And a girl that I was seeing at the time, she got spooked real bad 'cause she said that when she was in the bathroom putting on her makeup somebody was on the other side of the doorway in the bathroom. And it was like they were pulling on the door, and rattling the door, like they wanted to get in and she thought it was me. She thought it was me and she opened the door, and nobody was there. I was on the other side of the house. So that was it as far as, the extent there within my twenties and whatnot and really didn't see much.

But, a couple of times since then I had gone over to Elena's just to go say hi or whatever, and I've sat at the kitchen table talking to her. In the corner of my eye, I'll see something walk across in the backyard. Or I'll see something, a shadow, walking down the hallway. I'll look real fast, and she's like, "Did you see something?" I'm like, "Yeah, I thought I saw a shadow." And then one time we both saw the same shadow walking across in the backyard. Kara was actually with me one time when we were there, and we saw a shadow walking in the backyard. And was it a shadow that we saw, and then we got up?

[Kara asks first if I want her to speak, and I let her know I would like her perspective of experiences she's shared with Carl and Elena.]

Kara: Elena had been telling us that there were shadows going back and forth, and when we walked in, we were like, oh really? And then we looked at the back door and thought we saw a shadow. So, we walked up to the door and pulled the curtain back and we're looking back, and then the handle to the door rattled. We were both standing there, and there was nobody in the backyard. And we were just like, oh, okay...

Carl: After I grew up and moved away, I met Kara, and then we moved to an apartment on Vandiver. They had always talked about seeing and hearing stuff, which I didn't. The only time I ever did was one time I was watching TV, and it sounded like somebody was sitting on the leather couch. You know, when the sound of leather moves? Sounded like somebody was sitting on the chair. While I was lying across the couch watching TV, it sounded like somebody was sitting down. And then we moved to Burns and nothing ever happened on Burns. That was in that house, was pretty peaceful it seemed.

And then we moved here, and the two things I've seen here is, I saw—I was sleeping. I remember I was sleeping, and I could have been dreaming, but it can't be if Andrew and Kara have also seen the shadow person. Anyway, I felt like I was being watched and I woke up, and I'm looking down the—Our bathroom is in our master bedroom, and I'm looking at—I just keep looking in this area and I see a shadow person crouched down on the floor in the bathroom. And it sees me, and he starts crawling towards me real fast. And I just started screaming, like, holy shit! And I know I was awake, 'cause I saw this thing coming towards me and I started screaming. And I wake up Kara *[laughs]*. I wake up Kara and her reaction to me is like, *[makes a shushing sound]* "Just go to sleep, go to sleep, it's okay." Like it's, because I think she was just asleep and I'm like, but, I just thought...

Kara: I thought you were just having a bad dream.

Carl: I just saw something, and it was—And then I just couldn't sleep the rest of the night.

Jed: Were you able to move?

Carl: Yeah! I was able to move, because I felt this thing coming towards me, even I felt it get on the bed. And then I just jumped back, and I, you know...

Jed: It wasn't like the sleep paralysis, where you're trying to move your pinkie or something?

Carl: No. I was, I was—Because I remember I was awake, and I was just focusing, just focusing my eyes in the bathroom. And that's when, after focusing, I'm just looking and looking and then I see it. And when you talk to Andrew, Andrew was sleeping right here, we had the couch this way, Andrew said he woke up 'cause he felt like somebody was watching him and he said he woke up, and he said right here *[points to an area between the living room and kitchen]*, he said that he saw something just looking at him, and it was crouched down. And he said it was just looking at him and it just stood up, turned around, and just faded away.

Kara: Yeah, I saw that shadow person standing in the bedroom and just watching me sleep, and I jumped up and started kicking and screaming just like Carl did when he saw it. And then we had the incident where we heard each other calling each other.

Carl: Yes. We, I was upstairs taking a shower, and I heard—It was Kara's voice, plain as day. And I, she was calling me, and I'm like, "What? I'm in the shower!" Because I kept hearing her say, "Carl! Carl!" And anyway, I got out of the shower, I started drying off real quick, the best I can, and I came outside, and I said, "What?" And then—Kara'll finish this right.

Kara: I was in the kitchen and I heard Carl calling me, "Kara! Kara!" And he doesn't usually call me Kara, he calls me babe or something. So, if he calls me Kara, I think he's mad. So, I was just like, great. And I storm upstairs, and he's just coming out of the shower as I'm coming in the bedroom and we're both like, "What?!" And neither one of us had been calling each other. And we kind of just stared at each other for a minute, and I said, "Oh, hell no. There's not a ghost in my house." So, I storm downstairs, and I said, "Whoever's in this house needs to leave right now, you're not welcome in my house." And the motion sensor light on the porch went on, as if somebody had walked out the front door.

Jed: Was this after you had seen the shadow man?

Kara: No, that was before. That wasn't, not, we hadn't been living in the house very long when that happened.

Jed: When you saw the shadow man, what woke you up? Was it like the same sensation?

Kara: It was that feeling that somebody was watching you. Yeah.

Jed: Did you pick it up right away? Or was it looking around? Or...

Kara: No. I woke up, like focused right on it, it was standing kind of like, catty-corner to the foot of the bed. And it was just, it was standing up. It wasn't crouched or creepy, it was just standing there. And when I jolted and started kicking and screaming it just wasn't there anymore.

Carl: And I would say it was probably a year ago, when we were sitting here on the couch—Was it about a year ago? When we saw the orb? The ball? Come out of—?

Kara: It was about six months after my dad died.

Carl: Okay. So, we're sitting here on the couch.

Kara: It was about a year and a half.

Carl: Right. So, we're sitting on the couch and the TV was facing this way. The TV was on the side of the wall. We're on the couch, and all of a sudden, I see this ball that's coming out of this room going towards the TV *[pointing to a spot on the wall between the door to the game room and the staircase]*, and it goes up, like it disappears in the stairwell. And I don't say anything to Kara, and I just look, and then we both looked at each other. And one of us said, did you see that? And she saw it, too. And we were like—

Kara: The door was open, and it's pitch black in there when the light's not on, 'cause there's no windows. And the TV was right here, so we were basically like staring at the doorway. You know, 'cause it was right in our sight. And I, I see the ball of light, kind of like manifest? In the room? And it wasn't like bright, bright. It was dim. But, it was about that big *[spreads palms apart]*. It was flashing, like pulsing?

Jed: You say that big *[I try to mimic her spreading her hands apart]*, it was like about what, a foot across?

Kara: Yeah, I'd say about a foot across.

Carl: It was big.

Kara: Circular.

Carl: It really was so strange.

Kara: It wasn't just like this little wispy thing.

Carl: It wasn't a little thing that you see on TV. It was a ball of light. That was just so smooth—

Kara: And it was flashing, and it moved from the middle of the room, through the doorway, it went behind the TV.

Carl: Behind the TV.

Kara: And then it went up the stairs.

Carl: And I would say a little bit after that, not long after that, is when we saw that, looked like smoke or something.

Kara: It was a mist.

Carl: It was like a mist. It was so strange, same thing. Same spot and everything. And we can't be sure, but it was after her dad passed away. We always thought that it was her dad coming to see us or something. We don't know. We don't know. But something just the other day— This happened what, last week?

Kara: Last week.

Carl: I went into this room because I was looking for something *[points to same room the orb appeared from],* that's our game room. I went in there and I saw my hat that I use outside, because it's a big sombrero, when I'm cutting the grass or whatever. It was on the floor, and I reached to pick it up, and when I reach for it a gust of cold air came at me, and it hit my arm. It didn't come at my face, it hit my arm while I was reaching and uh... Didn't scare me. I wasn't afraid, it wasn't anything like that. But the door was shut, because I didn't want any cats going in there. So, I stood there after it happened and I was like, what was that? You know, in my head I'm trying to rationalize, I'm just trying to recreate a gust of wind coming through there, but can't, because there's an opening under the door so there's constantly air going through there. But I open the door a couple of times and I shut it fast, just to see if I can recreate some sort of, you know, air current, something in there.

Kara: But there's no A/C in there.

Carl: And there's no A/C in there, there's no air, you know. And I went by the vent to see if there's any air coming through the vent, and there's no air coming through the vent. I'm like, what was that? I just started thinking, because it was a—Jed, it was the weirdest thing. It was a cold whoosh. Because I was reaching for it, and it hit me right here *[gesturing toward arm],* and it was just the weirdest thing. But it didn't, I wasn't afraid. I even stood there for a few, because I tried to debunk it or whatever, and I couldn't. And not to say that it couldn't have been some draft that was building up or whatever. I don't know, but it was just the strangest thing. I wasn't afraid, like I said, and I even put away a couple of things while I'm in there. Because I go in there all the time to go play

PlayStation, and I'm never afraid when I go in there. So, whatever it was, I don't know.

Jed: Stuff like that ever happen to you before you were around Carl?

Kara: Yeah. I mean, not real—Let me think.

[She's silent a moment.]

Kara: I really don't think so. I grew up hearing a lot of ghost stories. You know, I'm a ghost story enthusiast. My mom would tell stories about her childhood, but... I don't think anything really ever happened to me until we got married. And then, there was just one separate incident when I was with my mom and Carl wasn't there. That was, like, the scariest thing.

Jed: What was that?

Kara: Well, I was helping my mom move out of her house in Brownwood and she was going to come live with us. So, it was just me and my mom, my dad was in the hospital. We were in the house just packing and fixing things that our realtor told us to fix so that we could sell the house. My mom had taken to sleeping in the guest bedroom 'cause she was afraid to sleep in the master bedroom. She didn't tell me why. We always had trouble sleeping there when we'd come visit. Just like, you'd see things out of the corner of your eye. My mom has, like, a ghost cat that follows her. Sometimes you would think you see a cat.

Anyway, she put me to sleep in that master bedroom. And I was scared to death. I just had the creepiest feeling. I didn't want to sleep in there, I was trying to sleep with the light on. And my mom's TV was in there, and suddenly the TV comes on by itself. And it's just, static? Like, and the volume was all the way up. I jolted out of bed, because it was super loud. I was looking for the remote control, because I thought maybe I rolled over on the remote. It was on the nightstand, so I turned the TV off, and turned it back on again. And... She had DirecTV at the time, so when you turn the TV on, it just says DirecTV. You know, with a black screen? There's no reason why it would be static. Like the TV never—

Like when do you ever see a TV with static on it anymore? It always is either just black or it'll say Spectrum, or DirecTV, or whatever. I thought that was really weird.

So, I ran out of there, and went and got in bed with my mom, and told her what had happened. My mom's in the other room, sleeping with the TV on and the light on. Because she said she can't sleep in the dark, and she has her two Chihuahuas in the bed. I'm scared to death. And then my mom's just sitting there like not—She wasn't asleep, she's not sleeping. And then her two Chihuahuas get up and walk to the corner of the bed and start growling at the bedroom door. And I'm telling my mom, "Do you see this? Do you see this?" And she's just got the covers up over her face. And then the bedroom door opens. There's nothing there. I was scared to death. I called Carl in the middle of the night, he told us just start saying the Lord's prayer, which we did. And I don't think I slept at all.

Carl: Something that happened about five or six years ago at Kara's mother's house. I have a hat, a Spurs hat, that I've had for years. It's my favorite hat. I even lost it in the ocean and I ended up finding it two hours later in the waves. Who, how, what are the chances of you finding your hat that gets—Anyway, my favorite hat.

Well, we're in Brownwood and I'm looking for my hat and I can't find it anywhere. We're getting ready to leave. I knew I had it right there in the bedroom with my stuff. It was just missing. I was like, "Mom, if you see my hat, put it away. It's around here somewhere." And Jed, I must have looked six times going back and forth. Look under the bed, look at—I mean, I looked everywhere for that hat for the longest time. And Kara's mom was living there by herself at that time, because my father-in-law was already in the nursing home.

And we went back, like I said, maybe six times later, could have been months later. And my hat was in the middle of that floor in that bedroom. It was just sitting there on the floor and I said, "Mom! What?" She came over there and she's like, what? She goes, "Oh look! There's your hat." And I said, "I know, I see my hat, but what is it doing just right there on the floor?" She goes, "I have no idea. I don't know how it got there." I said, "Mom, do you know how many times I've looked around this room looking for this hat, and here it is in the middle of the floor?" And she's like, "I don't know what to tell you."

Kara: It happened with Tom's wallet, as well. It disappeared, and then a couple trips later, it was just right there on the floor in plain sight.

Carl: Yeah.

Kara: But I don't know. I always thought it was kind of related, because my mom grew up in a haunted house. So, stuff happens to her all the time. Carl grew up in a haunted house, stuff happens to him all the time.

Jed: That's one of the things that I'm curious about, there are places where things seem to happen more often like the house on Sheffield, or at your mother's house.

Kara: Uh huh.

Jed: But then, there's also people that things seem to happen to more often than other people, and it might not just be at that location, and then it might be more than other people at that location. So...

Carl: You know, I think growing up and stuff, I've always been, I've just always had this feeling that I can, I don't know, sense things or something? I think even now as an adult I think I'm very intuitive of people's feelings and what they're doing. Me as a salesperson, I can pick up on people, the way they feel, and it'll change my whole dynamic of my sales pitch when I go to visit somebody, just—My being, knowing, what they're feeling at that time there. And I think that's a plus for me. But, uh... I think I'm really good as far as, you know, judging the way people's, you know, feelings and how they're—

Kara: When he decides he doesn't like somebody he knows in the first five seconds.

Carl: Yeah.

Kara: And they don't get a second chance.

Carl: That's probably true, too, but other than that, I can't really think of anything else that's happened to me over the years. I think living in that house as a child, I feel like the things that I've seen over the years living there, I think I feel like it kind of stole away a little bit of my childhood. You know, especially seeing that hag in the doorway. Even to this day, it's like one of the scariest things I've ever seen in my life. And I—

Jed: You couldn't see specific details because it was dark.

Carl: Exactly. But just that whole...

Jed: The form.

Carl: The feeling, and—I don't know if you ever have seen the Conjuring Part Two, and that one episode where that little girl is in the room. It feels like I can relate to that whole scene, because I've been there. I've been to where I've seen and heard stuff coming towards my bed, and I've felt being touched and...

Kara: Or where she hears the footsteps and then feels something breathing.

Carl: Yes. I feel like I've, you know, I've been there and it's just, as a kid sometimes it was horrifying at night. But other than that, it was a great place to grow up as far as the friends and stuff that you had, and all the fun that we had, too.

Kara: He's such a positive person.

Jed: Everything except the terror.

[Laughing]

Carl: But, anyway, I guess that's about it.

Jed: How about, like I told Dad, I can't ask Grandma anything. Did she ever tell you anything about things she saw or heard? Not just there, but any of the other places that you've moved?

Carl: Now, the thing that I remember about my mother is that we had where we heard the voices together. She must have seen stuff, too, because I would come home, and she would be blessing the house. And that happened several times that I would see her walk around saying prayers and she'd be blessing the house. So, I know that she must have heard or seen stuff, 'cause she was there by herself during the day when we weren't.

Jed: She just never told you about it.

Carl: I don't remember ever asking her anything about any. Like I said, we shared that one moment of hearing the voices, and she would get holy water to bless the house, and it was... Yeah.

Jed: Did she ever say anything about us kids when she was watching us?

Carl: No, I don't believe that she ever did that. I can't remember who it was, one of the nephews and nieces, that they would see something, or they talked about seeing somebody, or... But, no. I just know that she had to have seen or heard something for her to go around saying prayers and blessing the house.

Kara: Did you ever come home, and your mom was just hanging out outside? Like she didn't want to be in the house alone?

Carl: No. No.

Kara: That's what my mom would say, when she grew up in the haunted house? Like when she would come home, her mom was always on the front porch. Like she didn't ever want to be in the house by herself.

Carl: No. My mother, she was—When I would come home, dinner was already cooking or something. No, I don't think we ever talked about it. She knew, she must've, because she heard us talking about it. She heard everybody else talking about it. I just don't remember.

Jed: When you were living there by yourself, was there ever anything with the lights? Like in the kitchen or anything?

Carl: No. And you know like I said, I feel like it was Mom maybe protecting me the whole time I was there. I, uh, I didn't. Jed, I was by myself in that house, and for a year or whatever... I know for some reason after my mom passed away and after I moved away, that the house was empty for a time. And my mother had a Pekingese, her name was Princess, and my dad for some reason still had her in the house. That he would tie her up in the house, in one area of the house, and Elena would go over there daily to let her loose and let her outside and feed her, which was—I don't know why he did that. Thank God Lilly took her one day and she lived like a queen for the remainder, you know, how many years it was after that. I know she lived to be a ripe old age.

[Carl is referring to Princess being leashed to one area of the house. In truth it was not as restrictive as the current practice of crating animals, but as an animal lover it frustrates him. Moreover, the idea of her being left alone in the house specifically makes him uncomfortable because of his own experiences there.]

But, I know one story that Elena told me is that she... When she went over there to go check on Princess—Was it Princess or Diane? Any— Yeah, okay, it was Princess. That she went across the street, because this is when Elena still lived across the street. When she opened the door, she heard people just talking in the other room, and she heard Princess barking. When she went inside, all the pictures were turned, and she went, and she—That's when I think they got Princess out of the house. It makes me mad knowing that that dog was by herself in that house, for who knows how long. Yes, she was being taken care of, yeah, she was being given water, yeah, she had food and could move around, but she was alone, and that's what—It breaks my heart thinking about it. But, yeah... But other than that, you know, ask me more questions.

Kara: So, you were so afraid of the house that you thought it was cruel to leave the dog in there?

Carl: Yeah. I thought it was horrible, that she—I mean, they say that animals sense things that we can't, so who knows what she was seeing by herself. Can you imagine that little Pekingese by herself? That's horrible. Anyway. So, what else you got?

Jed: Who was it that they were sleeping and someone was tickling their feet?

Carl: That's actually Grandpa. And I think it was Grace, also.

Kara: And Tina.

Carl: Tina. Tina would stay there, too. Tina stayed with Elena; this was up until recently. You're going to have to get Tina's story on it, but I know when she was staying in that room. While she was sleeping in there one time the whole bed just went *[makes a sound and motions like the bed is moving across the floor]* while she was sleeping on it. While she was sleeping, the whole bed moves away from the, you know...

Jed: The wall?

Carl: The wall. And she was like, what? And then she got her feet tickled. Grandpa.

Kara: And now your dad's new wife. Oh. This is a story that we heard the other day. Is that Dad's new wife Nancy, while she's sleeping, she gets awakened at night by something knocking on the door—On the wall right next to her while she's sleeping. Three knocks, knock, knock, knock. And then it'll go away. Knock, knock, knock. And it'll like wake her up like that. And she says, if it's *[laughs],* she says, if it's his ex-wife, you know, "She's in for a rude awakening, because I'm not leaving anywhere." She's pretty funny. We like Nancy. But, uh, yeah.

ROSE & LILLY

[I met Rose in the kitchen of her home. Lilly is able to meet at the same time, so for their convenience I conduct the interview with both of them simultaneously. As someone who was periodically there while my grandmother babysat me, Rose provides more details regarding stories of myself and the supposed Flannel Man.

She'd previously said she hadn't had many paranormal experiences, so I ask her to begin by telling me about the phone call.]

Rose: This happened after Mom passed, not too long after. The phone rang, and I just remember reaching over and picking up the phone and thinking, who's calling at this time of night? It probably had been maybe two o'clock in the morning. So, I answered it and I said, "Hello?" And I heard, "Rose?" And I said, "Mom?" And she goes, "Yes, it's me, Mom—" No, she goes, "Yes, Rose." And I go, "Mom! Mom, where are you?!" I can't remember exactly what I said, but she just says, "Rose, I wanted to let you know that I'm okay, and I love you." And I'm like, "Mom, Mom." Makes me want to cry. And I go, "Mom, wait Mom, wait." And she's like, "I love you. I love you." And her voice just faded off. It's very emotional because I forgot about that. But here's the thing. The next morning, I woke up and I thought it was just a dream. My partner then, she says, "Hey, who called you last night?" And I said, "What?" She goes, "The phone rang and you answered it, but who was it?" And I said oh my God, you know, so... The phone rang, and I answered it... But I forgot all about that, Lilly.

Lilly: I didn't. That's one of the stories that I don't forget that we've talked about.

Rose: But as far as...

Jed: Well, the only reason I know about it is because Dad was telling me that he had dreamt that he'd spoken to her, got a phone call, and I think he had said that Elena had told him you'd had the same dream. What did my dad tell you about it?

Rose: You know what, I haven't talked to your dad about it, but I did talk to Elena. The thing about it is that it happened so quickly. It was almost like she was fading away as clear as when we started? But fading away. And all I wanted to know was, "Wait, Mom, where are you, Mom?" And she just started to fade away, the conversation faded away. But I was—Where did I live? I lived over on... Blackburn? I lived over on the West side at another house, it wasn't in this area. But you know, me and Mom were really tight. I mean, constantly together. So... you know, it just happened soon after, so I'm glad it did. But, at first when you wake up, you're thinking, oh, I dreamt about my mom, because I always thought about my mom. But for my partner to say, "Hey, who called?" Up to that point I think I really hadn't had any type of experiences like that in the house. Nothing had ever happened to me. Lilly—

Lilly: She was kind of a non-believer.

Rose: Yeah, I was always the one that like, "Nah, that didn't happen," or, "Maybe you were asleep? Maybe that was a dream." I'd always try to, you know—

Lilly: Justify it.

Rose: Yeah, whenever Lilly would tell me something happened, I'd be like, hmm.

Jed: How old are you guys in relation to Carl and—

Rose: Oh, I'm 56. Lilly's—

Lilly: I'm eleven years older than Carl. I'm going to be 58.

Jed: Okay, to me you guys are just... Like my mom, I didn't know how old she was, and she told me, and I was like...

[Laughing]

Lilly: How old is your mom?

Jed: I think 63?

Rose: Yeah, yeah. I always think of your mom as young, too.

Jed: Did Carl ever talk to you about things? Because Carl was telling me stuff, and I was under the impression that he was actually pretty scared there when he was young, and he kind of... Didn't grow out of it, but things stopped happening as he grew older.

Rose: I think maybe Carl might have told you that story about when he was in the bedroom. When he would sleep, he would always sleep with Mom and Dad. (To sister) Remember? I think that scared Carl a lot.

Jed: Yeah, it did.

Lilly: Yeah, but you know things happen at Carl's house, too.

Jed: Yeah, he told me.

Lilly: Did he tell you about the shadow person with Andrew?

Jed: Yeah. But, let's first talk about the things specifically that you saw. About how old were you—

Rose: At Mom's house?

Jed: No, the things that you experienced.

Rose: Oh! Well, really not too much there at the house, the only thing that I started to experience was a few years ago, maybe... What'd I tell you, about four years ago? I was getting out of work, that's when I had the rotating shift, and I got out of work probably about three something in the morning, because it was still early. Maybe even 3:45. I was getting out of my truck and I park right in the front of the house, right here with my white pickup truck. My routine is just to have my bag in the middle of the seat. I'll go ahead and grab my bag and put it on me, get everything like my hardhat in there. And from the corner of my eye, I saw a shad— A dark figure. I thought it was a person, you know? I just saw a dark figure walking. So right away, I turn, and I look catty corner that way.

Jed: It would have been on the sidewalk?

Rose: It would have been on the sidewalk, yeah, just someone walking on the sidewalk.

Jed: You were parked and would have been pointed in that direction?

Rose: Uh-huh, the person was coming from that—

Lilly: Across the street.

Rose: Exactly. My first thought was like, who in the heck is out at this time of morning? So, I grabbed my bag, I turned, and I look, and I saw that—I saw from the corner of my eye, so when I looked, nothing there. By the time it would have taken someone who did walk... those steps, at the pace that that figure was walking, not fast, not running, but walking? I got my bag, got my keys, I shut my door. Right here, this house. Catty corner the opposite way. Their basketball goal, you know, one of those portable ones? Just fell over *[makes crashing sound]*. Real loud. And I was able to turn, and with the light on that side I would have seen anyone running away, walking away, nothing.

Jed: There's lights in those houses that would have made silhouettes.

Rose: Uh huh, that I would have been able to see. Not just did I hear it, but it knocked over. It was down. My first thought was, who knocked it over? Then second, there's no wind. Nothing. Nothing to make that fall over. So, I grab my bag and I come in. That scared me, because I saw something walking. And then that knocking it over? And not anything being there? I felt that was meant to scare me, you know? And it did. So, I came in the house right away.

The other thing, this was in 2010 maybe? Yeah, I'm thinking maybe 2010. Aria *[her partner]* goes to Chicago, she's from Chicago so she goes and she's with her mom, and I was alone in the house and at the time I had a little dog. Sammy? And then I had a dog named Trishy. Trishy was a taller, white terrier. Sammy was a short little Schnauzer-something-terrier mix. You know, with the long tail? And he just always wanted to play. Like if he was here right now, he'd bring you a toy and drop it in front of you. He had a habit of holding these squeaky toys in his mouth and he would be squeaking the toy, that's how he'd get your attention.

So anyway, we were asleep and... I was asleep and Sammy would always sleep on the bed with me. And Trishy, because she was bigger and she just didn't like to sleep with me, she would sleep on the floor. Yeah, she would sleep on the floor on the little rug that I had on the side of the bed. So, my room is set up like this, Jed, where my bed is this way. The closet door is there, and my bathroom is there, on the left side of me.

Jed: The closet's at the foot of the bed.

Rose: Foot of the bed.

Jed: The bathroom is at the head of your bed, to your left.

Rose: Right, exactly. So, I'm asleep. I'm sleeping really good, but I wake up because I hear Sammy's squeak toy squeaking. Squeak squeak, his tail's wagging. Remember he had that long tail that he'd just whip around, and I feel the bed moving because of this. He's so happy, he's moving the bed. And my first thing is, "Sammy, go to sleep." You know, because what are you doing? I never even open my eyes. A couple seconds later he's doing it again. "Sammy!" Couple seconds later. "Sammy, go to sleep!" And at this point, because this's the third time I've had to tell him, that's when I get up. And I was going to move him or do something. But when I opened my eyes, at the closet, I see a white figure. I wouldn't say it's glowing, but it's light enough to where I could see it. It's almost like... Almost like a mist, but also a form.

I could make out the head, and I could make out an eye. You know? And it was almost like it was facing sideways. I could only see one side of it. And it seemed like it was kind of tall or raised. At this point, I'm looking and Sammy is looking right at it. He's at the edge of the bed facing this figure, squeaking his toy, wagging his tail. And whatever it is, it got his attention and he wanted to play with it. He wanted it to play with him. So, I'm sitting up in bed and my first thought was, okay, what is that? And I'm thinking, Trishy, what are you doing? And I'm thinking she's like maybe stretched herself up at first, because I see the white form first and she's a white dog. So, right away I'm looking at it, and I look down and I grab below, and I feel Trishy. She's laying by my side.

I start to look at it *[the misty form]* and that's when I see the eye, and I say that's not Trishy. I'm trying to figure out what this is, and it starts to move slowly across the room. Sammy is following it at the foot of the bed still, with his toy squeaking, squeak squeak, you know? I'm just sitting in bed watching it, too, and it's going across the room toward my bathroom. Sammy is following it all this time. I don't even think it woke Trishy up. I don't remember Trishy getting up or anything. But the form was—It went past me, and it went into the bathroom. Sammy jumped off the bed, he went to the bathroom door and stood there wagging his tail.

Jed: Was the door open or closed?

Rose: It was open, I always had the door open. And you know what? The thing is that my room wasn't pitch black. I always had a little light coming in through the—I have an outside light. And I think that I could see enough to where my eyes adjusted, and I could see the form, and then I could see Sammy, and then I probably felt him and saw him jump off the bed, and he's at the door. At this point, whatever it was it went into the bathroom. I felt like, well, of course I got to get up. I went over and I flipped on the bathroom light real quick, and there's nothing in there. Sammy's still wagging his tail, still the toy in his mouth. He walks in, he's looking at the bathtub, the shower. The shower curtain's closed and um, as scared as I was, Jed, my heart's beating, everything? I knew I had to go find out what it was, was it in there? So, I go in there and I just pull the shower curtain back. Nothing there, but Sammy goes up and he's looking inside the shower area, and then he's like, okay, it's gone. He turns around, just walks out, and goes back on the bed. And I'm wide awake.

I go and I make a phone call real quick, and I'm calling Aria and I'm like, something just happened in my room, I'm scared, blah blah blah. And she's, "Go to the living room, you'll be okay." And she's the one that said, if Sammy wanted to play with it, it probably wasn't a bad thing, but go in the living room and sleep in there. But after I thought about it for a bit, I'm thinking, okay, if I would have just got up and I saw something there, I probably would have just covered my head and gone back to sleep or something, because I'm thinking I'm dreaming. But Sammy wanted to play with it. Sammy jumps off the bed. He's waking me up. He goes into the bathroom. By this time, I'm totally awake. And that's the first time I ever saw, I think, a ghost. Because I had never seen a ghost before, or a figure, or whatever it was. I've never seen anything. And before that, I still had that um... That idea that people just saw things because maybe they weren't fully awake, or... Whatever.

Jed: Or weren't paying attention.

Rose: Or something. I mean, even with Mom coming to me, I felt that was different maybe? But actually seeing it, and having the dog physically see it and jump off the bed and all that, that's when I knew something was there that we just didn't see. Or just didn't think it was there, that it was actually there. And then seeing that thing, and then having that basketball goal knocked over. The noise was scary itself. That's when I know there's things out there that we don't... Always see? But they're there. So those are the two things that I could say happened personally to me. But as far as family members, I've always heard stories.

Lilly: Like when I lived on Sheffield. Remember I lived like a couple houses from Mom's house? Me and Carl were sharing a house and I'd always hear these kids playing. I would always take care of my yard, and I'm like, who's playing in my yard? And I would look outside and there was nobody ever there, and I could just hear giggling and giggling. And Carl even heard giggling and stuff. Then one day I was in the living room and I heard this little girl playing this clapping game *[Lilly claps a rhythm]*. I don't remember the game anymore, but I tell Carl, "Carl, what are you watching?" And I don't remember what it was, and then I said, "What channel were you on where those girls were playing the clapping game?

Remember this song?" And I repeated it to him. He goes, I wasn't watching nothing like that.

So, I looked in my bedroom and my TV was off. I said, "I heard these little girls going like this *[claps]*." And he goes, "I didn't hear it." I had told Grace about it. I was taking her to work and she came early because that's when they dropped her off, and she goes, "I'm gonna lay down on the couch until you're ready," and I said, "Okay." Then she said she went to sleep, and that she had a dream that these little girls lived in the house with their mom and dad, and she said in the dream she saw this man, that it was back in the days like The Little House On The Prairie days, that's how they dressed, and there was these girls and this man was writing in a journal.

He was saying that his little girls had passed on, and his wife passed on, and now he was sick, and it was a matter of time that he was going to go because they had died of fever or something? And that these little girls went up to Grace, and they told Grace, we're not here to hurt anybody, we just want to play with the dogs. And Grace's like, okay. So, when she woke up, she told me. And I'm like, okay. So, I would hear them.

One night I was getting ready to go out on a Friday, and I was in my room and I was putting on makeup. Then I felt them at my door, and I stopped, and I got chills. I'm not afraid of them, you know, 'cause I always hear them. I get chills, but not like scary chills or nothing like that, just chills like, I could feel their presence. I stopped, and I said, "It's okay if you're here and stuff, but I'm not ready to meet you." And then, right away the chills went away. And I never heard them again. And I, and I think by telling them—

Rose: But didn't you see the dogs playing in the living room?

Lilly: Yeah, but before all of that happened. Carl saw it, and I saw it. We would always see the back of a bare foot with a gown, a white gown, going into the kitchen. And I would always go to the kitchen, I would look, and there would be nobody home but me. Carl said he saw it, too.

One time, I went to lay down and I heard this noise in the living room, and it was like a woman's voice, but it was like a song. But not anything like I ever heard *[mimics a lullaby]*. And then I was like, did I hear that? And then my partner woke up, and she's like, "Who's that?" And I said, "What?" And she goes, "That lady singing." I said, "You hear that?" She goes, "Yeah, did Carl bring somebody home?" And I said, "No, Carl's not here." So, I got up and I went to the living room. Princess was sitting on the floor, looking up, wagging her tail, and Norman and Pugsley were trying to reach up. And they were like, you know, wagging their tails, but they're trying to reach up to the ceiling.

Jed: On their hind legs.

Lilly: Yeah. And there was nobody there. After that, I didn't hear that anymore.

[I followed up with Carl to see if he remembered anything like what Lily described...]

Carl: Lilly used to always hear a kid's song, but I can't remember what it was. She would hum it, but couldn't put her finger on it. One time she came into my room, and she was like, "Did you hear that?" "I didn't hear it, I'm sorry." I don't remember her talking about clapping, and I never heard it. But that was it. I was never uncomfortable in that house.

Jed: And the foot and gown?

Carl: I was coming out of a room and walking into the hall, and I saw the back foot of a woman wearing a white gown turning the corner. But I wasn't scared.

[We return to the interview with Rose and Lilly.]

Lilly: Another night the doorbell kept going off, and off, and off. And it was one of those ones that you put the battery in, and I kept going to go check, and I said, there's nobody there. My partner says, "Take the batteries out." I went over there, and it didn't have any batteries.

Rose: Oh shoot.

Lilly: So that freaked us out. I remember though, the dogs wanting to get to it *[whatever the dogs were looking up at]*, and there was nobody there.

Rose: I remember you telling me the dogs were playing with somebody in the living room. Even then I was still kind of a non-believer and I was like, they were probably just playing.

Lilly: At Mom's house, I would always wake up. When I was—I played with a Ouija board, my friend came over and played with the Ouija board and we were asking it stupid questions.

Jed: How old were you then?

Lilly: Like 13.

Jed: How long had you been at Sheffield?

Rose: I was just thinking we moved in when I was in the sixth grade, I was 11. We were there a long time. I'm 56 now.

Lilly: I was in the seventh grade. I don't know, but I would always be in my room. Me and my friend Elaine were playing with the Ouija board. We started asking it questions, and then it started saying, "You bitches," and it flew off the board. We're like, you did it, you did it. And then we—I had a cat, and that cat went *[hisses]* and ran out of the room, and the curtains fell. I mean, the cat wasn't by the curtains, it was at the edge of the bed and we were on the floor, and the curtains fell.

So, we're scared and ran and told Mom, and Mom was like, "What are you doing with that thing, go throw it away!" And so, I went and got the board and I went and put it in the trash. But after that, something always kept following me, and they—I would just like lay down, and it was like you're in that paralyzed sleep? Where you couldn't wake up. I could see the hall light on, and I could see Carl passing, or Matthew passing. And I'm like, help me, help me. And then I'd jerk myself up and I would get scared, but I would always see eyes just looking down at me. And holding me down. I would get scared, and the next day I would tell Mom, "Mom, can I change rooms with the boys?" And she goes, "As long you change everything yourself," and I said, "No, I will." So, the next day I would go and get the boys mattresses, the dresser's out, put them in the hall and then go put my stuff in, because I was afraid to sleep in my room and I didn't want to tell anybody why.

Jed: Which one was your-?

Lilly: I switched all the rooms, because it kept following me. You know until finally—

Rose: But it started with the first one...

Lilly: In the corner, where Andrew sleeps. You know, next door to Elena's. And then I moved to the one to the side in the front, the one next to the living room? And then it followed me there. And so—

Jed: There's the living room, the next one, and then the corner one.

Lilly: And so, I moved to the next one, the one by the living room. That's where the boys were. I moved their stuff and they changed, and they're like, "Why are you changing?!" Then it followed me there a little while later, and it would always hold me down, and it would just look, and I would snap up and it was, "This time, this time." I would be scared, and I would tell my mom and Mom is like, "No, no, no."

Jed: You'd hear the words?

Lilly: Uh-huh.

Jed: What kind of voice was it?

Lilly: It was just like a whisper.

Jed: Could you tell if it was a male or female?

Lilly: It was a male. And it would hold me down, like choking me or something? In the spring I would like to open up the windows, and there's burglar bars at the windows, but I would open them up, and I was sleeping in there and I heard, like—There's no dogs barking. The people next door had a dog and we had a dog, but I would hear like at my window *[mimics heavy snorting, breathing].* And I would hear like somebody's touching the screen. And then I was like—

Rose: She even woke up Dad.

Lilly: I was like, oh my God. And I kept hearing it. So, I just pulled my blankets off real soft, and then I got up and went and said, "Mom, I think somebody's at my window." Dad got up real quick and he got his rifle, he got the German Shepherd Beaver, and he went outside. When he was outside, I shut my windows and I locked up. I was already in bed by the time he finished checking everything, he goes, "There's nobody out there. Beaver didn't even make any noise, there's nothing out there." And I'm like, "Okay, okay." So he went in, and as soon as all the lights were off again, you could hear it like at Rose's room and the boys room, because the windows were open. And you could hear *[breathing sound],* it touching the screen. Like something was dragging, but I could hear it. I prayed to go to sleep right away and eventually went to sleep. But as soon as the lights were all off, you start hearing that breathing again at their window, and I said, well, they must be okay, because there's burglar bars. That's my way of thinking, but you could hear somebody breathing.

[I followed up with Carl to ask about switching rooms with Lilly.]

Jed: Do you remember Lilly wanting to switch rooms all the time as a kid?

Carl: Yeah, I remember that because... I know one of the things that Lilly told me was that... I didn't know because I was younger, you know, and I didn't know that she had played with a Ouija board. She said after she played with the Ouija board she started hearing, you know, growling and scratching at her door and at the window. And she just felt like something was following her all the time.

Jed: Yeah.

Carl: She told me that before. I thought that was pretty crazy. I was like, what are you doing playing with a Ouija board in the first place? That's creepy. But I don't remember hearing anything like that.

[We return to the previous interview.]

Jed: Would the sleep paralysis stop when you switched rooms?

Lilly: For a little while, and then it would happen again where I was like being held down.

Jed: You said you saw eyes at one point.

Lilly: Yeah. Kind of like cat eyes, but just eyes looking down at you.

Jed: But where?

Lilly: Above me. And they would always be like, "This time."

Jed: Just eyes unattached to anything above you?

Lilly: Right. Yeah. But, you know, a figure, but you couldn't see the figure, but I could see the eyes and I could feel being press down here *[points to shoulders]*. That happened to me a lot of times. So, it finally stopped following me.

Rose: Jed, do you remember anyone telling you about Mom hearing the spoon fall in the sink? In the morning we'd wake up, Mom would say, "Who's eating something at night?" And we're like, "I don't know, we're not, I'm not." She would ask us all, "Well, someone's eating at night, because I hear someone dropping a spoon in the sink." In the morning when Mom would wake up, there's a spoon in the sink. I remember for several days, maybe a couple of weeks, Mom would wake up and there'd be that spoon in the sink. And she was getting upset with us. So, she decided instead of waiting until the morning to ask, when she heard the spoon fall in the sink, she got up right away, and she was going to go catch one of us.

But sure enough, the spoon was in the sink and everyone was asleep, and there was no one there. She walked around the house looking. It didn't happen again. But it was almost like she had to get up and look around for it to stop. But she said every night she would hear that, the noise of the spoon dropping into the sink, and then she would see it in the morning. But it was like it didn't stop until she actually got up and looked. It was almost like validation, that something was actually happening. You don't remember that Lilly?

So anyway, remember a couple of Christmases ago, we're at Elena's house, and we were sitting by Mom's door. I was sitting here, and you were sitting down, and Jeanie was on my lap *[one of her nieces]*. I mean, remember, she was like leaning over? Not sitting on my lap, but leaning over? And she kept on looking into the room. Like, you know, just looking and then she would cover her eyes, and then uncover her eyes like—

Lilly: She was a little younger

Rose: Yes, she was younger, probably about four years. Yeah, because she just turned eight. She might have been about four. So, Lilly and I were sitting there, and I said, "What are you doing?" And Jeanie just pointed into the room. And I said, "What are you doing?" And by this time the back of my hairs were already standing up, because I'm wondering, what is she seeing?

Lilly: Because she's pointing to Mom's room.

Rose: And the light was off, there was nothing.

Lilly: You know that nobody likes to go to Mom's room, right?

Rose: She keeps pointing in there, and I said, "What are you looking at?" And she just points, and I said, "Do you see somebody in there?" And she shakes her head yes—

Lilly: Nods.

Rose: Yeah, nods her head. And I said, "Who do you see?" "A lady," she whispers, because all this time she's not telling me, she's just whispering. And I said, "Is the lady nice?" And she nods her head yes. And I said, "Okay, well if the lady's nice." And then Lilly says, "Close that door, please." So Lilly had Andrew close the door. But she had been doing that a while before I even noticed what she was doing.

And finally, when I looked down, she's looking in the room. And she's like, uncovering her eyes and covering her eyes, you know? So yeah, she saw something. But if I asked her now, I don't think she'd remember. I don't know, because we didn't talk about it again. She doesn't go to Elena's house a lot. Well, she did after school for a while. So I'm wondering if she might remember something. But she didn't ever—she hasn't mentioned anything.

Jed: Yeah.

Lilly: Because one thing about the hall at Elena's house, it's scary. And then Mom's bedroom. But the hall is scary. I get chills just, you know, going into the hall.

Rose: That's where you would stand Jed.

Jed: You're preaching to the choir here. *[Laughing]* So tell me when you noticed…

Lilly: You?

Jed: Yeah, you and Grandma. You just both noticed me, where were you?

Rose: I was… You know, I would go over there and I'd visit Mom, and you know where her table's at in the kitchen? We'd be sitting there. And I guess, you know, "Go check on Jed," or "Jed, where are you?" or something, and then we'd find you in the hall a lot, and you'd be looking down the hall. I remember mom asking you, "What are you doing?" "Looking at the man." And Mom was like, "What man?!" You know, right away. No, I think Mom was alone the first time you said that, now that I think about it. Because it freaked her out. She went room to room looking for a man, thinking that a man had come into the house.

And when I went over, I think it might have been the same day, Mom told me about you seeing a man in the house. And that she went room to room looking for this man, and there was no one there. I think that she had me check on you, and you're still in the hall, looking down the hall, and we're like, "Jeddy, come over here and tell us what this man looked like." And I think you might have already told Mom a little bit, but you described it to me. "Well, he has a long knife right here *[points to her hip]*. And he's wearing a shirt and pants, boots," and we're trying to get more out of you, like what color is his shirt? And I think you might have said red.

Lilly: Red plaid.

Rose: Yeah. Like you were trying to describe plaid, but you being a little kid—

Jed: I didn't know what that is.

Rose: Yeah, you being a little kid, just telling us red and black. And we're putting it together, like, plaid shirt? But what we remember is that you just said boots, boots and a knife. "A big knife, Grandma." And that's what scared Mom, that you had told her that there's a man in the house with a knife. She's like looking room to room. And when I got there, she's telling me, and she says, "Where's Jed?" And when I went, "Come on Jed, come over here," you're still looking down the hall. I went to go see what you're looking at, but there's nothing there. But I think you could see somebody, or you might have seen somebody again. But that's what I remember. Mom just thought it was a person in the house. And then after you described it, and then you said that you saw it again. I think you might have seen it a few times, right Lilly?

Lilly: Yeah.

Rose: More than once.

Jed: You'd said I wasn't trying to get anybody's attention.

Rose: You were quiet. You were quiet, a very smart kid. You know, you could explain things. You had a lot of detail, but you were not the kid to ever want attention. You know how some kids they want to just come and sit on your lap? They want you to be always involved, or they want to just be involved with what you're doing or whatever. You were never that kind of kid. So, you are not the one to go over there and be looking, and then just try to come back and tell us. We'd have to go, "What are you doing, Jed?" You know, and you would say looking at the man or whatever. You were just the opposite. Not trying to get attention. You were just doing this on your own.

Jed: I wasn't hiding it, but I wasn't volunteering it.

Rose: Exactly. But you know what? You were not afraid. I was going to ask Aria before she went, she had to go to Carl's house real quick. She was visiting with Elena, they were sitting at the kitchen table, and she said that she and Elena both saw someone walk right by the back door.

Lilly: Elena thinks there's a portal on her patio, because she says that she sees shadows all the time walking towards the back. So, she really thinks that there's something there. We always ask Elena why she doesn't get somebody to come out and check the house and stuff? She's like, "No."

Rose: Do you remember Mom getting the house blessed?

Lilly: Yeah, but Elena says that she doesn't call anybody to come check the house, because she's afraid she's going to upset them.

Rose: Yeah.

Lilly: So, she'd rather keep things the way they are. But the lights would always go off and on, she told you that right? The lights would turn off.

[I ask Lilly to describe her experiences.]

Lilly: When I lived at Tina's house, sometimes when I would go to bed, I would hear like a lot of people talking. And then I'd wake up and look outside and everything, and there would be nobody there. But that happened a lot. Or when I would go to bed, I would hear one of those old record players. What do you call them? Those old record players that was—

Jed: When you turn the crank to play?

Lilly: Yeah, that kind of music, from back then. I would hear the music playing. I would sit up and the music would stop. But then I laid down and you could hear it. And then somebody had told me, you're not supposed to disturb that, when you hear noises and stuff. The other night, I woke up and smelled something baking, sweet. And I'm like, thank you, Mom. You know, are you here? But you could smell that baking of something sweet. And I've woken to that smell before, you know, baking. They say that a spirit visits you and you smell things. But I've done that like three times where there's baking, where it even wakes me up. But then I see it's like three in the morning, and I'm just sitting there, and I could just smell it. And I'll check the house or whatever, but it doesn't scare me anymore. I'm more afraid of being murdered than I am of a spirit.

Jed: Were you the one that took Princess from the house?

Lilly: Yes.

Jed: Okay. I couldn't remember if it was you or Elena that actually took her out, because Carl said Grandpa used to leave her there alone.

Lilly: Well, Elena would go see her, but Elena would leave her there at the house. And I would tell Elena let Princess go, because nobody's there for her. Put her in the backyard and I'll go take her, say that she got stolen. No, no, no. Dad will get mad. Dad will get mad. And then finally Dad was going to go to Vegas and he says, can you watch princess for me? And I'm like, yes.

Rose: Yeah, but didn't it happen that someone went in, I mean not went in, but when Elena—

Lilly: Went in one time, all the pictures were on the floor.

Rose: Picture frames were broken.

Lilly: No, they weren't broken. They were just set on the floor.

Rose: No, she told me that they were all cracked up and broken. Pictures of all the grandkids were all put in a pile in the middle of the floor and broken. Elena goes in and sees this. And that's the day you went and got Princess, you just said I'm taking her.

Lilly: Yeah. Because she was there by herself all the time.

Jed: Yeah.

Rose: Yeah, you were upset, because the first thing is the police said, well, someone broke in and did this and that, you know. They looked around, no sign of anyone going in, breaking in, and you were upset. Y'all were upset, because when Elena went to go get her, she was under the table and Elena had to pull her out. And usually Princess was ready to go outside where she'd be wagging her tail waiting, and Elena would just untie her. Because they would leash her to the table. Dad would so she wouldn't walk around, but he told Elena go over there a couple times a day. Go let her out. But keep her tied, because she still wasn't potty trained or—

Lilly: She was potty trained, but Dad had this thing about animals being in the house, he didn't want her to walk around. And I'm like, well, how can you let her just stay there?

Rose: So, that day when Elena went to go get Princess, Princess was huddled under the table afraid. She had to literally pull her and when she was doing this, that's when she looked into the den area and saw all the broken pictures in a heap on the middle of the floor. She grabs Princess, runs to the house, and calls dad at work, that's when he was still working at Kelly I think, and said someone broke into the house.

Lilly: He wasn't living there.

Rose: He wasn't, he wasn't really living there, no. And that's when he comes and he said, "Just call the police, Elena." But when the police, the police were there before dad got there, and they were looking around and they said, "Did someone else have the key? We don't see any sign of anyone breaking in." So that's when you were really upset. I remember and you said I'm taking her. And you told dad I'm taking princess, so he didn't have anything to say about that. But by that time, he wasn't living there, remember? Yeah. So yeah, that was something that was scary to see. Did she tell you about that, about the pictures?

Jed: I haven't talked to Elena.

Rose: Oh, yeah Elena has got some good stuff.

[Aria arrives, and agrees to share the experience she had at the Sheffield house.]

Rose: I was telling Jed about when you were at Elena's house and saw the shadow.

Aria: Yeah, we were just talking at the kitchen table and it wasn't even dark out. Then all of the sudden, me and Elena both looked at the back window at the same time, and we just saw a dark shadow just walk slowly past the window. Of course we went up to go look to see what it was, and there's nothing out there.

Rose: So that's the only thing that you've ever—

Aria: That's the only thing at Elena's I've ever seen.

Rose: Yeah, but we don't spend a whole lot of time at Elena's, only during Christmas.

Lilly: It is freaky to be at Elena's house

Jed: Why?

Lilly: You just get like not a good energy.

Rose: Do you get that feeling?

Aria: No. Well, you know what, after that happened, I feel a little funny going over there.

Lilly: Like in the hall, or in Mom's room.

Aria: I don't know if anything specific, but just like a presence or something. You know. I never really realized it until that happened. And then I was like, wait a minute. Then it seemed like it turned on different senses, or I don't know what, but that's what it felt like.

Lilly: That's why being at Elena's, doesn't it give you the, you know, heebie jeebies now?

Jed: I mean, it's been years since I've been there. It did when I was small. I was telling Rose, and I told my mom too when I interviewed her, Mom would drop me off on the way to work at Grandma's and I would fall asleep in the living room. I don't know, what was I in, elementary school, middle school? There was the large couch, the blue one, I don't know what she has there now, and then across from it there was the loveseat I guess you call it.

So, it would be a matter of, did I want to lie on the loveseat where my back would be to the hall, but I couldn't see it? Or did I want to lie on the couch so I could at least see. I don't actually have memories of when I wasn't uncomfortable there, because anything other than that, I was just too young to recall not being afraid. Like you're talking about, you know, now the bathroom is creepy and stuff and—

Lilly: Just going down the hall.

Rose: In the daytime, yeah. Like I told Jed, that whenever I take Elena shopping, and we're taking the groceries in and I have to go to the restroom real quick and she might go outside or something. I feel weird. You know, being inside the house by myself. I just want to finish up real quick and then go look for her. Or I'll even say, "Who's home?" "Oh, Andrew's home." But even still, you know, he might be asleep or something. I just want to finish up what I'm doing. And, you know, leave or sit in the kitchen where—

Lilly: That's the only spot that you feel—

Rose: I think I feel comfortable in the kitchen area sitting down at the table. Other than that, the rest of the room…

Lilly: And do you notice that like, when you're in the kitchen, the hall always looks a little dark, even during the day? It just looks dark, you know? But that house gives me the heebie jeebies. Dad even asked me if I wanted to live there and stuff. And I said no.

ELENA & ANDREW

[I met Elena at the Sheffield house where she lives. I am actually unnerved when I arrive at the house and step inside, not due to any external influence, but because of my memories of the feeling of being there as a kid. However, I'm surprised once I'm inside that it just feels like a house.

Elena takes me to the back bedroom that was my grandparents', where she has set up chairs and small tables since it is the quietest room. She lets me know Andrew is sleeping, and I should speak to him before I leave.

There is a lot to go over, so I just ask her to start with the earliest items she can recall.]

Elena: I think, um... Well, when I was 18, I was going to work downtown, and I got off the bus and this lady came out of nowhere and she just put her hands on my shoulders, stopped me, and she said, "Honey, you have an aura that illuminates so much light." And I was like, okay, what's an aura? Because you really don't hear anything like that. So, when I got home, I looked it up. Back then we didn't have what we got now, technology. Everything you had to look up in a dictionary or go to a library. I was looking it up, and I was like, I wonder if that's why I experienced some of the things that I've seen. And it all started when we lived in, uh...

Jed: You said this happened when you were 18, so what was happening before that?

Elena: Well, yeah, that was when I was 18, and so I let it go. But, this lady, the way that she looked at me, I kept saying, what does that mean? I started thinking back on things that happened, so then that had to start when I was 12. We lived in Hurst, Texas, and I remember walking to school in the mornings. In the distance, I'm saying like maybe seven blocks away, I would see this black truck, and I'd see a very tall man in a black suit. I could never see his face, but he was always standing there in that same spot. His truck was parked there; he stood by the truck so I'm assuming it was his truck. And he would just stare at me. But I saw him for... I don't know, it was for a very long time, and then we moved so I didn't see him anymore.

Jed: How far would you say, like on top of a hill, how far away—?

Elena: It was like down the street. And I'm saying like seven blocks away from where I was standing. You know, going to school.

Jed: Would you just stop seeing it as you—Was it like in the direction you were going? Or behind?

Elena: As I was walking, it was like I would just always look to the left and there it was. I would see him. It was like he was parked there, but it was like he was watching me. Like I said, I could never make out his face, but he was a very tall, slender man. But I always wondered, why does he dress like that? You know, he looked like, I don't know. Maybe alien? I don't know. I couldn't figure it out. So that stayed like that until we moved.

When we moved to San Antonio, I didn't experience anything anymore. It wasn't until we went to the Philippines. I was 14, no 15, just turned 15. We were in the Philippines and walking to school is when I started feeling like somebody was always walking behind me. I could never figure out what it was, but I felt it. I remember telling my mom, "I feel like somebody is watching me and walking behind me all the time." And she said, "Well, maybe you need to go to church." So, I went to the church there and I talked to a priest, and they tell you to say all these prayers. I did that. But I remember one night I had gone to bed, and I woke up and I saw a dark shadow. A very tall, dark shadow in the corner. My doors were closed, and they locked. I heard the lock. And I remember screaming, you know, because I saw it. And I just couldn't make out the face, but what I saw—You know how you have, umm, what do you call it, Death? The sickle? He was holding that, but I couldn't see the face. But he was right there. I remember screaming and my dad and my mom came, and they were trying to open up the door. Nothing, they couldn't open it.

Jed: Was the door open to start with, and you heard it click, or it was closed then clicked?

Elena: It was already closed, but I heard it click. They couldn't open the door. And I remember I was screaming, I was so scared, Jedediah. I sat there, I couldn't even move, I sat there. And next thing you know, it just like disappeared. But it stood there watching me. I remember crying and crying. I said, okay. I knew something...

Jed: It was still there while they were at the door trying to get in.

Elena: Yes. And so finally the door opens. It clicked, and my dad and them walked in. And I could never make out why that happened, or how it happened. So, it still continued for a good while. Every day—

Jed: That feeling?

Elena Uh-huh. That I had that feeling that something—That there was a presence there. But I just could never see it. I'd pray every night and just try to go to sleep and not even think about it. Time went by and then everything stopped. I didn't see anything or hear anything. And then when we moved, we came back here. We lived here in the house. When we moved here to this house, when my dad bought it, I slept in the corner room in the back. And—

Jed: The one in the—

Elena: Where Andrew- Yes, in the front. Yeah. And then—

Jed: How old were you?

Elena: I was 17. We brought a Ouija board into the house, we started playing with the Ouija board. And then after that, that's when we started feeling things and hearing things, you know, because we would ask a lot of questions. And it wasn't until later that someone said you should never have brought that into your house, because you open the door to spirits.

And we started, um, I started hearing things. I started feeling like there was something there, like in the closet? You would hear like a scratching sound. I started hearing that. That's when I started seeing things. I started seeing shadows.

And I remember when I moved out. No, no, no. Before I moved out, before I got married and moved out, I just always had that eerie feeling. Okay, I opened the door to something, and it's not good. And after that, my sisters—I don't think they all saw it? I know Grace did. Grace and Lilly. Tina didn't experience anything till later. But when I moved out I didn't see anything, but I was always afraid. Always. I don't like to be alone. I really don't. Because I feel like when I'm alone, that's when I sense and I feel. So it, it just stayed that way. When I got married and I had Andrew, everything was okay. Until my mom got sick, and I lived on the corner, right here *[points across the street]*. And I would come, you know, and take care of my mom and help out.

Jed: Nothing ever happened in the old—In that house?

Elena: No. Nothing never happened there. I didn't feel anything or sense anything there. It wasn't until after maybe a year, year and a half later after my mom passed away. The house was empty here for a long time. My dad wasn't living here. But my dad calls me up one day and he says, "Can you go let the dog out?" And I'm like, "What dog?" He says, "Princess." I said, "Dad, you still have mom's dog here?" What he did, I don't know if you ever remember my mom used to have a table in the corner? She had a TV there? I don't know if it was there when you were little. I don't even know if you remember. She had a TV there. My dad had Princess, and it was a little Pekingnese, he had Princess tied up. On a leash, but you know the leash was caught underneath the leg so it wouldn't take off.

Jed: So the dog wouldn't roam the house.

Elena: I didn't know that. I didn't know that the dog was even here. And so every day I'd come, but it would cry Jedediah, and my dad didn't want me to just—He would always say, "Okay, go let her out, let her in, give her water. I'll be there and I'll feed her." And I didn't know all this was going on until I call Lilly and I say, "You know what? I didn't know that Mom had a dog." I knew she had Princess, but I didn't know what happened to her afterwards. Because I wasn't living here anymore.

Jed: Yeah.

Elena: And so Lilly came and she picked up the dog, and she told my dad, I took Princess. But before all that happened, I remember coming one day to let Princess out. And I heard voices. As soon as I walked in the living room I heard like a lot of voices, like a lot of whispering. And I stood there, and I was like, what was that?

Jed: Like, you stood in the...

Elena: I stood in the living room for a few seconds, trying to figure out where were these voices coming from?

Jed: They didn't stop when you came in.

Elena: No. No. So, I walked to the den. And as I walk in, I had this chill, a real bad chill. Everything just hit me real cold. Then I remember getting Princess and taking her outside. I didn't even want to come back into the house. But I came back in, I tied her up, I went back home, because I was getting ready to go to work. And that's when I had called Lilly and told her about Princess. And Lilly says I'm going to come get her. That afternoon, or the following day, I came back again to let her out. And I don't know if you remember, or if you even remember seeing pictures all on the wall, here *[motions toward the back of the room]*?

Jed: On the backside?

Elena: Yes. Mom had a lot of pictures there. And I came in... All the pictures were turned upside down. And how? Don't even ask me how that happened, but the pictures were upside down.

Jed: On the wall still?

Elena: On the wall. And in the corner, she had a big picture, and that was in the center of the den, on the floor. You know, like the glass part? And the glass was broken and everything, and I'm like, how did that happen? How did a picture come from there, end up here? Close, in the front.

[I asked Elena later if she recalled what the picture was, "All I remember is it was a picture of some of the grandkids, when you were little. That's it."]

Jed: How far away did you say that was *[referring to distance where the picture belonged and where it was found]*?

Elena: Okay. Say for example, you see there? The corner there? To right here.

Jed: So, like—

Elena: You see right here in front of your feet.

Jed: So, like 15 feet?

Elena: Yes. So, I got Princess, I brought her in. I ran home to tell my dad, I was going to call him up and tell him everything that I saw. But as I was reaching the front door of my house, my dad was coming round the corner. So I ran back over here and I told him I heard noises when I went in. The pictures are all turned upside down. He goes, "What do you mean the pictures are all turned upside down?" I go, "You'll have to see for yourself." I don't know if he remembers, but he started looking around. Started looking around outside, see if anybody had broken in or anything. Nobody. Nobody had broken into the house. The house was still the same. So I didn't want to come back here anymore. Lilly came and got Princess, and so I didn't come back here until... I don't know, it was the following year. I was going to move.

I had only moved there to help out with my mom. And my dad says, "Well, why don't you just move into the house? It's empty. Nobody lives there." I was real iffy about coming back here. Tina had lived here with her husband. She wasn't here that long, though. Like I said, the house was empty and I was looking for another place to live. So when I moved here, I think it was maybe a month after I was here? It was really a nice day, like fall weather? I remember having the windows open. And you know the little racks that you buy for your dishes? To put your dishes after you wash them? I had a little one and I had put it on the table in the kitchen. I had some hangers there because I was hanging clothes outside. And you know, it was just one of those days, real pretty.

As I was folding clothes, I heard this loud crash. I turned and all the hangers that I had on the table were all on the floor in the kitchen. Like, just scattered. So I stood there and I said, "Okay, whoever did this, stop it. Right now." I picked everything up, and I put the hangers back inside the dish rack. As soon as I turned around, continue folding my towels, again it happened. So I got really mad. I was scared, but I got real mad and I said, "Stop it already!" After I picked everything up, as I was setting it down, I say, "I mean it, don't touch it." It didn't happen anymore.

But then, you know, I would hear footsteps. We would hear the doors slam. Tina came one day to have coffee with me, and we heard a door slam in the hallway. I don't know which room it was, but we heard the door slam. Ever since I've been here, I've been hearing things and seeing things. I remember one night I was going to go to bed and I ended up cleaning my kitchen. I just gave it a good cleaning. That next morning, I got up—I had a glass that I would measure water for my coffee, and it took three glasses to measure out the water I used for my coffee pot. That morning, I got up and I see three glasses all lined up. Water was filled all the same. None was higher than the other. It was all the same.

I stood there like, what's this? I didn't want to use that water for my coffee. I emptied them all out, but I asked Raymond *[her husband]* when he woke up, "Did you by any chance put three glasses of water here by the coffee pot?" He said no. I was still puzzled how that got there, so I said, okay, I'll have to ask Andrew. Andrew got up and I asked him if he had set three glasses full of water for my coffee pot. He said no. I just was like, I don't know, maybe in shock? I had no idea. It's like I froze there for a minute and I'm just thinking, who did this? You know? It didn't happen anymore after that. So that's when I said, okay, someone's playing tricks on me. Someone's messing with me.

[The interview with my mother appears later with the rest of her family, but she was the first person I interviewed. After the interview with Elena, I had mentioned the glasses of water to my mother, who then recalled the following.]

Jed: Okay, go ahead and tell me what you remember. Just like before, what happened with the glasses?

Wanda: Yeah. I used to drop you and Gerald off in the mornings, before I went to work. You would take the bus from there *[the Sheffield house]*. Your grandmother had gotten up to open the door, I went to the kitchen to get a glass. I said, "Were you going to drink this water?" She goes, "No, there's always a full glass of water on the counter. I don't know who leaves it or why it's there." I go, "Oh, okay." So, I threw it out and got me another glass of water. I said, "So it's always here?" She goes, "Yeah, there's always a glass of water on the counter when I wake up in the morning." And I hadn't thought of it until it came to me. Like, wait a minute. Yeah. She said it was always there. It gave me a creepy feeling at the time, but it's like, who leaves water...?

Jed: Did you see it at other times?

Wanda: Yeah, there was times that I'd wake up, because we had to stay there for a while, while we were having our house worked on. And there would be a glass there, but I didn't think anything of it. If it had water in the mornings when I would get up or whatever I'd just throw it out. It's like, I don't know who's leaving water in a glass. It'd be on the counter, next to the sink.

Jed: I kind of remember we stayed there, but—

Wanda: That's when you used to, in the room that we stayed, that's when you used to have your invisible friend.

Jed: I was just assuming that it was when I was much younger and they were watching me, but that's also—

Wanda: It was around the same time. Yeah. When they were watching you, you'd go in there and they'd say, "He's always talking to his invisible friend."

Jed: How old was I when we were staying there, when we were getting our house built?

Wanda: Five or six.

Jed: I'd forgotten about that. I guess when I asked you if you'd ever seen or experienced anything there, I just kind of meant when you were picking me up or dropping me off, but I forgot that we lived there, too.

Wanda: Yeah. It always felt like you might be watched or something. I'd only go in there to sleep, I never just sat there.

Jed: Which room did we sleep in?

Wanda: You know when you go in? The first to the right, the one that used to be Carl's.

Jed: Yeah.

Wanda: That's where you would play with your invisible friend. That's all I remember.

[We return to the interview with Elena.]

Elena: After that, I could see somebody walk by me, or I'd see somebody walk outside. I always say I have a portal outside in the backyard. Another night my son Daryl, he was in high school... Maybe he was a junior? I was cooking and I had a recliner in the den, so he was watching TV in the den and I was sitting in a chair that faces the back door. I never sit in the chair where my back is to the door. That day we had the curtain open, and I sat down and saw a girl walk by. Daryl had company that day, he had two of his friends, but they were watching TV in his room.

We were watching a movie. Then I turned like this *[looks over her shoulder]*, to see if somebody was behind me. There was nobody there.

And when I turn, I see Daryl, his eyes were real wide and he's just staring at me. And he said, "Mama, did you see something?" And I said, "Did you?" He said, "Yes." I go, "What did you see?" He said, "I saw a girl." And I said, "Did she have long hair?" He goes, "Yeah." And I said, "It looks like she was in the alley, walking in the alley, right?" But to us, it's like she walked in front. We both got up, we walked outside, we didn't see anybody. We walked to the back gate, looked up and down the alley, we didn't see anybody. But we did see a girl, and she was probably... She looked Native American? With long black hair. That's what she looked like to me. We both stood there, and he looked at me, and that was the first time he saw something.

Me, I've always seen something. Twice I've seen a guy walk by and he wears a white T-shirt. You can't see his face, but he always walks like he's coming from the front gate and coming to the side like that. Because by the time that we look out the door, there's nobody there. I've even walked to the side of the house and I haven't seen anybody. So, things like that are what I've experienced. I just haven't had anybody sit and appear in front of me. But I can feel them. That they're there? I see them from the corner of my eye. Or I'll feel cold, like sometimes I feel cold like somebody just walked right by me, I feel that coldness.

[You will recall James also sharing stories of their mother experiencing cold spots in the house.]

Elena: I've even felt like somebody touched my legs, and all of the sudden I'll have that icy feeling on my legs. I've seen a little girl. I was sitting in the living room one night and I dozed off, but I opened up my eyes and I see a little girl. She must have been about three or four, and she had gold curls. She was wearing like a long night gown, and she's leaning on the couch like this, just looking up at me. And I looked at her—

Jed: Like on the arm?

Elena: Yeah, she was looking—I was sitting there and she's like this, just looking up at me when I open my eyes.

Jed: Like on the—

Elena: In the loveseat, I was sitting on the loveseat.

Jed: Like putting her elbow on—

Elena: Yeah, right there on the couch. On the cushion of the loveseat.

Jed: On the cushion that you're sitting on, looking up at you.

[I put my chin in the palms of my hands and lean forward on my elbows, looking up at Elena.]

Elena: Yeah. Literally looking up at me. And when I opened my eyes and saw her, it's like she got startled. She looked at me, and she took off running down the hallway, and then she was gone.

Jed: Which hall?

Elena: In the hallway here in the, in the...

Jed: The front of the house?

Elena: Yeah. I've had my son's friends come over late at night. Everybody used to hang here. One of my son's friends, Jacob and Daryl's, which I call him my son, too, his name is Mason. He came one night, and he said, "Elena, who's that little girl that's in the front yard?" I go, "What do you mean?" "There's a little girl in the front yard that's by the wishing well." I had a wishing well that Noah had made me. And I said, "What time was this?" He goes, "Two o'clock." And I go, "God, you guys always stay up late." He said he came over here and it was two o'clock in the morning, he sees a little girl standing by the wishing well. So, he went to the back to tell the boys who's the little girl? When they went to the front she wasn't there, she was gone.

Jed: Yeah.

Elena: We've heard stories from other people here in the neighborhood that hear children and see children. I think Lilly might have mentioned that when she lived here, two houses down? She used to hear children in the house when she was there. So, I'm saying that everybody has seen something. Well, certain people. I don't know. Some people don't believe. And some people, you know, they—I always say they have that gift, you know, what we pick up. What else has happened here?

Jed: When you said you used the Ouija board, how soon was that after you'd moved in?

Elena: Oh God, we were probably here about a year? Probably about a year. Yeah. Because you used to sit there when my mom was talking, was taking care of you. You were always talking to somebody. Always. My mom used to ask you, "Jeddie, who are you talking to?" And you would tell her, "The man." She said, "What man?" She says that you would say, "The man." And she asked you one day, we're sitting at the table because she was going to feed you kids. I think she had you, Avery, and Andrew, and Lucas.

[I understood this to mean that the events she described that involved me predated their use of the Ouija board.]

And I remember you were standing there, she had a recliner there, and you were talking. I asked my mom, "Who's he talking to?" "He talks to a man." And I remember asking you, "Jeddie, who're you talking to?" You said, "Jasper." I said, "Who's Jasper? What does he look like?" And you say, "He's real tall, and he wears jeans, but like old dirty jeans, and some boots." And I said, "What kind of boots? Cowboy boots?" You say, "No. They have shoelaces." You would go like this *[mimics hands back and forth over the feet]*. "They have shoelaces." And I said, "What does he wear?" And you said, "A shirt." And then, I don't know who was wearing a flannel shirt, and you said, "Like that, that kind of shirt." So, it was a red flannel shirt. And you said it was checkers. And I said, "Okay, what does his face look like? "And you had said you don't always see his face, but you could hear him talking.

Mom used to say, "He talks to somebody." So, I said okay. But when I moved in here, I did see... I remember walking to my room and the bathroom door was open. And you know like if you kneel down and you're going to rinse your hair, you don't want to get in the shower, but you're washing your hair? You just kneel down?

Jed: Yeah.

Elena: I saw feet *[through the doorway]*. When I saw that, I stood there, I took a step back, and I turned to look in the bathroom. There was nothing there anymore. But I saw feet, big feet. Like, you know, like this *[spreads hands, maybe a size 13 US]*, because somebody was kneeling over the bathtub. So, I didn't think anything of it. Another time, I saw somebody walk by in the hallway. I was in the kitchen and I just happened to turn, to look in that direction. You know, like if you're going to the living room? And I saw somebody walk by, kind of fast. I saw the flannel shirt. And I thought, this is what Jedediah saw. But I couldn't see the face. Oooh, I got a chill. He was tall. He was tall, but I could see he was like, real broad. And all I saw was the shirt. That's what I saw. I just let it go.

I started taking care of kids here. I noticed all the little ones that I had— Mason, the one that saw the little girl, I started taking care of his daughter who is a year old. And Andrew has a friend named Ethan, he had a son that was a year old. He asked me to take care of his son. The following day is when I got the call from Mason saying he needed a babysitter. So, I said yes. And it wasn't until that evening I started thinking, what did I put myself into? I've never had one-year-olds, and two of them at the same time! They came, and I noticed that the little ones were constantly looking up. They were like this *[strains neck back]*, always looking up. So, I would observe. And I'd say, "Who are you looking at? What are you looking at?"

One was already walking, he was running, that was Liam. Kelly wanted to be right behind Liam, she was crawling and it didn't take her but a week before she started walking. But they would always look up, or they would look down the hallway, the two of them. It's like they stood, and they were like this *[staring]*. I said, what are these two little ones looking at? What do they see that I don't see? I didn't feel anything, but they were constantly looking down the hallway and looking up. I said, okay, whatever they see, it's nothing that's frightening them.

So, then I started taking care of Jacob. The kids were already growing. They were already going to start Pre-K, so Jacob was 7 weeks old when Hailey brought him to me. And the other kids that I had here, Jacob I had on my side the whole time. Everything I did, he was always on my arm. Then he started walking, and I said, "Jacob?" And I walked from the kitchen, right there going to the living room, and he's on the couch just like laughing and talking. I say, "Who are you talking to?" And he points *[in front of him]*. I look, I don't see anything. But he's just smiling the whole time. I said, "Okay, will come and eat lunch, tell your friend you got to go. Come and eat lunch." And he just came to the kitchen. But even Jacob, before he started walking and I had him in the walker he was always looking up, like the other two. He was always looking up, and he'd smile. I used to say, "Is Grandma watching you? Grandma's looking at you?" I used to tell him that.

Then I had this friend of mine who asked me if I'd babysit her two kids. One of them was nine years old, the other one had just turned four. Harper, that was her name, she was the same age as my granddaughter, so I introduced her to my granddaughter. But when I started taking care of her, I noticed that when she'd go to the bathroom, she'd turn on the hall light. And she never wanted to go to the bathroom by herself, so she would ask Scarlett to go, my granddaughter. I asked her one day, "Why do you always turn the hall light on when you're going to the bathroom?" She says, "Because it scares me." I go, "What scares you?" She goes, "I don't know, but something scares me."

Jed: How old was she?

Elena: Nine. And then later on, we're in the other room and next thing I know she's like this. She does this *[leans to look past me]*. I was always observing the kids, and I say, "Ari, do you see something?" And she said, "Yes." I go, "What do you see?" She goes, "A lady." I said, "What lady?" And she goes, "The one in the picture." I said, "What picture?" She said, "The one you have on your wall."

 I say, "Go and show me which lady you're looking at." She pointed to my mom. And she goes, "I see her." I said, "Does she scare you?" She says, "No, I just see her." I said, "Okay, so you see my mom. Just as long as she doesn't scare you." I figure, okay, she senses and she sees things. And she told me she has since the day she walked into the house, that she felt something. I said, "I'm not gonna let anything happen to you. If anybody bothers you, you tell me, I'll tell them to go away." Before the kids used to come over, I would just say, "I have kids coming over, so please leave them alone." I was constantly talking out loud. I wanted them to know that they're not going to scare anybody.

Tina one night came over here, and at that time she had two little Chihuahuas. That's all she had. She asked me if she could spend the night here. She didn't want to be at home that night. I told her yes, you can sleep in the master bedroom on the bed. Ray fell asleep in the living room, on the couch, and I went to bed next. Next thing, I look and Tina's standing in my doorway holding her Chihuahuas. And she says, "Can I sleep with you? I said, "Why?" She told me she got up, she went to the bathroom, and she thought she heard voices in the bathroom. She went back to the bed, and she said she was just laying down, getting comfortable, when she felt somebody jerk the whole bed. Just like moved it away from the wall. She got scared, grabbed her dogs, and she went over here said she didn't want to sleep in there anymore. I said, okay, so she slept with me and the next day she left. She never came back to sleep again. She does come to visit, but she herself said that when she lived here, with her husband, that she was in the room and she heard someone whisper her name. And I told her that had happened to me.

One morning I got up to get ready for work, and I sat on my bed. I didn't want to turn on the light yet, but I just sat there, and I heard a man's voice whispering my name. When I turned, I thought it was Ray. And I said, "Ray, are you awake?" But nothing. Then I heard "Elena" again. I got that chill, and I just grabbed my stuff and went to the kitchen to put on coffee. I was thinking, okay, who's calling my name? And I started thinking about Tina, that she heard somebody call her name. But she said after that, nothing ever happened. Only when she was here that she heard the door slam when she came to visit.

Other things have happened here. Umm, Aria. Aria is Rose's other half. I call her her other half. She came to visit one night, and it was probably about 6:30. It was getting dark outside. We both were sitting here in the kitchen, and we both heard a knock, a hard knock at the door. Like three knocks? And we both looked at the window, because my curtains are kind of shear so you could see if somebody's at the window. We didn't see anybody. Then I said, "Aria, you want to get up with me? You heard that right?" And she said, "Yes." So, we got up, we opened up the back door. There was nobody. Nobody. But the knock was loud. We didn't see anybody knock. We didn't see anybody.

Jed: Was it like a single knock?

Elena: Three knocks. We heard it, but when we heard it, there was nobody there. And then Aria looked at me. A short while later, she said, "You know, Elena, I think I'd better go, because I have things to do at home." And I said, "Thank you, Aria. Now you're going to leave me here by myself *[laughing]*." So, she left.

I didn't want to come back in the house. Only because I felt something, you know? I just felt something real eerie. So, I stood outside. Ray had gone to the store. I called neighbors around me, it just so happened nobody was home. Everybody was out doing something. I was like, great. I finally walked in the house. Ray came home and then he says, "What's the matter?" I said, "You know I always hear things and see things." He goes, "Yeah."

Well, after that, time went by, you don't hear or see anything. I remember hearing Ray yelling, and I said, "Why are you yelling?" He said, "Why are you knocking at the door? I told you I'd be out in a minute." "I wasn't knocking at the door." He was taking a shower and he heard somebody knocking. And I said, "I didn't hear anything." He said, "Yeah, you were knocking hard." "It wasn't me." So he just let it go. Maybe a few weeks later, I'm sitting on my bed in my room, Ray's taking a shower. This time I heard a knock on the door. I got up, came to the doorway, I looked, I didn't see anybody. But I did hear Ray say, "I'll be out in a minute." I didn't say anything. I waited 'til he came out, and I said I didn't knock on the door. He says, "Yes, you did." I said, "No, I didn't. But I did hear it. I didn't see anybody, though." And he just, like, scratches his head, he doesn't think anything about it.

So like I said, we've all seen and experienced so many things in this house. Just like I was telling you on Friday, when I went to the football game, I walked in and Ray said, "I just heard your voice, like you're talking on the phone to somebody." And I go, "Where?" He goes, "In our bedroom." And I said, "Well, it wasn't me *[laughs]*." And he scratched his head. So he's experienced things himself, probably not as much as I have, because I've experienced more, even sitting outside on the porch. I felt like somebody was sitting next to me. Like, smoking, maybe a pipe? Like, tobacco? I smelled it. I've smelled cologne, maybe old-time cologne? But I can't make out the scent that I smell.

I remember a night that I was sitting outside, and Andrew and his friend Mason were just coming in. I said, "Mason, did you see anybody?" And he says, "No." And then he sat next to me and I said, "Mason, is there somebody standing there? Look at the reflection from Sylvia's *[a neighbor]*." You could see the pole from my front porch. I said, "Do you see somebody standing there?" And he said, "Let me go look." He gets up, and he goes, and he looks, but by the time he gets to the front gate, 'cause you can see, and I'm looking at the window, then it's gone. But it looked like somebody was standing there, you could see it through the reflection. But another time Mason did see somebody run.

I've seen somebody, like a shadow? If I'm sitting in the living room, like a shadow run by, like going to the back. And then you run to the back door, and there's nobody there. And so, all these things that I've seen, but nobody has ever hurt me. I've just felt like the presence, or always sitting next to me, behind me—In the shower! I remember taking a shower one night, and I saw like a shadow go right in front of the shower curtain. I opened up the shower curtain real quick thinking, did somebody come in? There's nobody, but I saw it. Like somebody just walk by fast.

And so—Ugh, that gives me a chill, too. Some things give me chills and some things don't. I don't know if the girls told you or mentioned it, but when Mom was alive... You know we used to take turns sleeping with her. We would fight to sleep with my mom because my dad worked the night shift at Kelly. I remember one night my mom had the bed right here. It was right here. And this probably was like... I'm going to say three in the morning? We both heard this loud sound like a... Like a plane! You know? Like an engine of a plane. We heard it so loud. I remember her and I sat up on the bed, and all of a sudden, the whole room was like an orange cloud. I couldn't see my mom, but she was there, because—

Jed: Were the lights on?

Elena: The light? No, everything was dark, but you see we heard the sound and all of a sudden it was like, like, everything was in a bright, orange fog in the room.

Jed: You could see the room then?

Elena: Yeah, I could see—No, I couldn't see the room. I just saw fog all around me, but orange. But I said, "Mom, are you there?" She goes, "I'm right here." And I said, "Mom, I can't see you." She goes, "I'm right here." And I was—I said, "What's going on?" She said, "I don't know," and I remember telling her, I said, "I'm scared, what's going on?" She says, "I don't know. We're okay. We're okay." And then all of a sudden, Jedediah, the fog just cleared out like something just sucked it all out and the room was clear again. And me and Mom were still sitting there, and we looked at each other. We got out of bed to look outside. There was nothing. But we heard like an engine. So, what was it? I tell my mom, "Were we abducted or what?" Because how do you explain all that? How long were we even like that? We don't even know.

Jed: You said like a plane engine?

Elena: It sounded like a plane, like, like a...

Jed: Like a jet?

Elena: Just loud. It was loud, you know? And I just remember seeing like bright orange, that the room was lit bright orange. Lit it up. But it was a bright orange fog. But how long we were like that? I have no idea.

Jed: That sound like an engine, there wasn't an impact or anything. Did it just fade away?

Elena: It faded away, yeah.

Jed: And that's when the orange—

Elena: Everything.

Jed: Faded away as well?

Elena: Everything. Everything faded away. It was like we looked outside, there was nothing. Not even cloudy or anything like that. It was clear outside. But we could never explain that, me and Mom. We just don't understand how all that happened. Or how long we were like that. But we do both remember—Well, she's gone now, but I remember looking at her, trying to move. It was like our bodies were frozen. But we could hear each other, you know, talking. I don't even remember if I even could turn my head to look at her, I just remembered that I was like—It was more like a shock what was going on. We didn't know what was going on.

Jed: And you talked about it afterwards?

Elena: Yeah, we did, and then she didn't want to talk about it anymore. But, somebody brought something up, and I said what me and Mom saw. And they go, "When did that happen?" I said, "Well, I'm surprised Mom didn't mention it to you." But, yeah, things like that. And like, like today... I got this thing where I get up every morning, it's like the same time. I get up at the same time, at 3 o'clock, and I will walk the whole house just to make sure everything's okay. Sometimes I hear something, that's why I get up. And I'll look. I carry *[laughs]*, I keep a hammer by my bed. I keep two big sticks by my head, by my bed. And as soon as I hear something, I jump up.

There's another time Ray woke me up one night. He was coming to bed, because he usually falls asleep watching TV. So he was coming to bed, and I remember he crawled into bed and then all of a sudden I saw like a bright, really bright light on my dresser. I have a little cabinet on my dresser. It's really small with little French doors. And I saw, it looked like a ball of light. But not real big, it was like this. But it was so bright.

[The bedroom we are in is at the back of the house and not directly visible to the street. The windows all have curtains.]

Jed: Like the size of a fist?

Elena: Yeah, but I'm like, where's this light coming from? Is it coming from the outside? So I looked towards my window. There's nothing. I'm looking on my wall, and Ray's already going to sleep, I'm trying to wake him up. But he was tired and wasn't going to wake up. So I sat there, and I'm looking at this light, and the light gets bigger, but then all of a sudden it got small. It didn't frighten me, it kind of gave me like a warm, good feeling? And I sat there, and I watched it as the light got smaller, and smaller, and then it was gone. But I looked, thinking that it was coming in from the outside, like illuminating, coming in? But it wasn't. And I can't explain that either. What was it that I saw? Why?

Jed: Was it like the way light looks to us on a flat surface? Or was it giving off its own light?

Elena: You know like when you turn on a flashlight? And then, you know, it got bigger and then all of a sudden it just got smaller, and smaller, and then it was gone. Like that.

Jed: Yeah.

Elena: Oh! Two more things! Jacob came over one day. He had brought me some flowers and I put them in a vase he bought me when he was 16. It was in the center of the table in the kitchen, and we were in the living room, him and I, we were talking. All of a sudden, we heard glass breaking, like something just shattered. We both got up and came to the kitchen. My vase was on the floor, lying on its side. The flowers are still in there, there's still water in there. And Jacob picked it up, he goes, "Mom, didn't you hear glass break?" I go, "Yeah."

We both heard it. It was so loud, Jedediah. He goes, "What the 'F'?" I said, "I don't know." So, he sat there, I think he was just more puzzled? Jacob doesn't really like to talk about ghosts either. Anyway, shortly after that he leaves. Whenever something happens, somebody leaves.

Then around Christmas, I was putting up decorations. I had this one decoration; you could put a candle in the center, and it was a two piece. You had the bottom, you set the candle in there, and the top was like the shape of an umbrella. But it had like little windows where if you put a candle, you could see the light illuminate through the little windows. Well, I had that up in the center *[on top]* of my refrigerator so everybody could see it. One day, I was by myself and I hear glass break. So, I'm looking around. Did someone just break one of my windows or what? I'm going through my house, looking through my windows. I come in here...

Because I was in my room. That's how loud I heard it. I'm hearing impaired on one side, but I heard this. I couldn't tell you exactly where the sound was coming from, that's why I started investigating. Okay, where did the noise come from? I walked from my bedroom down the hallway, I come into the kitchen, I go to the back. I didn't see anything.

Nothing was broken, nothing disturbed. This was before my dad moved in. Then I go back the same way I came. Nothing. Everything's still intact. I check the bedrooms, everything's okay. I don't see glass broken anywhere. Then I come back the other way, and then right there on the floor I saw that top part of my little decoration, all broken.

I had the kitchen blocked there at the time, so I come back around to the kitchen and I take a step back and I'm looking and I said, okay. That *[the main part of the decoration]* is still in the center *[of the refrigerator]*. How did that top part come off and land on the floor? Because *[the main part]* still was in the center, not moved. I just started sweeping everything up. And you know, who would do this? Why? Why did you do this? The bottom part was still in the same spot, but how did the top—? Because the top kind of had to twist it a little bit, to put it on? I can't explain how that happened.

Matthew and I heard this when we were both in high school. I was 17, he was 16. I remember we were sitting in the den watching TV and we could hear footsteps! Actual footsteps like somebody just walking really hard on the roof. I remember us waking up my mom and telling her, "Mom, we hear something!" And she said, "Oh, it's nothing." So, him and I, we'd go outside and walk to the back gate to see if we could see. You know, to see if we could see anybody on top of the roof. We didn't see anybody, but we heard the footsteps.

One of our cousins, Abigail, came here. She has twins and they're in high school now. Her son wanted to use the bathroom. I said, "There's a bathroom here you can use." And he goes, "Is this the room?" Because we had mentioned it to him. I go, "Yeah, this is the room that Andrew has experienced things." So Andrew's sitting on the chair in the corner, Carl's sitting on the couch, and it's me, Abigail and the other twin, and Kara and her son. We're all sitting at the table, and then all of a sudden— This door stayed open maybe about that much *[spreads hands apart]*. All of a sudden, we heard that door slam hard. Well, Abigail jumped up, and she opened up the door, her son was sitting on the bed right here. She said, "Are you okay?" And he came out of the room looking scared. I said, "You didn't shut the door, did you?" He was just like this *[shakes head side to side quickly]*. And I said, okay. And Abigail just looked. And Kara said, "I tell you." Because Carl used to see someone come out of this closet right here.

Jed: Yeah, I remember it had the curtain on it.

Elena: Do you remember anything? You were small.

Jed: When I got to the point where I could remember stuff, I guess I wasn't experiencing anything anymore. So, no, I don't remember much really. I guess there's two things that... I was so young that I don't, I don't know how much I can trust them? Because young kid memories. They both happened in not the corner room in the front, but the next one in the middle.

Elena: Oh, the middle one, yeah, that's where Grace, the first bedroom to the right, that's where Grace saw—She was asleep. I think she went to take a nap in the room, and somebody was tickling her feet and she kept saying stop. She thought it was one of Gerald's friends. Or Carl's. And she kept yelling for my mom, "Can you come and get the kids' friends out of here? His friend is tickling my feet." Or something like that. Grace probably will tell you differently, but from what I've heard, she says that my mom went in there and asked Grace, "Where is he?" And she said he ran in the closet. When my mom opened the closet, there was nobody there. So my mom asked Grace to describe him. Well, the way Grace described him is like, he had short blond hair, wearing the wire-rimmed glasses? Round? But that he had, I don't know, maybe like old-time knickers, something like that. That's what Grace saw. Umm, I don't know what other stuff Grace has seen, but only what I've experienced.

Jed: You mentioned the thing that happened here, with the orange fog and the sound of the engine, have you ever seen anything in the sky, anything like that?

Elena: Well, one thing... You know, when I was 17, I did see a UFO. We were living at the apartments at Kelly *[military housing]*. I forgot the name of the apartments. That's where we lived when we came from the Philippines. I went to the movies one night with a friend of mine, and we came out and we saw something. It was funny because I go, "Why are we seeing this? This is a military base." And we see something zigzag in the sky. I remember telling my friend, "That was like the shape of a diamond." And my friend goes, "Yeah." And then we see it going like this *[makes a zigzag motion in the air]* real fast. And then it just went straight up real fast, and it was gone. We ran home.

Jed: How old were you?

Elena: Seventeen. Because I had just turned 17 when we came from the Philippines.

Jed: When you say you could see it was the shape of a diamond, it was lit up?

Elena: Yeah. We saw the colors, we saw a lot of red. We saw orange? And the way it was spinning. But we could see it zigzag. But the spin. And that's when we saw it, we saw it shoot up real fast and it was gone. Just like that, gone. It was maybe a few seconds, but we both saw it. That was the only time I saw something like that. Then the experience we had here. That's why I always say I think me and Mom must have been abducted or something, because how do you explain... And even when you watch TV shows, have you ever seen TV shows on alien abduction? How some say they're like in a fog or something like that?

[I followed up with Carl to see if he had any recollection of Elena or his mother referencing the orange fog.]

Carl: Well, it was during the day and she just said the room got real— They heard a noise. Like a real loud noise, like an engine. Almost. She said that the lights in the room got so bright, you know, and her and Elena, they just couldn't move. And then it was just gone.

Jed: When did she tell you that?

Carl: I was maybe in high school, or middle school.

Jed: How did that even come up?

Carl: I don't remember. I mean, but you made me remember when you said something about an engine. And I still remember Jed, when you said something about a real loud engine I was like, hey, I remember Mom telling me something about how they were in the room, and the room just got really bright, to where they couldn't even see each other. I remember my mom saying that she couldn't move or something. And then it was just gone.

I don't remember if it was a fog, or just a bright light or something, but I can remember my mom telling me something about her and Elena and a loud noise and they couldn't see each other.

[We return to the interview with Elena.]

Elena: Sometimes I don't want to come in this room by myself, Jedediah. If I'm in the house by myself, I will not come in this back room.

Jed: Yeah.

Elena: No. But if somebody is here, I will come back. One day, I don't know what I came in this room for, and right there *[points]*, where the fan is? I was standing there, and Ray was in the living room, and I saw like a white shadow go right by me, real fast. And that scared me. I don't know why it scared me, but I got out of the room so fast and told Ray. Because whatever I was doing, I dropped it, and I went to the room and I told Ray just go back with me into the room. I can't remember what it was that I was doing.

Ray walked in here and he goes, "What'd you see?" And I told him, I even told my dad. I said, "I saw something in your room, and it went by me. I actually saw it go by real fast, but it was white." Other times when I see shadows, I see them from the corner of my eye. Like go right by me. Or, I feel like if something's near me, and if I feel something cold, then I know something's there. I don't know if you ever felt anything cold around you, or you ever picked anything up? I mean, do you ever feel anything around you, like when you're alone?

Jed: I've got a heck of an imagination, and so I've never... I have to assume without seeing, or hearing, or feeling anything specifically, that, you know, if I'm... Fear is going to make me feel things. But one thing I told my mom about, was how I was afraid of the dark. She's like, I didn't even realize that. I was like, yeah, I'd prefer to leave the lights on. Like when I travel in hotels and stuff, I leave the bathroom light on, TV, sometimes the light.

Elena: I do, too, I still do to this day. I leave the TV on, the bathroom light has to stay on. Only because I know that when it goes dark, that's when I see things.

Jed: You said you see shadows—

Elena: I see shadows peeking around the corner. I've even felt when I'm lying in bed, you could feel the mattress move like someone's coming into bed. So, I prefer to have lights on. If nobody's here and it's late in the afternoon, say six o'clock on, I will turn on the lights. And it's not because I'm scared. Because I start to feel like somebody's there. Sometimes I'm constantly like this, looking *[over her shoulder]*, you know?

Jed: Yeah.

Elena: Yeah. I don't know.

Jed: The funny thing is, when I was in Fort Worth, I realized that I wasn't afraid of the dark in that house. My preference would be to have the door closed, have the curtains drawn. But I actually fell asleep better when it was pitch black. There was a TV with a cable box in one of the bedrooms, with the light from the numbers? The room would be so dark, that if I woke up in the middle of the night the light from the numbers was enough to—

Elena: Illuminate.

Jed: The entire room, yeah. My eyes adapted to it. So that's how dark it would be, and I was comfortable, and that was my preference. But there's other places where I don't like—

Elena: Maybe it's because you feel something. I don't know if this ever happened to you, but it's happened to me watching TV and all of a sudden, the channels just start changing. And I'm like, okay, stop already. Or I remember one night I was watching TV in the living room by myself. And you know when you turn the volume up, how it comes up?

Jed: Yeah, and you can see the—

Elena: Yeah. The little lines. These were so large on the screen. Everything was just so big. So I turned off the TV. I turned it back on, and it was gone. But it was just like all of a sudden, it was there, like if someone was turning the volume up, but everything was so big.

Jed: Yeah.

Elena: I don't know if it's something to scare me, but, it does. I always tell it I'm not afraid, but then there are times, yeah, I am. I'm not afraid if somebody's here. But if I'm alone, yes. Then I start to get scared. I don't know why, but, because—

Oh! Another time, too, my dad and Nancy were sitting there, and we were here. It was like maybe 10 o'clock in the morning. My grandkids were sitting on the couch here in the den, and it's sunshine outside. We hear the knock again, on the back door, another loud knock. We all look towards the back door, and I said, "Do y'all see anything out there?" They go, "No." You could see right there through my curtain. Scarlett, my granddaughter, gets up and opens up the curtain, and there's nobody. But I told Dad, "But y'all heard that right?" Nancy, she was like this *[makes a face with big eyes],* "Yeah, we heard it." I said, "Okay, I'm not just imagining. I'm not hearing things, y'all heard it."

But other than that, you know, we have our days. Like I told you, Ray on Friday heard somebody talking. He thought it was me.

Jed: Yeah.

Elena: And I told him, "Matthew and I did walk in front of the carport. You sure you didn't hear us there?" He says, "No, I didn't hear Matthew's voice, I heard your voice. You were talking, and it came from the back room." And I just left it that. I didn't even want to go in my room after he said that. But I went in there and—Now the one thing I do, is my light stays on a lot in my room. Because when you look down the hallway, when the light's off, it's very dark. And, like I said, I don't like the dark. I don't think I really liked the dark since I was little, and I've always had to have a light on. And what, I'm 62 years old? And I'm still needing to have the light on.

Jed: I don't remember anything happening, or why I would be afraid of the dark. I mean, one of the first real books I read was a Stephen King book. People said that it's because of the stories you read and watch. Like that's what I was afraid of. I don't know.

Elena: And the thing about it is I don't remember really watching a lot of scary movies or anything. Oh, I didn't tell you. Another time when we were in the Philippines, my mom said, "Elena, go to the car and get your dad's fatigues out of the car." Well, the house that we lived in on base was a pretty big house, but when you walk out, you walk out the door and it's a screen porch that went all the way around the house. You have all that screen porch, the floors were real beautiful wood. You open up the double doors, you go outside, you're on the screen porch. Then you open up the door to the screen porch and then there were stairs that went down, and then it's a sidewalk. But there's no light. It was dark.

See, that's another thing, it was dark. I didn't want to go by myself to the car. We didn't have a driveway or anything, we parked the car right there on the street. I asked Tina to go with me, but then my mom called her for something. I ask Lilly to go with me and then they call her. So, my mom finally said, "Just go get it!" I walked out and went downstairs, and just before I was going to open the door to my dad's car, a ball of fire just appeared right in front of me. Just hovering, floating, right in front of me. A big ball of fire. And I thought that this only happened to me. I just recently found out that it happened to Matthew, too. I didn't know that.

[After my interview with Matthew, he shared his experience for the first time with Elena.]

Jed: He told me about that. What happened with you?

Elena: With me, the ball of fire appeared right in front of me, but just hovering. Just right in front of me and then all of the sudden it was gone.

Jed: Between you and the car?

Elena: Just like you and I are right here?

Jed: Yeah.

Elena: Just like where you're at. It was right in between. And it just hovered there. It wasn't close to my face, but just there. But it was—

Jed: Like two or three feet in front of you.

Elena: Yeah. And I'm looking at this, it's like I froze when I saw it.

Jed: Where did it come from? Was it just suddenly there?

Elena: I got there, and all of the sudden it just like appeared right in front of me. And I'm like, I remember I wanted to turn and run, but I couldn't move. I just stood there, just staring at this ball of fire. But the next thing you know, it's gone. I opened the door, grabbed the fatigues, and I ran in the house. I told my mom I don't want to go out there anymore. I don't want to—Look at me, just thinking about it *[shows goosebumps on her arms]*. I didn't want to go out there, that's when I was experiencing all those things and I didn't know that Matthew had seen it until he told me.

Jed: Yeah.

Elena: That's so weird. I said, "You know what Matthew—" Look, I'm getting teary-eyed. I said, "All this time I thought it was just me." It's weird. I'm not crazy, Jed.

Jed: Yeah. It's like, I asked Carl, too, about Grandma and if she ever told you or him things that she might have seen, here or in other places and he said I don't think she did. And I was like, well, it would make sense, you don't want to scare your kids.

Elena: My mother did used to see—She was told when she was little that, through the Mexican belief, you have your Lechuzas, you're Llorona and all that stuff. All those stories that you hear. My mother did say one time, she said that... I don't know who was sick there at the house? I remember that she said she was a little girl, and she kept looking in the window and she said there was a lady there. I don't know, with my grandmother or... I don't know. But then all of a sudden, she says that she heard somebody behind her, "Go away." You know, like a woman? And she said she ran. Because what they would bring when somebody was sick or something, they'd bring in the curandera, you know, to cleanse.

I think my mom used to say that they would hear like, when you find coins and you're playing with them, that you could hear that in the house. I don't know if my mom mentioned it, I remember hearing that one of my uncles caught a Lechuza. But I don't know, it's just something when I was little that I heard. And it's just stories that you hear, you know? I remember my mom saying that they could hear voices in my grandmother's house.

And you think about what settled around there, what was there before? Like here, I had a neighbor that used to call me up. She'd say, "Do you hear kids playing outside?" I said, "No." She says, "I hear kids, I hear someone knocking on my door." She said she'd go outside, she'd look all around, look inside the house, and not see anything. And I tell her we've all experienced that, the knocking, the laughing. I've heard whispers. And they say that when you hear whispers and all that, that you really shouldn't hear it. Try to...

Jed: Pretend you don't hear it?

Elena: Yeah.

Jed: I didn't realize you were hard of hearing in one ear.

Elena: Yeah.

Jed: But it's still loud enough for you to hear.

Elena: My hearing throws me off, my sound. But before I lost my hearing is when I used to hear things, but now that I only can hear on one side that's even worse, because sometimes I don't know where is it coming from? I can't tell. Ray'll say over there, and I'm looking in the opposite direction.

Jed: Yeah. Because the only way you could tell direction of a sound is by having two ears. If you can't hear out of one ear, there's no way to tell.

Elena: You know, I'm a reader. I love to read. But it's got to be really quiet. I don't know if you can do it. You could be in an open space or library and read, but you could still hear people? Or, any place where there's noise. It has to be quiet if I'm going to read. Sometimes I'm in the room and I can have the TV on, but I would turn the volume down. I have to have the TV on. And that's another thing. The more light, the better for me. Even in daytime.

Oh! I'll tell you one time when I did get hit by somebody. I don't know if you ever heard of the VFW downtown? I went with Tina there. She was going to meet some of her co-workers from Fort Sam.

Jed: Is that like the two story—?

Elena: Yes. And I heard that it's haunted in there. I didn't know that. Well, I remember they had picnic tables outside, and I remember that there was a band that was setting up, they were going to play. Tina said, "Let's go get us a drink." So we walked in and we're at the bar and she says it's haunted upstairs. I said, "No, it's not." She goes, "Yeah, it really is. This place is known for it. You want to go up there?" I go, "No, I do not want to go." I will not even go to a psychic. Don't ask me why. So anyway, we got our drinks, and at the same time I'm just looking up the stairs. And I'm just like, I'm not going up there. We go back outside, we sit down. And we're sitting, you know, she had her friend sitting on one side, some on this side. I'm sitting on the end. And all of a sudden, someone hit me so hard on the shoulder. I turned, there's nobody there.

I'm like this, touching my shoulder, because it hurt. I got hit really hard. Tina looks at me, she goes, "What's the matter?" I say, "Someone just hit me." She says, "What do you mean?" "Like someone just went like that *[punches her palm with her fist]* and hit me hard." And she says, "Well, I told you it's haunted here." But now I'm like this the whole *time [holds the top of her arm]*. And her friends all look at me, and she tells her friends somebody just hit me. And they're all like, uhh. You know? And then they go back to talking. But I'm sitting there like this, and I'm just looking and holding my shoulder because my shoulder was sore from the hit. After a while, Tina said, "Are you ready?" I go, "Yeah, let's go." And she goes, "Oh my God, today is Noah's birthday. I bet it was Noah who hit you." And I said, "Probably did." So, before we left, I said, "Sorry, brother. Happy birthday. If that was you that hit me, I'm sorry."

But Jedediah, I got hit so hard, I never got hit that way. That's the only time I ever experienced something like that. Someone hit me. And they say that sometimes that spirits will attack you. But, was somebody trying to get my attention that day? Was it my brother? This is what I say, "If you're here, let me see you." But nobody has ever appeared in front of me. The only thing that I've ever seen clearly is the shadow in the corner of the house in the Philippines, the ball of fire, the white shadow that went by me here in this room. And then, what I've seen from the corner of my eye that goes right by me, dark shadows or something trying to peek in and look in the bedroom. And the smell of perfume, of smoke, like if someone is smoking a pipe, even a cigar. I've had that. The man calling my name. The glasses filled with water, the shatter of glass. You know, those things.

Jed: It's funny how when you have these things happen often and you experience them, like everybody I talk to eventually says, "That's all I've experienced." And it's all relative to the degree and the amount. But the funny thing about it to me, is when you say that's all that I've experienced, most people I would imagine maybe would have had one or none of those things happen to them ever.

Elena: And I've had several.

Jed: And you've had them not just here. Like at the VFW, at the Philippines. When you were in Hurst.

Elena: Yeah.

Jed: Like everybody had assumed it was just the haunted house, and it might be—

Elena: I always say is someone following me? Does someone follow me?

Jed: Well, they're not all the same experience.

Elena: No. But like I said, the one thing that did scare me was when I was 12 and I used to see that man every single day. Until we moved, I used to see him. Did you ever see the movie Poltergeist? Did you ever see the man in that movie, that was real tall and he wore the black suit? It was something like that, but this tall man stood by an old, beat up, pickup truck. I'm talking like the very first pickup trucks that came out. Something old like that. He just stands there, but I could never make out the face.

Then I started thinking, was it my grandfather? Would my grandfather be watching me? A great grandfather maybe? My grandfather before he passed away, I was real close to him and yet my grandfather didn't speak any English. So to this day, I don't remember how we even made conversation. I don't remember. But I do remember being with my grandfather all the time. My cousin, who is maybe a year younger than me? She's the same age as Matthew. She used to cry and get so mad at my grandfather because my grandfather wouldn't let her in the room with us. And she would run and go tell my grandmother, and I was closer to my grandfather than my grandmother. She was mean to me, my grandmother. And my grandfather, I remember him saying, "She's just so spoiled." But, I'm trying to think, Jedediah, and I don't know if I've blocked this out, how did I, how did I talk with my grandfather if he spoke no English whatsoever?

[It's not unusual for children to learn a language while they're young and then lose it as they grow older due to dis-use. For instance, Noah and James spoke Greek as children, but could not later in life.]

Jed: You didn't speak Spanish?

Elena: I don't remember. But I remember him so clearly. I remember when he got sick, I was 11. And he told me, "I'm going to be leaving. When I leave, I don't want you to cry. When you go to the funeral home and you see my body, I don't want you to cry. I want you to smile, because I'm going to be in a better place." He died in the house at my grandmother's. I remember everybody was there to see him, and he wasn't really talking. He was like if he was sleeping. I remember I walked in there, and I sat on the chair, and he opened up his eyes and he said, "I'm leaving now. Okay? Don't cry, remember I said smile. You smile at me and be happy." And I just looked at him. Just when he was saying that, my mom walked into the room, and my mom saw that he was talking to me. After he said that to me, he closed his eyes, and my mom told me to leave the room when she was trying to wake him up. He didn't wake up. It was shortly after that my grandfather passed away.

[We began speaking about Matthew's experiences being touched at his house.]

Elena: Sometimes when I'm here, you feel like someone brushes their hand around here *[shows me on her arm]*, and you turn all of the sudden and there's nobody there. Last night I was in my room, and I feel like someone did this *[touches]* on my head. Then I start looking, and I'm like, did a bug fall on me or something? But there's nothing. Or, you just have that smell. One thing I do smell sometimes, it's like when you light a match and you blow it out?

Jed: Like sulfur?

Elena: Like sulfur, yeah. Sometimes I smell that. Oh! Let me tell you another time. The little girl, Harper, the one I told you about? We were sitting, and this was maybe a month ago, we're sitting here at the table and we're playing Connect Four. I'm sitting on this chair, the one that I don't like to sit in because your back faces the back door? Harper was in the middle, and we're playing, and all of a sudden we both looked at each other, and I said, "Did you see something?" She goes, "Yeah. I just saw somebody." And I said, "You saw somebody walk by *[she indicates the hallway]?*" And she goes, "Yeah." I go, "Me too." But what I saw, and she saw it too, this person's a man and he's wearing like a flannel shirt, but it's more of the green with the brown. But all you see is this part *[motions to the neck and below]*. You don't see the face the way he's turned. It's like he's blocking his face.

Andrew was in the living room watching TV, but I didn't want to get up and say anything yet. After we finished the game, I went to go look and I was like, did I see something or was it Andrew going by? Andrew was sitting in the living room and I looked at him, he goes, "What's the matter Mom?" "Oh, me and Harper just saw somebody walk this way." He goes, "Are you kidding me?" "Yeah, we saw somebody like actually stop and then walk real fast." And he just looked at me and shook his head. Was that the last time I saw something? I think that was the last time. They come and go.

Jed: Things seem to just happen, just come and go. There's not like a pattern, in time of season, years. It just happens.

Elena: Yeah. There was another time, too, I didn't tell you, when Rene came from the Philippines. I mean, not the Philippines, from Hawaii? And he brought his wife Becca and his son Wade. Wade was probably about two years old. The bed was over here on this side and I remember walking in, and Becca was lying on the bed. And I said, "What are you doing?" And she was going to school at the time. She goes, "I'm just studying." And I laid on the bed, and all of a sudden, I hear, "ta tah ta tah ta tah..." I said, "What's that noise? It sounds like someone's bouncing a basketball."

I looked out the window because my neighbors had a basketball goal right there. I said, "There's nobody there, but let me go check." So, I went to the front room, opened up the door, nobody. I came back and I laid next to her, and I could hear it again. This time I heard it like it was here in the wall. And I said, "Becca, do you hear this?" She goes, "Yeah." I said, "Is there anything else that you hear in this room?" She said that she heard the door handle to the closet jiggle like someone's trying to come out. And I said, "What do you do when you hear that?" She says, "I just cover my ears." We didn't talk about it anymore, but she said this room gave her the creeps.

Andrew when he moved to the corner room, he woke up one night and he was standing at my doorway. He said he felt like someone was pushing down on his chest and he couldn't get up. And I looked, and his neck was all red. And then, as he turned around, he had like scratch marks down his back. And I went and I put holy water in his room. That's one thing I carry, I keep that in my room all the time, holy water. I started putting holy water throughout the whole house. That happened to him, but he says he doesn't remember anything scratching him. But I saw the scratch marks. He only said he felt someone pushing down on him, that he couldn't get up, couldn't breathe.

Jed: Funny thing is, I asked Lucas about it, if anything ever happened to him, especially since he stayed in that room. He's like, no. Nothing ever happened, he slept fine.

Elena: Yeah. Not everybody has felt things. There's another word that Lilly uses, you were on my mind, I was just thinking about you… What's that word you use? Telepathy. Yeah, telepathy. She says we were thinking about each other. But it's not the first time, it happens a lot.

Jed: Dad said it used to happen, things like that, with your mom.

Elena: With my mom, whenever she fell down, I felt it. I remember one day I woke up and my knee was so sore, I couldn't explain it. I'm like, what the heck? Am I going to have arthritis, it's starting early? And I got here and my mom, she was telling me she fell down on her knees. I said, "Mom, I think I feel your pain, because every time something happens, I feel your pain." But we never talked about it. There's a lot of things my mom didn't like to talk about. Because like I said, what me and my mom experienced, what we used to tell her, what we would see... I don't know if my mom ever saw anything. I don't know. The brothers and sisters have told you if she ever experienced anything.

Jed: I don't think she told anybody if she did. I think Carl may have said he would come sometimes when she was blessing the house, but she wouldn't say why she was blessing it. Just part of the normal course of things, she would be blessing the house.

Elena: If she saw things, she didn't tell us about it. You know, but Carl like I said was very young when he experienced something. You were very little, you know, and used to talk—You would talk to somebody!

Jed: What was I saying?

Elena: You carried a conversation with this person. We would see you sometimes, you'd be, "Uh huh." But it's like you weren't afraid. You were never afraid, but you would actually talk to somebody. You were never afraid, nobody hurt you, let's put it that way. I think you have your evil spirits. You got some that will attack, you got some that don't. But other than that, anything here like hurting us? No. I think scaring us? Yeah, they do a pretty good job scaring us. Other than that, things come and go. One day I might hear anything, in the next few days nothing. I tried to record something yesterday *[with her phone]*, I really did, but nothing. And it's strange and I thought, you know what? I wonder if it's because all the kids are gone? I have no kids now *[she's no longer babysitting]*.

[We began talking about how we would be taken to garage sales as children.]

Elena: I will not go to garage sales anymore. I will not bring anything home, because you don't know who ever had the stuff last. Was there something evil in the house? Were they a bad person? And we're bringing it into our house. And you don't want that. I saw that on a show I watched years ago, "Don't ever bring anything into your home that belonged to somebody else, because you don't know what you're brining." And I didn't think about that, that's true. You don't know what you're bringing into the house. So every time someone says you want to go to garage sales, I just pass. Because most of the stuff I did buy, I got rid of. Because I don't know. But I think what we did, is that we opened the door when we played with the Ouija board.

Jed: I wonder. Or if it just took that long of you being here. Like you said, when the kids are here—

Elena: I have seen orbs on my phone when the kids are here.

Jed: I wonder if the house was empty for a little while, and it's coincidental—

Elena: But how do you explain before I moved in and the pictures being upside down? Things like that I don't understand. You know, the glass that we hear, the shatter of glass and that nothing was broken, but then things are moved, and they are broken. I wish I knew who did it. You know?

Jed: Yeah. There's too many occurrences, from too many people, to totally discount that something happens here.

[We are finished with the interview, and I am on my way out the door when Andrew walks in. Elena asks him to share some of the things he's seen. He's just woken up, but he's willing. I pull out my audio recorder for an impromptu interview as the three of us stand in the kitchen.]

Andrew: The two weirdest things that ever happened to me... One time my buddy Joe was here. We're playing a game *[in the bedroom]*, he's sitting here, I'm sitting over there *[motions to either side]*. And like right here, right on the other side of the wall, you just hear *[gently taps his* *fingers on the wall]*. It's just like real faint, though. He pauses the game and goes, "What was that? You heard that right?" I go, "Yeah, it sounds like someone's knocking." So, he figured that it was just the pipes, you know. But, then like four or five minutes later, you hear *[slams his palm against the wall]*. And it's right here *[beside Joe]*.

Jed: Wow.

Andrew: I go, "Dude, the shower's over here *[points to the other side of the room]*, that's where the plumbing would be." And then, maybe like ten minutes later, it was *[slams his hand against the wall four more times]*. I was like, "Oh, crap." That was freaky. One time I woke up, going to the bathroom, come lay back down, and it looked like there was someone standing right there. Like, I don't know, maybe like 6'8", 6'9", somewhere around there. It was pretty freaking tall. It's dark, and you're just like, what the hell? I was waiting to see if it was just my eyes to adjust. And it looked like it just started fading away. But it looked like it shrunk down, then just like disappeared.

Jed: Almost like a TV, how the image shrinks to the middle *[the old cathode tube TVs]*?

Andrew: Yeah, exactly like that. Another creepy thing was, it sounded like someone was on the roof. But like someone dropped from the tree. And you heard "dun, dun, dun!" Like someone running across the roof. The girl I was dating at the time, we heard the thing land, we both looked up, looked at each other. That's when you heard the "dun, dun", and you could follow it with your eyes. And it sounded like maybe about two feet before the wall, like, they jumped. You know, you can hear that slight...

Jed: Yeah. I know exactly what you're talking about.

Andrew: And that was it. She looked at me, I looked at her, "Did you hear that?" She goes, "Who's outside?" *[Laughs]*

Jed: I mean, the first thing you'd think is an animal falling out of the tree, but then the sound of like—

143

Andrew: Yeah. That's what I initially thought, like maybe it's an animal. Maybe it's a cat or something.

Elena: But the footsteps were hard?

Andrew: But the footsteps sounded just way too heavy.

Jed: Like a roofer up there? That's what I think of.

Andrew: Yeah, but then it sounded like someone running. It had to be someone tall, because the length of stride in between each sound, it's like, "boom... boom... boom" *[draws out a long beat between each sound]*. I went, "Whoa, what the hell was that?" It was three footsteps, actually. And I don't know, that was weird... Every now and then you would hear this *[fingers drumming on the wall]*.

Elena: I told him that! That was what Becca heard.

Andrew: Yeah, you would hear that. Nothing else really.

Jed: Did you see—

Elena: I told him the day that Abigail's son came in here to use the bathroom. We were all sitting in there, and remember the door slammed shut? Were you here?

Andrew: Oh yeah! That was weird! It was kind of crazy, 'cause we're all sitting there, and it's probably like this—

[He takes us to the main bedroom door, pulls the door back and slams it shut.]

Elena: Loud.

Andrew: About that much force. And Abigail jumped up real fast, her son just sitting right there.

Elena: He was shocked. His eyes got real big.

Andrew: I didn't know he was in here. I was talking to Carl. He comes walking out and has like a real blank face, "Y'all heard that right?" even

144

his mom, "You didn't shut the door did you?" He just shook his head. It was loud.

Jed: What about the corner rooms *[in the front of the house]?*

Andrew: Do you remember when I woke you up that night *[to his mom]?*

Elena: Yeah.

Andrew: I go, "Check my back, check my back.".

Elena: Oh yeah, and you had the scratch marks!

Andrew: It looked like—

Elena: Remember it was red on your neck, too. You felt like someone was pushing down on you. But didn't you also say you saw somebody like on top of the table, like there was somebody squatting or something looking at you?

[Andrew doesn't answer right away, he stares at the ground trying to remember.]

Elena: I remember you telling me, it's like somebody was—

Andrew: It wasn't me.

Elena: Yeah, you were in the room and you said you opened your eyes and it was like someone was staring at you. It was like standing on your TV tray. And just looking at y-

[Andrew looks up at me suddenly.]

Andrew: Have you ever seen... It's Christopher Walken, Eric Stoltz... The Prophecy!

Jed: Yes.

Andrew: Remember how they would sit *[in the movie their characters would squat deeply, their knees at their chest]?* It was kind of like that. But, you know, you wake up, and you're like, what the hell was that? And you're like, okay, that was just my mind. Umm, you see things out of the corner of your eye. But it's just like shadows. It could even be the daytime, you're walking *[does a double take toward the hallway corner].*

Elena: Do you remember that time we went to Schlitterbahn, and we came home, and you were outside?

Andrew: Ooohhh! God!

Elena: Tell him about that.

Andrew: I forgot about that. So, I'm at the desk *[in the bedroom],* I'm typing a paper. I get up, go to the refrigerator, grab a water, come back in. When they're gone, they'll leave the TV on. But I noticed that the TV was off. I didn't have any music on in here, the only thing that was running was the A/C. So, I take a break, walk out again. I go outside and smoke a cigarette, and I come back in. And I hear people talking. I'm like, okay, well, it's the TV. I come back in here *[bedroom],* and it took me like two-three minutes to snap. The TV's off. So, I walk out, I get to about right here, a couple feet outside the doorway.

[He steps into the doorway of the bedroom, a few feet beyond the threshold.]

Andrew: And I hear... It's a female speaking to another female, and it's a little bit louder than a whisper *[mimics soft, unintelligible murmuring].* Then I walk out, and it stopped. I'm like, okay, I'm hearing things. I went outside, smoked another cigarette, came back in, and I heard it again! But this time, I hadn't shut the door where the actual latch caught *[when he'd walked into the bedroom and closed the door behind him].* So, I just opened it real slow, to about right here *[cracked open].*

Jed: Because you heard it again.

Andrew: I heard the voices again, just *[murmured whispers].* And it just stopped. I was like, all right, that's it, I'm going outside. Then I called them, I called Stacy and I asked her, "Hey, where are you guys at?" She says, "We're on the way. You okay?" I go, "Yeah, I'm cool." So then when they pulled up, she goes, "Oooo, what happened to you? What did you see?"

[Laughing]

Andrew: I said, "I heard something. I heard people." That was the second time. The other time when I was in the shower *[again in the main bedroom]*, I heard it again, but it was louder. Like a conversation, but it was like me being here and speaking to someone in the living room. And in the shower, I'm hearing this. I turn off the water. Nothing. So I turn it back on, start showering. I open up the shower curtain, and like as soon as I step out of the tub, you can hear it. And it, it sounded muffled. Like someone's on a CB radio or something.

Jed: Yeah.

Andrew: And it, it just kind of like, slowly started fading away. And I was the only one here. It just sounded muffled, like "rawr rawr rawr". It started getting further and further away, and that was it.

Elena: Can you go over something real quick with him, the time when Carl was at school and you and Lucas were here, and he was in the shower, and you were doing dishes?

Andrew: So... Lucas was there....

Elena: Y'all were in high school?

Andrew: Yeah, we were in high schoo—No, we were in the eighth grade. I'm standing here *[at the kitchen sink]*, and it's just like this *[turns on water and pantomimes washing dishes]*. And I feel a tap on the shoulder. But it's a light tap. I mean, it's just kind of *[gently taps his own shoulder]*. I thought it was Lucas. I go, "What do you want, Lucas?" "*[As if from behind him]* Hey, come in the shower real quick." I said, "What?" He goes, "Come here." I go, "Hold on." Then it's like he yells, "Now!"

I turned around, nothing. I'm like, what the hell? At the same time I turned around, Lucas is coming around the corner like this *[annoyed]*. He's standing here, he goes "What do you want?" I'm like "...What?" He goes, "Why are you banging on the bathroom door?" "I didn't bang on the door, why did you tap me on the shoulder?" We both just had that blank face. "Alright, let's get out of here."

Jed: You heard him yell, he heard slamming on the door—

Andrew: Not slamming, but just more banging.

Jed: But you didn't, you would have heard—

Andrew: I would have heard the door open. I would have heard the handle.

Elena: The handle squeaks.

Andrew: You would have heard that, but I didn't hear that. But then again, the water was running.

Jed: Yeah.

Andrew: I was doing dishes in the sink, so I could have missed it. But it was just one of those things where... I mean, when he comes around the corner, he's wet. I was like, I wasn't banging on the door. Well, I didn't tap you on the shoulder.

Elena: I was telling him about the other day when me and the kids were playing the game, remember I went into the living room and I go *[makes a face, looks around quizzically]*. You said, "What?" And I said, "I thought I saw you go by, somebody stopped right there and then took off."

Andrew: Yeah, wasn't me.

Elena: But I didn't know someone had touched you.

Andrew: It felt like a tap, but a tap and a graze. It wasn't like real real light, you could feel a little bit of pressure.

Elena: Yeah, I told him I got hit on the shoulder. I actually got hit hard, and that was at the VFW Downtown. When I was with Tina? And Tina said, "It's haunted here."

Andrew: The thing that really trips me out is that... In this back-corner bedroom, you can be sitting there, lying there, and it feels like you have a hair, a long hair, go across your forehead *[pretends to hold something and lightly draw it across his forehead]*. Then you'll feel it on your neck. It starts getting frustrating. I'll look around, see if there's any spiderwebs or something. What the hell's falling on me? I'll be watching TV, I'll feel it at my ankles. It's just like, like—If this is your ankle, it feels like this *[lightly runs his fingers up his leg from his ankle]* and then you'll feel it like that. So, when you feel it moving, you're like, ah, shit, what's crawling on me? Then you look and turn on the light, and nothing's there. Little grazes. I mean, other than that you hear little sounds, but you start to distinguish, okay, that's that. If you open up the back door, open up the front door, these doors rattle.

Elena: I told him we have a portal on the back porch.

Andrew: Well—

Elena: That I've seen.

Andrew: The thing is, people have seen someone walk by. The silhouette of someone. I've never seen it.

Elena: I told him about the knocks. See how you can see through the curtain? So you would think you could see someone, right? Even at night when the light's on. You could see someone, like their shadow. But, and this is how loud the knock was, you hear someone go like this *[knocks loudly on the back door]*. Like that, and we all automatically turn, and there's nobody there. I say, okay, if you're here, just let me see you.

Andrew: Why do you say that? Don't say that. That freaks me out. Let me see you? I don't want to see you.

Elena: I want to see it.

Andrew: Let someone else see it, not me.

Jed: Did you ever see anything floating in one of the rooms? You know, how for years we'd hear how Uncle Matthew and Beaver heard a baby crying over there.

149

Andrew: Hearing the baby crying, walking in and seeing a woman, and she has no eyes. Just black holes for eyes.

Jed: That's the funny thing, and why I'm asking everybody specifically what they saw and heard, because getting it straight from Matthew was, they heard it, and he and Lady went over there, and I think they heard a baby crying. Lady was scared and hid behind him, but they didn't see anything. But that was it. It was Lady, and not Beaver.

Andrew: This is another version of the story.

Jed: Yeah, that exactly! We've always asked for the story, but then it gets repeated.

Andrew: Yeah, you just don't remember it right.

Jed: Right. Like when Elena asked what Matthew told me about a certain thing that happened in the Philippines, because it turns out she experienced the same thing.

Elena: I just recently found out the same thing happened to him.

Andrew: What? The ball of fire?

Elena: The ball of fire. He saw it, too, in the Philippines and I didn't know that, he just told me a few weeks ago.

Jed: Probably because I'd asked him about it.

Elena: And I was like, "So you saw it, too?" He goes, "Yeah." I said, "Okay, I just thought it was me." Because I told Jeddy the things I experienced in the Philippines, seeing the dark, dark shadow in the corner of my bedroom by the door. Feeling somebody always walking behind me, I'd turn around and there's nobody there.

Andrew: You just sensed that there was a presence?

Elena: Yeah, right behind me. Walking right behind me. Then my mom telling me I need to be good, go to church, talk to a priest. Then the priest tells you to say all these prayers. I even joined the choir there at church. Now to just get all of this out. But I was telling him all my stuff started when I was twelve.

Andrew: Jed, I forgot about this—

Elena: Yeah, you forget things until you're asked.

Andrew: I can't remember what year or grade I was in, but I was up late, and I was in the middle room.

[He walks us to the hall in the front of the house, specifically to the tall heater set in the wall between the living room and the first bedroom.]

Andrew: When you walk in there's a little desk right there, and I was typing on the typewriter. Yeah, old school. So, I kept hearing bangs on the wall, and I kept thinking, what is that? Is that Dad? I didn't hear any more, but then you hear that little *[thrums his fingers on the wall]*, but it's real faint. Then I heard this *[runs his fingernails across the wall of the front hallway]*. Fingernails scratching on the wall.

Jed: Yeah.

Andrew: But it wasn't hard, it wasn't real deep. There wasn't a lot of pressure. But it started like, maybe a couple feet behind the door *[from the direction of the living room]*. I'm hearing it over here and I'm following it as it's coming around the corner. And it's coming around here, and you hear like *[runs his fingers past the heater]* and you hear where it hits here *[points to a specific spot head high on the wall just past the heater]*. And it comes right on the door—

Jed: Across the heater?

Andrew: Well, like, it didn't scratch it on the heater...

Jed: It just went past it.

Andrew: Like you could hear it was on this side *[points to one side of the heater]*, then it was this side *[points to the wall past the heater]*. You heard two bangs and you could tell it—You're like sitting in a chair right here *[just inside the door]*. When you hear this *[puts fingers hard against wall]*, and it starts *[drags fingers across the wall, stops, starts again and finally hits the door with his hand, hard]*, that's when you're like, whoa, what the hell was that?! I got up, I come out, look around. And she *[Elena]* goes, "Andrew?" I go, "Did Dad just go to bed?" She said, "Dad's been in bed." I go, "Did you hear that? That scratching on the walls?" She goes, "We better not have rats or squirrels or something." But it turned out, that was probably one of the first things that happened that really freaked me out.

SANTIAGO FAMILY ANALYSIS

Before I delve too far into the Santiago family, I need to point out that Elena is an outlier in the total number of events she reported. She is one of two individuals in the Santiago family who have lived in the Sheffield house for significant durations, as teenagers and adults, and she lives there still. No members of the Cortez family who had reported events in the Telford residence still live there. So, and this is purely conjecture, if she is for whatever reason more likely to have a paranormal experience, and such experiences are more likely to occur at the Sheffield residence, it would not be surprising that she has the most reported experiences.

The time the Santiago family spent at Sheffield was mostly during their teenage years, some more, some less. Unfortunately, I don't have specific timeframes regarding that. However, as mentioned above, Elena and Carl were the two that lived there the longest for 17 and 16 years respectively at the time of these interviews. While the total number of years spent there is nearly the same, Carl spent more time there as a teenager and young adult, while Elena lived there still at the time of the interview. Elena and Carl's reported number of childhood events is similar at seven and nine respectively, but Elena had fewer childhood events at Sheffield compared to Carl with four and nine respectively. However, Elena has by far the most total reported events from either family as an adult at 27. The Santiago family reported 30 events as adults at Sheffield overall. As a result, I will sometimes present information where Elena is included in the results and then present those results without her as well. The goal being to discover similarities and differences in the data with and without her present.

There were 104 total paranormal related events described in interviews with the Santiago family. The average and median numbers of total events by individuals were 13 and 10 respectively, with Elena having the most total reported experiences at 34 (Figure 1). The events reported are heavily weighted to having occurred during adulthood, but it is evident the effect that Elena's reported events have on the scoring.

	Total Events	TE as Child	TE as Adult
Elena	34	7	27
Carl	18	9	9
Lilly	10	2	8
Matthew	10	2	8
Tina	10	2	8
Andrew	9	5	4
James	7	0	7
Rose	6	1	5
Average	13	3.5	9.5
Median	10	2	8

Figure 1

Additionally, the total reported events overwhelmingly occurred overnight at a roughly 3 to 1 ratio on average per person, and roughly 8 to 1 when compared by the median number of reports per person (Figure 2).

	AVG by Person	Median by Person
Day	2.5	1.5
Night	8	8
Unknown	2.75	1

Figure 2

As will be shown below, the numbers of reports by Elena influenced the averages, but not the median numbers of reports (Figure 3).

There were 70 total events described in interviews with the Santiago family excluding Elena. The median numbers of total events by individuals, as children, and as adults all remained the same (Figure 3). The visible difference in total number of events reported (Figure 1) and the differences in the average number of reported events with and without Elena (Figures 1 and 3) would lead to consideration of possible reasons for the discrepancy, namely location as a variable.

	Total Events	TE as Child	TE as Adult
AVG by Person	10	3	7
Median by Person	10	2	8

Figure 3

Finally, the averages and medians of reported events by time of day became more similar (Figure 4). Elena and Carl had the most events where they were unclear of the time of day with 9 and 8 respectively. The individual with the next most reported events where it was unclear what time of day the event they were describing occurred was Matthew with 2. This is interesting in that Carl and Elena are the two individuals that spent the most time at the Sheffield house. Since Elena and Carl reported the most total events generally (Figure 1), it may be that the more events a person were to experience, the less likely they would be able or inclined to differentiate certain details of the experiences.

	AVG by Person	Median by Person
Day	1.29	1
Night	7.14	8
Unknown	1.86	1

Figure 4   Excluding Elena

The most total events for the Santiago family occurred at the home on Sheffield with 57, followed by their other own residences at 40 (54 percent and 38 percent of events respectively). If you remove Elena from the dataset, the proportion of experiences at Sheffield versus the other residences owned by the interviewees is nearly transposed and becomes 38 percent and 52 percent respectively.

Smells were only reported by two individuals, Elena and Lilly. Elena had experiences smelling smoke on one occasion, and sulfur on another. There are many mundane explanations readily available for these olfactory experiences. For instance, smells carried on the wind or hypnagogic or hypnopompic hallucinations (hallucinations that occur when a person falls asleep or wakes up respectively).

There were 20 total tactile experiences reported, with Elena reporting the most at 7. What set Elena apart in this category is her 3 reports of feeling cold gusts of air, whereas only two others reported that sensation even once. However, even disregarding this specific type of experience due to natural environmental causes, she would still lead with 4 reports, followed by a three-way tie between Matthew, Carl, Andrew. Of these four individuals, all of Carl, Andrew, and Elena's reports of being touched (3 each) occurred in the Sheffield house.

	Tactile
Elena	7
Lilly	1
Andrew	3
Carl	4
Tina	1
Matthew	4
Rose	0
James	0
Average	2.5
Median	2

Figure 5

There were 42 experiences that can be described as auditory in nature by the Santiago family, with average and median numbers of reports near 5 (Figure 6). Elena had the most by far at 17, followed by Lilly and Andrew. In general, reports of the noise subset of auditory experiences were common in that all but one of the Santiago family reported hearing something in this category. However, Elena reported six times as many experiences of unidentifiable noise than the next highest totals. Elena's total number of reports of auditory experiences are consistent with the others except in the noise subset (Figure 7). If you remove her reports of noise, her total reported auditory experiences fall between the average and median number of reports at 5. All of Elena's reported experiences of noise, all her auditory experiences in general, occurred in Sheffield.

	Auditory	Noise
Elena	17	12
Lilly	6	1
Andrew	6	2
Carl	5	1
Tina	4	2
Matthew	3	2
Rose	1	1
James	0	0
Average	5.25	2.625
Median	4.5	2

Figure 6

Elena reported experiencing hearing loss, but her reported experiences with unidentifiable noises and voices both precede and are subsequent to her hearing loss. Additionally, she stated she had experienced things like the sound of unidentified glass breaking while in the company of others who at the time corroborated hearing the sound with her.

Carl and Elena both seem to recollect the same event where they heard footsteps on the roof when they were teenagers. However, Carl describes these footsteps as running, while Elena describes someone "walking really hard on the roof". Andrew then similarly describes hearing someone run on the roof years later as a teenager himself, and while in the presence of someone he was seeing romantically who at the time corroborated the experience. This is an example where, as we look for and consider the similarity of experiences between individuals, we need to consider if items such as vocabulary and inherent personal bias limit the expression of that experience, and as a result unnecessarily limit our focus of inquiry. Put more simply, if we take statements by experiencers too literally, we may miss opportunities to make connections between their experiences and those of others.

The category of vocalizations, chiefly talking and mimicry, is where auditory experiences were significant. For example, if you remove the reports of noise experienced by Elena as an outlier, 16 of the remaining 29 total auditory experiences are vocalizations of some sort. Sheffield had 5 and 4 mimicry and talking reports respectively. Carl reported a case of mimicry experienced by him and his wife at his home, while Tina reported 2 distinct experiences of mimicry at her home. Notably, the only other report of hearing talking was when Lilly lived at Tina's home, although this reportedly happened while Lilly was falling asleep.

	Vocalizations	Mimicry	Talking
Elena	4	3	1
Carl	4	0	2
Lilly	3	1	2
Matthew	2	1	1
Tina	2	2	0
Andrew	1	0	0
James	0	0	0
Rose	0	0	0
Average	2		
Median	2		

Figure 7

Observed experiences were the broadest, encompassing seeing items move, having items move in the absence of a witness, the appearance of humanoid figures, and otherwise uncategorized items seen. Defined more generally, it could be described as a change in the environment that is visually identifiable.

There were 61 reported observed experiences, with Elena leading all reports with a total of 24 (Figure 8). If Elena is removed, the average falls from 7.62 to 5.29, while the median remains nearly the same at 4. Carl then becomes the individual with the most total observed reports with 11. In both the categories of observed movements or changes and observed human figures, Elena reported significantly more experiences than the next person, Carl.

	Total Observed	Object Changed or Moved	Human Observed
Elena	24	8	7
Lilly	4	2	1
Andrew	2	0	0
Carl	11	3	4
Tina	4	2	0
Matthew	5	0	3
Rose	4	2	0
James	7	0	2
Average	7.62	2.13	2.13
Median	4.5	2	2

Figure 8

Human figures were seen more often by the Santiago family than the Cortez Family (Figures 8 and 17). Men were seen in the Sheffield house, with multiple reported sightings of a man in a flannel or checkered shirt. Carl reported seeing a hag (to be reviewed in the discussion of experiences near sleep below) within the Sheffield home, while Elena reported being within the house when she saw a Native American woman in traditional dress run through the alley behind Sheffield. Only two individuals reported seeing a child, Elena saw a blonde-haired girl at Sheffield, while Matthew saw a dark-haired girl (repeatedly) in his home. Both children appeared to be aware they were seen.

Matthew and Elena shared similar experiences at the same residence in the Philippines. Matthew reported an orb in his room appearing to watch him, while Elena described a ball of fire appearing before her. It's unclear, and impossible to say, if they were describing the same object. Elena and Carl both reported seeing orbs in their homes as adults. James reported seeing a ball of flame in the sky of West Texas that is probably more accurately described as an unidentified flying object.

Everyone in the Santiago family save for Matthew reported seeing a shadow of some sort, with a total of 13 such sightings. Elena led the mentions with 4, but three others were tied at 2. It's debatable that when Lilly says she saw the eyes above her whether she was describing a shadow figure versus disembodied eyes. Additionally, Rose and Matthew both described dark figures that were humanoid in that they wore clothes (per my understanding of their descriptions), but the features of the figures were indecipherably dark. Oddly enough, both of these sightings occurred in the early hours of the morning in the respective driveways of their homes.

	Shadow
Elena	4
Lilly	1
Andrew	2
Carl	2
Tina	2
Matthew	0
Rose	1
James	1
Average	1.63
Median	1.5

Figure 9

All of Tina, Lilly and James's mentions of shadows occurred near sleep. While Rose's reference to a shadow was not near sleep, Carl, Elena, and Andrew reported seeing shadows both near sleep and while wide awake. Carl and Elena also reported seeing shadows pass by at the Sheffield house, with Elena specifically stating, "I see shadows peeking around the corner." Every one of the Santiago family interviewed reported at least one event near sleep, with four individuals reporting 3 events (Figure 10).

	Near Sleep
Elena	3
Lilly	3
Andrew	1
Carl	3
Tina	3
Matthew	1
Rose	1
James	1
Average	2
Median	1

Figure 10

Sleep paralysis is a state when waking or falling to sleep where the mind is aware of its surroundings, but the body is unable to move or speak. Some have surmised that it is from this paralyzed state that the specter of the succubus and incubus arose, and it has again been theorized that many of the threatening shadow figures people describe are the result of hallucinations experienced while under the effects of sleep paralysis.

Turning briefly to Lilly, the events she described after using the Ouija board occurred near sleep and in conjunction with paralysis, and her report didn't appear to indicate anyone else heard the noises she described. While Carl corroborated Lilly wanting to switch rooms and her having mentioned the Ouija board, he did not appear to recall anything like the sounds she described. But again, Carl too had his experience with what he described as the hag in a situation that may have been sleep paralysis. These and other similar experiences by the family may indicate that at least some of their experiences were due to sleep paralysis, and the apparent prevalence of sleep paralysis in the family mandated additional research.

In the journal article "A twin and molecular genetics study of sleep paralysis and associated factors," researchers "found that self-reports of general sleep quality, anxiety symptoms and exposure to threatening events were all associated independently with sleep paralysis (Gregory, 2015)". Gregory also found in their study of twins that sleep paralysis was moderately heritable. Approximately one fifth of respondents reported at least one experience of sleep paralysis in a 2011 study reviewing the lifetime prevalence of sleep paralysis (Barber, 2011). What this could mean is that the Santiago family, living in the same home and under the same pressures, may have been more likely to experience sleep paralysis than is typical based on their inherent genetics and external factors.

Eventually, the questions I asked were broad enough for the subject of UFOs (unidentified flying objects) to arise. UFOs were not a subject I asked about when I began the interviews, but they were by the end simply because of how common an experience they appeared to be. This is an example of the questions asked, and what I told everyone I was interested in learning about initially, influencing how those being interviewed responded. Even in interviews where UFO sightings were mentioned, UFO sightings were not an initial topic of questioning. As a result, there was not much follow up. The topic was treated as an extraneous matter, as one might argue UFOs and the paranormal have nothing to do with one another. Regardless, as the people I interviewed became more comfortable, they began sharing more experiences beyond ghosts.

While reviewing the data, I noticed a vague correlation between those who had reported a mist or fog of some sort at some time, and those who had reported seeing UFOs (Figure 11). Seeing a mist of some sort was particular to the Santiago family. The only respondent from the Cortez family to use the term used it to describe a flying figure that might better be described as translucent rather than a mist. Similarly, Matthew described one experience in his home as a heat wave, which could also describe a form of translucency.

After noticing the correlation, I contacted Carl and Matthew (the latter based on his heat wave comment), and both confirmed they had previously seen UFOs. In that follow up conversation Matthew described the heat wave as consistent with my understanding of translucency, or refracting light. When asked to describe the size and shape of the heat wave, he stated there were actually two, about two feet apart, each about three feet high. Rose was the only Santiago who reported seeing a mist-like form that didn't report seeing a UFO. However, when asked further about the experience with the mist-like form, she said she felt it seemed more alien than ghostlike, as it was so foreign in appearance. I am not arguing causation, but at least an interesting coincidence. On the other hand, it could be that the observation of lights behaving oddly in the sky is much more prevalent than we are aware, and so can be correlated with any number of items if you try hard enough.

	Mist	UFO
Elena	1	1
Lilly	0	0
Andrew	0	0
Carl	1	1
Tina	0	0
Matthew	1	1
Rose	1	0
James	1	2
Average	0.63	0.63
Median	1	0.5

Figure 11

It was reported in a number of interviews that as a small child I would say I saw a man with a checkered shirt in jeans, like a lumberjack. This is consistent with other reports shared on the Strange Familiars (Renner, 2018) podcast where a similar lumberjack-looking man dubbed the Flannel Man was seen in homes and locations where the man's presence would be out of the ordinary. It would be understandable if one were to assume these were influenced by the cultural zeitgeist of Flannel Man reports, but these accounts are easily over 35 years old. Far earlier than the listeners of Strange Familiars and other podcasts brought the image to the public consciousness.

While I don't want to dismiss the accounts shared by Elena, Rose, and Wanda where I describe seeing or speaking to something matching the description of the Flannel Man, they were not tabulated as experiences.

After all, I can't deny the possibility that my imagination of the time played a part in them since I have no memory of anything like the accounts they describe. It is possible I overheard someone mention a dream or experience of their own and inserted the description into my play. The frequency with which other small children seemed to stare off into space in that house as reported by Elena and others gives one pause, but it is difficult to draw any conclusions from children that are unable or barely able to speak and cannot communicate their experience.

Aside from secondhand stories about myself or other children, only Elena and Carl reported seeing the man in a checkered shirt, or flannel, directly. While James related a story of his mother having spoken to "the man with all the hair," the words he attributes to his mother don't directly reference a man in a flannel or checkered shirt. Purely based on what he said when interviewed, it's possible he conflated multiple descriptions he'd been given over time and assumed or misremembered it was the same apparition. This same perspective could possibly be applied to Elena and Carl's reports. Both Carl's experiences of seeing a man outside his room or crossing the hallway occurred when he wouldn't be much older than 12 years old. Elena, however, shared 2 experiences as an adult where she saw a man matching the description pass quickly in the hallway.

So, leaving the exact description aside, what is just as interesting to me is the repeated figure of a man whose face can't be seen, whether viewed head on or from the side, and whose face at times is absent altogether. This is something I'd like to consider further when I look at similarity of experiences between the families. Specifically, I realized when reviewing Carl's interview that it was unclear just where the man in the checkered shirt whom he saw was standing in relation to Carl, before Carl ran out of the room. Or, what he meant when he said he couldn't see the man's face. Carl made himself available for follow up questions since the interview, and I reached out to him again for clarification.

Carl shared that the man he saw was standing outside his window, and so Carl was only able to see the man from the waist up. Carl confirmed that the parts of the body he could see were clear, as much as anyone standing outside his window would normally be. It was only the face he couldn't see. I asked for more detail here, what exactly did he mean? Was the face absent, blurry? Carl stated the face was blurry, out of focus. This contrasts with the body Carl could see clearly, and he did not indicate there was any kind of obstruction preventing him from seeing the face.

CORTEZ FAMILY

The maternal and paternal lineage of the Cortez family are both traced back through Mexico, more specifically Piedras Negras in the state of Coahuila in the case of their father. Their mother's parents were from Goliad, TX, but there were no more details readily available about their origins.

As will be described in the interviews, their father traveled from Mexico by himself to live with family in Eagle Pass as a 13-year-old. He never spoke English, but he was a talented carpenter and was able to support his large family. Upon marriage their mother stayed home to raise the children, a necessity due to their number.

I do not have detailed information about their mother and father, my grandmother and grandfather, but my memories of them are that they were kind and hard-working people. I still remember my grandfather walking me down the street to pick out cookies and sweet bread from a small local bakery, the specific image and taste of which I still crave today.

Like the Sheffield house, when the Cortez family moved into the Telford house the oldest child had already left home. The house was across the street from a church and was visibly old by the time I became aware of my surroundings and visits there. It had a pier and beam foundation, and there were parts of the floor where you could see through to the ground below.

Not just the house, but I am told the neighborhood was senior citizens when the Cortez family moved in, the neighbors retired teachers, and the Cortez family the only children. As will be described in the interviews, the original house is no longer there, although a new home has been built on the same property.

See the family tree below. Joseph and Melissa are twins, both stated they could not recall having any paranormal experiences as a child or adult and were not interviewed. Paul, Elijah, and Connie were not interviewed.

These are left in the order of the interviews, as the interviews tend to build on and refer back to previous interviews with the other family members.

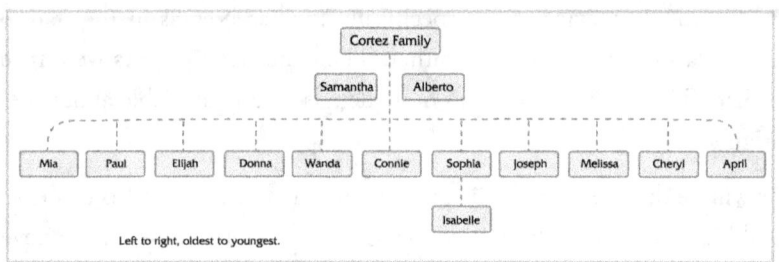

WANDA

[The first person I interviewed was my mother, Wanda, as at the time she was the only person I knew would agree to sit down with me. She is seated comfortably, surrounded by her dogs. I briefly tell her my goals with the interviews, and she begins to fill me in on the background of her family, barely giving me time to start the recorder.]

Wanda: —Which was Grandma, my mom's mother. And she said when they first came across, when they were girls—Because there were a lot of girls from their family, and her father, my grandfather, his brother married my grandma's sister. So, they were both married to brothers and sisters, and they came across on wagons. They were on wagons back in their day, so she learned how to sew and everything. She says even back then there was stuff that they couldn't explain. She was very religious, too, and she used to say that children had virgin's souls, so they could still talk to and see the saints that we couldn't see, the angels or otherwise. And she said that she had seen some stuff in her childhood that they believe were witches and they—What did they call them? I always get those names wrong. Chalusa or something? It was like Chalusa, but it's a Mexican name. It was a witch that would turn into an ugly bird form or something, because they used to say that if you woke up bruised and stuff, it was that the witch was attacking you. And my grandma from Eagle Pass used to say that's true. My mom's mother, which was Luna, she had her small two-bedroom house and she had four kids. Her kids had already grown up. In that house, she had one room, the bathroom divided the two rooms, and you could hear a ball bounce. When I was with her during the day it didn't bother us any, and I looked at her and she goes, "It's just the ghost in that room."

Jed: How old were you?

Wanda: I was like nine. And I'm like, "Ghost?" And she goes, "Yeah, it won't do nothing to you. It's just a friendly ghost." I was like, okay. Then I was coming out of the bathroom and the rocker, she had a rocker in that room, was rocking. And the ball was bouncing, and bouncing, but I was the only young kid there that day. And she goes, "Were you playing with the ball?" "No." "Okay, go sit down." When I got older, I said, "You really have a ghost in there?" She goes, "Yeah, you can feel him looking at you. A child and an adult. But they won't bother you. They're not evil." But I was scared to stay in that house if it was nighttime. Because you would hear the noise of people walking and whatnot. But she would say her prayers, and she said she didn't think anything of it.

And then as we got older, I guess I was 10 or 12 because I was already living at home. We were at our house, and Mom and Dad, they had to go pick up Uncle Paul and Uncle Elijah from work. It was the middle of the night, and April was a baby. So, me and Aunt Donna were there. We were the oldest in the house, all the kids below us were sleeping. In that house, we didn't have very many rooms. You had one big living room, big kitchen, big back room. So, you had like three beds in a room. I was mad because I was fighting with Aunt Donna. I went into the back room and Aunt Donna stayed in the living room. In the living room, there was a window on one side, and two windows on the other side of the room. Then as you go through there, there's a kitchen you'd have to go through.

I went into the other room and I was pouting, and Aunt Donna goes, "You better stop lighting matches. I'mma tell Mom when they get home." And it got real quiet, I said, "I'm not lighting matches, you are." She goes, "No, I'm not." So, I come back in the living room with her, and we're sitting there. She goes, "Really, you're not?" I said no. And then in the window by April's crib, the curtains started blowing like there was a breeze coming in. We didn't have the windows open. We looked at each other and we started saying our Father who art in heaven. We went and got April out of the bed and put her with us. We're lying there, and then when Mom and Dad got home with the boys, we told them. Dad always used to say, "If you're fighting with each other, something's going to happen. It's evil coming out. Y'all need to stop."

But in that house, you would always hear a baby crying. And you think, well maybe it's the neighbor next door. But the neighbors next door didn't have any kids. And the neighbors that were on the other side were as old as we were. But you'd hear it like it was right in that room. And they used to scare us half to death.

Jed: This is the house that I was familiar with, the one across from the church?

Wanda: That was the only one you were familiar with.

Jed: Yeah, this is a different one?

Wanda: This was a different one. This was over there on Amanda. They already knocked it down. It was the small little house that Mom and Dad used to have on a half-acre. And back in those days we had an outhouse. We didn't have a bathroom until Dad finally attached one to the house. But yeah, you could hear things. Uncle Paul always used to walk in his sleep. They used to have to watch him because he'd sit there and then you could lock the door and put all kinds of locks on it. He'd unlock it, go around the house, come back in, and go back to bed like nothing.

That's when we found out from Mom that Dad had said when he was little, he came to the states at 13 from Mexico, he had left one time from the house, and he was mad as hell. He used to fight with his sister, because she was wild and he was always trying to keep her in the house. He was cussing and everything else. As he was walking, he said that there was a man behind him throwing bricks at him. All dressed in black, throwing bricks at him, and he got mad and he turned around and told him something, picked up the brick to throw it, as he got it up in his hand, the brick disappeared. The guy threw a brick at him again and Dad went to pick it up again, cussing at him, and it disappeared. And it happened three times, and the third time it scared Dad half to death that he ran home. And Mom said for three days he couldn't talk. He was just scared to death. So, Dad was a real believer.

Jed: How old was he when that happened?

Wanda: 16 I guess, 17, and it scared him. Dad was one that—He always had his little cross with him and stuff. But Mom said he never spoke about it. He would never sit there and repeat it or anything like that. He was scared. He himself said that had to have been the devil.

Dad's sister would go to a fortune teller in Mexico across from Eagle Pass. Mom used to say, "No, no, I don't want to know the future and I don't want to hear anything." Everything would scare her. And Dad was just like, nope. He just made sure that he paid for everything that he did. He helped people for whatever he could, because he believed that what you do right for somebody else will come back around for you. If you do evil, it was going to come back to you, so he didn't like to do anybody any wrong.

We were having problems with our little house on Amanda, so we moved up a couple of houses to rent a house from one of Mom's and Dad's friends. We were living in there, and Dad wasn't home yet, he was working. I think he was working in Louisiana. He used to go with the company that he worked with to go build houses in different areas, usually Louisiana or something like that. So, he wasn't home. We were at the house and Uncle Paul and Uncle Elijah were fighting with each other. They were running down the street, they're chasing each other. And Aunt Donna was in another room sleeping.

We were in the living room, and I don't know where Mom was, or if she was there or what, but, we saw this big bird up on the electrical poles. And it's like, "Hey, c'mere, look at this bird!" We're seeing it, and it was just watching the house. Like, what is that? And—Oh! It was called a Lechuza! That's what it was called. Lechuza. And they said, "Is it one of those?" I said, "I don't know, I've never seen one." We're standing there looking, and we go to wake up Donna. *[mimics shaking someone]* Donna, wake up. *[Mimics someone waking slowly]*.

She woke up, she goes, "There was a man over me holding my neck. I couldn't wake up, he was choking me." But there's nobody here, and she said, "No, no, he was standing right there, he's standing right there." And so, we had started saying our prayers. We go to the living room and Elijah and Uncle Paul run back, and they were mad. He goes, "Well, Elijah punched me in the ear." Blah blah blah, they're fighting. "Well, what happened?" "We were fighting over at the house, and all of a sudden we smelled sulfur." And they ran back home, scared to death. And then there was two of those Lechuzas, or birds, hanging—I mean, they were big, they were just—I've never seen a bird that big.

Jed: There was one at first.

Wanda: There was, then there were two.

Jed: It wasn't an owl or something? Or a vulture?

Wanda: We've never seen the owls. No. These were bigger. That's why it scared us so much, because we were so young.

Jed: You've seen owls and buzzards.

Wanda: I've seen owls and buzzards. Yeah. Because even then at one time when we moved out to FM 78, I mean Pfeil Road where we bought a house, I was driving to work one morning and I swear I saw this thing standing on the side of the road about this big *[sticks her arm out below shoulder height]* and it would just look out past it, and I go, what the heck? And look in my mirror and there's nothing there. Like, I'm just seeing things, it's too early in the morning. Maybe that was an owl. What would that owl be doing on the side of the road? That's like—

Jed: Like how tall?

Wanda: Three feet, four feet tall. And I knew it was an animal, but it looked like a bird just sitting there.

Jed: But four feet tall sitting there.

Wanda: Yeah, just—Yeah. Three, four feet tall, an' I was like, okay, that an owl? I've never seen one get that big. Why would it be on the side of the road? Because again, it was just sitting there. You know what I mean? It was like a giant thing. Well, I look in my mirror and there's nothing there. And there's cars behind me, so I was like... I'm just seeing things, hallucinating.

[After follow-up questioning, she was sure it was some kind of bird because while it was taller and thicker than any bird she knew of, she could see the texture of feathers and what she described as two large black eyes when she passed. She couldn't see any other features, and no sign of carrion that it might have been feeding on.]

Wanda: So, yeah, we sat there and watched it for a while. We're sitting there and, "Where'd it go?" All of a sudden, they disappeared.

Jed: All of you saw it? So ever since then, you've never seen any type of bird that looked like the two birds that were on the line?

Wanda: No, never. And I have never known anything to be that big. It scared us, because it's like, is it an owl, is it a vulture? No, it's too big. Because we were all of us standing at the screen door. Back then you had screen doors, you had the main door open. And you know, just the reflection of the streetlights, those are big.

Jed: Was it at night?

Wanda: It was at night. Yeah. It was already like 10, 11 o'clock at night. So, it was already dark. We sat there, "Hail Mary full of Gra—" That's the only time we sat there and said our prayers. We said, "See, Dad says quit fighting, this is why it happens." Those are the only things I can think of right now.

Jed: The thing with April, was that at night, too, or in the afternoon?

Wanda: That was at night. Because they used to work in the Argyle. They would get off at 12, 1 o'clock in the morning. So that was in the middle of the night when they would sit there and have to go get them.

Jed: How old were they?

Wanda: They were already 18, 19. They were still in high school, but they were working. Aunt Mia had moved out to Philadelphia already, New York, with one of our Aunts. Me and Donna were the oldest girls in the house and the other kids were sleeping. Everybody was sleeping, it was me and her that were awake. We were supposed to watch the kids and not open the door to anybody, because it was so late. When that happened, we looked at each other, because we didn't have any fans on.

Jed: And y'all had the...

Wanda: The windows closed. We had everything closed.

Jed: Did you have the, I know you didn't have central air, the wall mounts *[window units]*?

Wanda: We had nothing. All the windows were closed, because if you had any, it was—I think it was during the winter, actually. All the doors were closed, the curtains—We always closed the curtains. You couldn't see in. When the curtains actually blew from the window, we looked at each other saying, "Did you open the window?" It was like, no. So, right away we went to get the baby out of the crib, because we didn't know what was going—And the thing is—That's what I forgot to tell you. The thing is, you could hear like, wings fluttering. Like if a bird was there, and it's like in a cage? You could hear fluttering. It's like, oh my God. So, we got the baby out of there in a hurry. But then they kind of—Well, after we started praying it kind of settled down and...

Jed: Same neighborhood that... The earlier house?

Wanda: Yeah. Yeah. Same neighborhood. It was on Amanda.

Jed: Was she old enough to stand at that time, or?

Wanda: Yeah, but she was asleep. I think she was like between six months and a year. She was fast asleep. It was only me and Aunt Donna that were awake. And, uh, the baby—Sometimes you'd hear voices in the kitchen and the baby crying. Well, you know, in another time at the other house, we had seen—

Jed: Still at Amanda?

Wanda: Still on Amanda, in the house up the street. Where we lived was 1655 and the other house was like four houses up. Dad was renting that house until he fixed something or the other. You could see what looked like a giant fire in the backyard. That house had a garage detached from the house, but it looked like a fire behind the garage. We went out to see, and there was nothing there. It looked like there's a fire, because you see the red...

Jed: You didn't see the flames, but it was behind the shed?

Wanda: It was behind the garage, and you see the redness, like it was a fire back there, so, it was like...

Jed: Like flickering?

Wanda: Yeah. And it was, it was like—So, Dad went and looked, and it was nothing. One of my grandmas says, 'cause Mom had told her, she says, "When you see that, usually it means that there's metal or gold or something buried there." I go, "I'm not going to dig it up to find out if it's not." But we could never figure out what it was. Dad went out there to see if the shed was okay and... No fire. And it wasn't the neighbors, all was quiet and dark.

Jed: Did it stop before he went out there, or, could you see?

Wanda: It stopped before he went to see.

Jed: About what year was this?

Wanda: This was also in the '70s, because April was born in 1965. And we stayed in this house for about five years, I think, then we moved back to our old house. Yeah. But we moved back to our old house, because at the same time we felt that there was—Livin' in the house that we rented from their friends, Dad and Mom felt like there was evil or something there. 'Cause it seemed like nothing was ever working for us, everything was going wrong. We moved back to our old house and stayed there until Paul got out of the service. Mia was in New York. Paul got out of the service and our house was getting worse, and so Paul decided, okay, I've saved some money, I'm going to get y'all into a bigger house. Dad didn't want to move. We moved into the house on Telford and Dad stayed for a week or so at the old house, and he says, "Okay, I'm moving in with y'all." But yeah, that other one was... I've got to think of what my grandma used to tell me all the time. I didn't see Dad's family too much, because they were in Eagle Pass. And us younger kids couldn't talk as much Spanish, so they didn't want to see us because they couldn't communicate with us. So, they only seemed like they would take Paul and Mia. We would see the Luna grandmother more than the other ones.

Jed: So, the Eagle Pass ones weren't the ones who spoke English?

Wanda: The younger kids spoke English; we only spoke Spanish up until a certain age. Like I was speaking Spanish until I was in kindergarten, and then the schools made us stop. You had to sit there and learn English and they wouldn't let you speak two languages, so they put you in Head Start and you had to stop. And you couldn't talk Spanish at home anymore. So, the two older ones, which is Paul and Mia, were the only ones they used to take to Eagle Pass all the time because they could still speak Spanish. The only grandparents we saw were on Mom's side. And the ones that saw them the most was Elijah and Donna, until they started getting bigger and then they didn't have time. They didn't want to go over there.

I would go with Mom and visit her for weekends to get away from everybody in the house. But she's the one that used to tell me how it was in the past. She was the one that would sit there and tell me if something went wrong, we did some evil to somebody else, always expect it to come back to you. You always have to be fair, and everything else. Because Grandma on Mom's side, Luna, she actually had nine pregnancies, but only four of them lived. The very last one that had died was of some illness or something she says, and so she had a lot that... You know. And back then she said the women had to do everything. They'd have to wash clothes, to take care of the kids, cook, and they just did whatever they were told. But there weren't a lot of medicines and stuff like that. So, they couldn't understand some of the stuff that was happening or anything. As far as illness and stuff, they didn't know how to treat a lot of things. She used to say that there were things that they would see they couldn't explain, but they wouldn't ever talk about it. Just because it was... Who would believe you anyway? I've gotta think of all the things she'd tell me, because I used to love to ask her questions.

Jed: She'd tell you specific things?

Wanda: Yeah, she liked to talk. Because we'd get up at four o'clock in the morning. That's when I started getting used to getting up early. That and the fact there were 11 kids in the family. You'd better get up early to get in the shower before everybody else. So, when I'd go and stay with her, she'd get up at four, make coffee, go outside tend to her plants and whatnot, come back in, cook breakfast for Grandpa, and continue her day like that. And then she'd sew, or crochet, and on like that.

Jed: How old were you and how old was she?

Wanda: She was already in her 60s, I think, because she was already— She was in her fifties, because I think when I first went to her house Melissa and Joseph had their one-year-old birthday party there. And that's when I was old enough to know, I think nine or ten, to know about the ghosts and stuff.

Jed: The stuff at her house with the rocking chair and the balls, was that day, night, all times of the day?

Wanda: It was day and night. Mostly in the day you'd hear it. At night you'd sometimes hear the rocker rocking.

Jed: And the footsteps at night?

Wanda: Yeah.

Jed: But the ball you'd hear during the day.

Wanda: During the day.

Jed: You could see...

Wanda: I'd see the ball bouncing *[she later said the ball appeared to have been dropped from around knee high]*. You could see the rocker rocking.

Jed: When you saw the rocker, was it day or night?

Wanda: It was daytime, because I had taken a shower, I'd gotten dressed and came out of the room and the rocker was rocking. And I said, "Grandma were you sitting in there?" And she goes, "No." I said, "The rocker was rocking." She goes, "Yeah, it's the spirit in there." And I looked at her. I said, "Does it do it often?" She goes, "Yeah, it doesn't do no harm, though. I think whoever had the house before must have died here with a young one, because you'll hear the ball bounce sometimes." And I go, "I know, I've heard that." She goes, "They won't do you no harm. They're not the evil ones."

Jed: So that was like 1965?

Wanda: Yeah. April was born in 1965. And Melissa and Joseph they had their one-year-old birthday party over there. Yeah, because Grandma and Grandpa would have different ones of us go spend the night with them, like two or three of us kids. I know one time I went over there, I got so scared I didn't want to stay. My dad had to go and get me, because I cried and cried. I couldn't go to sleep.

Jed: Why?

Wanda: I was scared in the house. It was nighttime, I didn't want to stay there. It was like—

Jed: Cause of all the sounds in the house.

Wanda: I think so, it's like... Because she would have us sleep in the living room, and there was—They had their room in another room, and the other room is the one where you'd see the stuff move. I said I wanted to go spend the night, they go okay, but we're not bringing you home. I said okay. Luckily, they didn't live too far, because I cried and they had to call Dad and tell 'im to come get me because I wouldn't go to sleep. I was crying all night. It was like, every time I was falling asleep, I'd hear the rocker move, or somebody standing—I felt like somebody was standing over me. So, Dad came and got me. I never did go back and stay at the house at night. I'm like, no, thank you.

Jed: So, she was a young girl in the early 1900's then?

Wanda: Yeah. She was younger, they were young, so—Well Grandpa, my grandfather, he died when he was 83 I believe, or maybe older. I forget how old he was. Because Dad, your grandfather, died at 83. Mom died at 76 years old. That's when I started realizing, okay, there are certain things that you can't explain, certain noises and stuff. And they used to scare us. Grandma used to say when sometimes you'd hear those dogs howl real ugly? Someone's died and they feel it, that's why they howl like that. Because we used to have animals all the time, our dogs. We didn't ever have any cats. Mostly dogs and goats. Those are the only ones I can remember right now on Amanda. I'm trying to remember others. There was another one I remembered. Great Grandma's... My mind went blank.

Jed: Well, which house were you at when you said Grandma was sick and she saw someone?

Wanda: Oh, this is the one on Amanda. I stayed home with her that day, because she was running a fever, really sick. But Mom had so many kids that she said, "No, I ain't going to the doctor, I'm not going anywhere, I'm fine."

Jed: How old were you?

Wanda: I think I was ten. My grades were better, I was the middle child, so I could miss more school than the others. So I stayed home and I was watching her, and she was lying on the bed. I thought maybe she just had fever and was delirious, she goes, "'Wanda, open the door for the man, he's knocking." I said, "Mom, nobody's knocking." "Yes, he's at the door, open the door." I go, "Mom, there's nobody knocking." I got up and looked out the window. I said, "Mom, there's nobody here." She goes, "It's a man all dressed in black. He's at the door, open the door." I said, "Mom, there's nobody here. I'm not opening that door for anybody." And she's like, "Mija…" and she turned back around to go to sleep.

I started saying my prayers and I just got back in bed with her. I was next to her, and when she woke up, I said, "Mom, are you okay?" She goes, "Why?" I said, "You told me to open the door for the man at the door." She goes, "I said that?" I said, "Yeah." She goes, "I thought I was dreaming. I seen a man there." I said, "Yeah, I know, you said he was all dressed in black." She looked at me, I said, "But Mom, there was nobody there." She goes, "I must have been really sick." I said, "You seriously scared the heck out of me. I had to start praying." She goes, "I'm sorry. But now that you're telling me this, I really did see it." I said, "I know, I thought you were sleepin', but I looked at your eyes and they were awake." She goes, "I guess I was sicker than I thought." I said, "I think so."

All I did was pray, and went and got her Rosary, lit a candle. Your great grandma, Mom's mom, Luna—Both grandmas were religious, but Grandma Luna is the one that always had her little mantle with her saints and stuff. She would say her prayers every morning, every night. She'd light her candles and Mom didn't have a spot to do that, but every now and then she'd have a candle like on the stove and stuff like that. And she had her crosses. But it's like they say, put a cross on your door to keep the evil out.

And I thought, man, that scared the heck out of me when she keeps saying open the door, there's a man dressed all in black. It's like when they say people are close to death, they start talking to the dead people on the other side. That happened when Dad started talking to his deceased mother and father, and saying, "Oh, look, here they are right now." And when Mom was almost dying one time and she was on the verge, she said it's true. She goes, "If you say I was almost dying, I was talking to my mom."

Jed: When was that?

Wanda: When Mom went into a coma, I think ten years before she passed away? She passed away in 2001. Ten years before that, she had gone into a coma. She fell and hit her head. She had two blood vessels

183

that burst, so she was in a coma for two weeks. That was another one. She was in a coma for two weeks when she had her liver turn from hepatitis C, to cirrhosis of the liver. And even then, she said when she'd been in a coma she could hear everybody talking, but she couldn't say anything. I said, oh, so it's true, people can hear you when they're in a coma, they just can't speak. The other time was when she had the blood vessels that burst. When she was in the hospital, she said, "I was pretty close, but Grandma and them said it wasn't time. I could see the light." She goes, "You can see a light, and it was real peaceful, but she said, 'No, you have to go back, you're not ready yet.'" And she goes, "And I could see her. I could see Grandma and Grandpa, they all looked happy." I said, "Well, that's good to hear there's another side."

Jed: She saw her parents, and your father saw—

Wanda: His father, yeah.

Jed: —His parents?

Wanda: His parents, yeah. They say when you're dying and you're really on the edge, you can hear, you can start seeing your family, the dead people. They're there waiting for you. You look at them *[the people on their deathbed]*, and it's like they're already deceased. You know it's getting close.

Jed: It's like a lot of the stuff that happened to you, that you saw or heard, was kind of around the same time period.

Wanda: Yeah, it was! It was weird.

Jed: What was the street across from the, uh…?

Wanda: Uh, Telford? That one. There was a presence there, also. But it was, that was also in one room.

Jed: The back room?

Wanda: No, that was in the front, the first room. We had the living room, bedroom, dining room, and the back room. But that one room in the front is the one where Mom would sleep, and times that you would sleep you'd feel somebody watching you. And I thought it was just me at first, and then Mom said, "No, I do feel I'm being watched sometimes in there." But you know, nothing ever really happened. You just felt like there was another presence behind your shoulder, or somebody standing behind you. To me it didn't feel evil. I don't know if anybody else felt it, but it would feel like there was somebody there, at all times, in that one room.

Jed: How old were you by that time?

Wanda: 15, 16. Yeah, I was 16 years old, at least.

Jed: I thought something happened to somebody, in the back-corner room.

Wanda: I'm trying to think, because after I got married to your dad, I stayed there. Before then, Mom had that living room, the girls had the back room. We had one bed and the back washroom. It was called a washroom, we had a bed in there, also. And that had windows all around, but I can't think of anything back there.

Jed: You never saw people or anything like that.

Wanda: Uh-uh.

Jed: Except for the birds.

Wanda: Except for the birds. I never saw people. Every now and then I'd feel as if there's somebody in the house or something like that. Like, I might have seen a flash of someone coming by, like a ghost. But not so much that'd you see the ghost, it's just like, corner of your eye, peripheral vision, something passing. Sit there and turn and there's nobody there.

Jed: But you never really heard or saw anything as an adult?

Wanda: Uh-uh, not that I can think of.

Jed: You said, at the old house—What did you tell me? The one we sold.

Wanda: Stephen's *[her nephew]* the one that saw one. There, I always felt that I'd see somebody. The house I bought used to belong to the guy's father. His family was living there. He said it was his mom's house and he wasn't gonna keep it, so that's why I bought it by taking over payments. But I never saw anybody. Every now and then I'd feel like somebody walked past me, and it was nothing. But that's about all I ever felt. I was surprised when you told me that room always scared you, that back room.

Jed: But I always thought I was just afraid of the dark. There's been some houses, apartments, where I was totally comfortable. Like my preference was sleeping in the pitch dark, because I got to sleep easier.

Wanda: Well, and then when I moved out, after I broke my elbows and came here, Stephen was staying there. He said that he just felt very uncomfortable in the house. He was scared, and he would burn his candles, because he felt that there were ghosts there. I mean, I guess I felt like sometimes somebody would be watching me, and I'd tell myself there's nobody here except you.

Where I really felt there was something is when I'd see the dogs growl at a door or something. It'd be wide open and they're just growling like there's somebody standing there. And there's nobody there. I'd see them and it's like, something's going on. I only saw them do that a couple of times. But I just kind of put it out of my mind. It's like it must be a ghost or something if y'all are—Because they say dogs sense things first. And the whole house will be closed, it'd just be us and they'd be like at the door, just growling at nothing there.

Jed: It was day, night?

Wanda: It was at night. A couple of times during the day. But it's like, what are y'all growling at?

Jed: Would it be multiple of them *[dogs growling]*?

Wanda: Yeah, it would be a couple of 'em. I'd have to get up and go see because they're growling, and they'd run to the room, and they'd just lay there with me. Like, okay, guess something just scared you. I never really felt scared in the house. You figure, I did live there since I was 40 years old by myself. I just had me and the doggies.

Jed: So, 20 years?

Wanda: Yeah, 20 years.

Jed: Did those things happen early on in the 20 years? Later, in the middle?

Wanda: Early on in the 20 years. It just never bothered me.

Jed: And it never happened again? The dogs never got bothered again?

Wanda: Uh-uh. That was the other thing, too. At the one on Sheffield, your grandma's house? In that one, every now and then you would feel like somebody was watching you. But I'd be in the other room and you'd be talking in the room, in the front room. Because they had a living room, and bedroom, and two other small bedrooms to the side. And then a bathroom. So, when we had to stay there while they were building our house, we were living and sleeping in that one room.

Jed: How old was I?

Wanda: You probably were like five. And you would be talking and talking, and playing and laughing in the room. And then I'd go in, "Jed, who are you talking to?" "My friend." "Your friend?" "Yes." I said, "Okay. Well, be good. I'm going to be in the kitchen if you need something." "Okay." And Grandma says, "He shouldn't be talking to a friend." And I said, "Everybody has an invisible friend."

Now, one time I asked, "Jed, how old is your friend?" "I don't know." "Is he little like you, or bigger than you?" "He's bigger." "Really? He's bigger than you?" "Yes." And I said, "You don't know how old?" "No." I said, "Is he as old as Daddy?" "No. Maybe. But he just talks to me, makes me laugh." I said, "All right, you can keep talking to him, but if he's not nice, don't talk to him anymore." You said okay and went back to coloring. They would say, "He shouldn't be talking to 'em." And I said, "They grow out of it eventually. How are you going to have him stop talking to an invisible friend that you can't see? All you can do is keep him safe." Because I couldn't see anybody, and you'd be talking and talking away.

Jed: Who was telling you I shouldn't be talking to it?

Wanda: Your grandmother. "He shouldn't be talking to any invisible friends." "He always talks to his friend," I said. And I thought it was a little boy, and that's why I asked you how old is he? "He's a man." So, I started getting you out of the room so you wouldn't be in there all the time. And then Rose was always coming over and that's when she started teaching y'all school.

Jed: I remember that.

Wanda: Yeah. But you were always, you'd be playing in that room, but talking to the invisible person.

Jed: Was it just that room or in other parts of the house?

Wanda: It was mostly in that room that I remember you talking to him in.

Jed: Which room was it?

Wanda: That first living room. The living room and then the first bedroom. Right in front of the bathroom.

Jed: In that first bedroom in front of the bathroom is where I have that weird memory of, like, a guy with a beard and a plaid shirt. But it's, it's weird because the memory—Like I studied psychology and know memory is fallible and everything else like that. The longer it goes, the more difficult it is to remember exactly, if anything. And if what I'm trying to remember is when I was like five or six years old, that's even worse.

Wanda: I know.

Jed: But the image I have is like a shadow or silhouette on the wall, but not... a shadow, because I could see that there was a plaid pattern on the shirt.

Wanda: Yeah.

Jed: So, in my memory, it's like, I don't know if it's what I actually remember? Or the only way my mind can make sense of it. Because I can see a shadow with a beard, and a plaid shirt against the wall. It doesn't make sense to me, logically, but like that's—

Wanda: Yeah. Yeah. That's the room where you always used talk to him. In that one room by the bathroom. That's where Matthew used to sleep, too.

Jed: Did I ever describe it, or give it a name or anything?

Wanda: No. I have to think on that one.

Jed: Elena said that I told her a name, but I would want to see if I told anybody else the same thing.

Wanda: No. I don't know.

Jed: Because I had thought that I was the only person that really saw something like that. And then when I talked to Elena, she told me, "Oh no, other people saw him, too." And like, they still kind of do every now and then. And I was like, "Well, I really have no wish to go back to that house then."

Wanda: Well, the good thing is it was never, you've got to think of it, it wasn't an evil one.

Jed: That's true. I mean, it was always so uncomfortable for me. Like when you dropped me off there to go to school? From then, through high school, and visiting as an adult, it's just always been uncomfortable. I didn't like going to the bathroom—

Wanda: *[Laughing]*

Jed: Going to the back rooms, getting anything from the room for anybody. Going down the hall, I was just not comfortable anywhere in that house.

Wanda: Wow.

Jed: I mean, yeah, by all accounts I liked it...

Wanda: You were a young kid, that's why.

Jed: But I wonder why—Dad told me a story about Grandma hearing us kids laughing and being loud while Grandpa was asleep. Then going in there and us looking at nothing above the bed and laughing and talking, and us saying that "he" was making us laugh or something. So, I wondered what she was telling you guys. But she never told you anything like that was happening.

Wanda: Uh-uh. Because I had seen it where you would be talking and laughing. Every now and then you'd feel like there was a presence, but it didn't... You know, I just always shook it off.

Jed: Did you see me talking sometimes, like—

Wanda: Yes.

Jed: I was looking at something?

Wanda: You were looking at something in front of you and you'd be talking. You'd be looking up.

Jed: Like looking up at someone, like if someone was taller.

Wanda: Taller than me. That's why I'm trying to think of what the name was, but I'm bad on names and I forget 'em. I don't know if it was Tony, maybe?

Jed: So, when I was talking to someone, was that during the day? During the night?

Wanda: That was during the day. It'd be during the day, any time of the day where you'd be by yourself or something in the room. And sometimes, you wouldn't want to go to sleep at night. You'd fall asleep, finally get to sleep.

Jed: But I was never afraid.

Wanda: You were never afraid.

Jed: Was I afraid of the dark?

Wanda: When you were little?

Jed: I didn't become afraid of the dark until these things stopped happening, huh?

Wanda: Yeah, you didn't become afraid of the dark until later, because I didn't even know you were scared of the dark. I'm not sure if you started wanting to have a night light on. I couldn't sleep with a light. I never did like sleeping with a light on. You'd sit there and keep me awake. I don't know if I used to have to put a light out for you and Gerald. Because Gerald for the longest time couldn't sleep by himself. He'd crawl in bed with us. I don't remember.

Jed: Did that ever happen with Gerald? At any of the houses?

Wanda: No, not that I remember, no. I don't ever remember Gerald having a silent partner, a friend.

Jed: Or things that he said he saw or heard when he was a kid, that he might not remember now?

Wanda: Gerald wouldn't say anything. Gerald was one that talked very little about anything. I never remember him talking about, hey, I seen this, or Mom that. If he was scared or something, he wouldn't say nothing.

Jed: Well, I see why he wouldn't.

Wanda: Yeah. He wouldn't tell me.

Jed: I think he wouldn't want to make you worry about anything.

Wanda: Probably not.

Jed: Even then, he was—

Wanda: He's always been very protective.

Jed: Trying not to make you have to worry about anything, because you had enough to worry about?

Wanda: He was always—Gerald grew up too fast. He had to always take care. He felt at an early age he had to take care of me. And then, he took care of you. He's always been the protector. He wouldn't day a lot of things.

APRIL

[I meet April at her home, her granddaughter Evelyn in the other room playing. It's a two-story house in a new subdivision wherein she is the first tenant.]

April: It started when I was little. I was in elementary, so I guess I was like Evelyn's age, between five and seven. Maybe a little older. I would sleep with Mom, and I used to wake up because I felt something. I'd wake up and there was a man standing next to the bed, and he was all in black. You couldn't see his face or anything. And I used to wake up Mom and tell her, "Do you see the man?" And she said, "No, I don't see anything." And then he'd be gone. This happened like every night, and I was scared to go to sleep. Mom gave me a Rosary to put on and she said to say the Hail Mary and I wouldn't see it anymore.

So, before we went to bed, we always said our prayers. I started sleeping with the Rosary and I stopped seeing him. But it was happening often. I would see him, and then Uncle Elijah would see him in his room. I would see him standing by the bed. Elijah would hear him and see him in his room, but by where the heater was. Not standing directly by his bed. Then he would hear him. He had told Mom, and Mom said, "Well, April seen something."

Anyway, after I started sleeping with the Rosary and Mom blessed everything, I stopped seeing him. But, in Mom's old house there was always something or another going on from the time I was small, up until high school, and even after I moved out, because you would hear noises in the kitchen. Like dishes rattling, or you could hear whispering voices. One night I was asleep, my hair was long at that time, and I could feel somebody actually pulling my hair to where it was hard enough to pull me, like I was hanging off the bed. I was pulling myself to pull away, and they were pulling me back, and then I woke up. And I was hanging halfway off the bed. I got scared, I was like, what was that? When Dad was asleep, they used to pull the blankets off him.

I was getting ready one time when I was in high school. Mom and Dad were going to H-E-B and they had just left. I walked out, locked the door, and saw them drive off. I was getting ready in the restroom and I heard pounding on the door. "April, open the door!" Mom's voice. And I said, "Okay, Mom, hold on." "Hurry, open the door!" I'm like, "Okay, I'm coming!" I'm literally talking to 'em. I get to the door, nobody's there.

Jed: That was the bathroom door?

April: No, the front door. I was in the bathroom. I went to the door thinking, okay, I'm rushing, and she wasn't there.

Jed: These were all the same house?

April: All at Mom's old house.

Jed: Which house was that?

April: Telford. I was like, aww man, playing tricks again. So, then I went back, and then I heard it change from Mom's voice to Dad's. I'm like, okay, I know nobody's there, I'm not even gonna—

Jed: You started hearing Grandpa's voice, too?

April: Yeah. Yeah. It got to the point to where I was scared, but then I already knew. You know what I mean? It was just messing with me. We heard somebody in the kitchen, like they were putting up the dishes. Nobody. It wasn't nothin'. Oh, one night me and Mom were there by ourselves because Dad took off. When he was mad, he'd take off walking forever. We were in my room, and we heard him at the door, "Vieja!" That's how he used to call Mom. We went, he wasn't there. So, me and Mom got scared, we went across the street to the neighbor's house. But it was always doing stuff like that, either playing jokes or just trying to scare you. Plus, one time besides the hair, I felt somebody like this on my feet *[touches her feet]*. There was always stuff like that.

Jed: Was it while you were awake or while you were sleeping?

April: While I was going to sleep. Sometimes I was half asleep, half awake. Like where you're just drifting off? Then you would just hear like *[makes whispering noises]*, like people talking like that? Like you hear them, but you can't tell what they're saying. Like people on the corner or something and they're whispering? You can hear that.

So, one time me and Cheryl were there, and I think the dishes were moving again or something? And they used to have at the old house the glass cabinet doors? You could hear where they would shut *[slaps hands on cushions]*? Anyway, we got scared so Cheryl said, "Come on, let's go to Miss Haddock's house." So, we went next door and stayed at Miss Haddock's house.

And uh, let's see. I don't know if I already had Brian *[her son]* and I was living with your mom? Or it was right before that, because Dad was there. Mom was getting scared, because it started messing with her. She'd be in the room and then she'd see a quick shadow go by her. She could feel the shadow go by. Like, you know how when somebody walks by you real fast and you feel that breeze? She'd feel that. Then she'd be in the front room, and she could see the shadow walking back and forth in the kitchen. So, she called us one day, "I'm scared, come home." We went home, and I remember Aunt Cheryl got a priest out there a couple of times to bless the house, because there was so much stuff going on. I think they told Cheryl there was something in the house, or something like that? Cheryl could tell you more. But, yeah, Mom was getting really scared because she kept seeing the shadow and she would hear noises. She was scared.

Jed: When was that?

April: That was—Let me see.

Jed: That was still on Telford?

April: All this happened on Telford. I think up until the house was condemned probably. Because you would still hear noises and stuff like that. And I remember we had Fluffy *[April's dog]*. This was after Dad had passed. We took Fluffy over there, Fluffy was little, he kept barking and growling in the dining room. We'd say, "Come here, Fluff," but he would go to that dining room and just growl and bark. And it wasn't Dad, because, you know, he knew Dad before. It was like, you know when dogs are scared of something or don't like something? That's what he was doing in that dining room.

[Her granddaughter Evelyn is curious and sits with April to listen.]

Now here in this house, even though we had it built, I was scared 'cause I kept hearing things. Brian wouldn't even be here, and I would hear him walking. I'm sittin' there, oh, Brian came back home, I didn't even know. So, I get up and I look, no, his car's not here. What the heck? One time me and you *[to Evelyn]* were lying on the bed, remember? You said, Nana, Daddy's home. Because you could hear when someone's upstairs; you could hear walking around in his room.

Jed: Does the floor creak or something when you're underneath it?

April: Yeah, you feel and hear the walking and stuff. So, I'm like, what the hell? And I would hear things during the day *[April worked remotely]*. I'd gotten scared, because they'd go to school and I would hear things, like people talking. What the hell, did Brian leave his TV on? I'd go up, nothing. I'm like, what's going on? I don't know if I had talked to the neighbors before, but they said this used to be an old burial ground years and years and years before they started building out here or something. 'Cause it's brand new, how am I hearing all this? Then I thought, well, they say that sometimes if you go to a cemetery, you can bring unwanted ghosts back or something like that? When you leave the cemetery, you should always say a prayer and say they're not wanted or whatever.

Then I told Brian, and he would hear talking and stuff, or he would hear me calling him. I told him, "You know what? We're going to repaint your room." Because he had his room real dark. I said, "You've got to repaint your room to a lighter color, clean everything out, and I'm going to go up there and I'm going to clean the whole house, and bless it." So,

I've got the holy water and before he painted it, I went in there, cleaned it, and blessed it. I had my Rosary on, and I kid you not, while I was blessing his room, Jed, I was getting goosebumps on my arm. It just felt eerie. After I blessed it and opened all the windows and painted it? Didn't hear it anymore. 'Cause it was only coming from his room, you see? I didn't hear it no more. I don't know if he brought something in from somewhere, or somebody put something on him? I don't know. But after that, he was sleeping good and we didn't hear that noise.

But one night I was working upstairs, it was late at night, and I had the video camera on because Evelyn was little. I had the camera down here and the monitor up there so I could see her. Sophia was sleeping down here on the couch. I was watching and Evelyn had woken up, so I went and got her, took her upstairs and she was upstairs with me. Then I looked on the monitor, right? Because it's going off. I looked again and said what the heck is that? Is that a face? Jed, the face was so freaking clear. You know what I mean? You could actually see the fa—I mean it wasn't in color or anything, 'cause it's black and white. But you could see the shape of the face, the hair. It looked like it might have been, maybe in the '70s or something? That old hairstyle, or maybe even before? But you could tell, and Chris *[April's husband]* was asleep on the bed. I said where is that at? I'm seeing things.

So, I said, okay, Evelyn's not down there, so what's goin' on? I came down here, turn on the light, looked at everything. 'Cause it was coming from that one corner, and that one corner I had, uh, that thing I gave your mom? That you put at the end of the bed *[basically an end of bed chest]*? I had blankets on there, and I was like, well, maybe it's the light. I turned off this light and I went back upstairs, and it was still there. I came downstairs and woke up Sophia. I said, "Look at this." And she goes, "What?" I said, "What's it look like to you?" She goes, "What is it, a picture?" I said, "No, look at it." And she goes, "It's a face. What do you have it on in the room?" I said, "I don't. Watch, I'm going to go turn on the light. I'm going to look again, then I'm going to turn it off, tell me if you see it." She goes, "Yeah, it's a face. I can see a man." He was looking at Chris. Chris was knocked out asleep. It wasn't Evelyn, because Evelyn was upstairs. So, he's watching Chris.

I went in there again and turned on the light, and I think that I woke up Chris or something. Then when I turned it off, she said it was gone. But you could literally see the face. You saw that the hair was like parted to the side, and it was full. He had like a little mustache, like this *[motions fingers across the length of her lips]*. It was a black and white fuzzy picture, but you could see the face. What was weird about this one, was this didn't scare me. I told Chris, "What did your stepdad used to look like? You need to ask your mom if she has a picture." Because I still could see that face in my head. I didn't get an eerie feeling like there was something bad. Chris was kind of feeling sick that time. I don't know if it was his dad looking at him, watching over him? Because it wasn't a scary feeling. When I saw the picture, I was freaked out, but I wasn't scared about it like the other incidents that were going on.

What else...? That was it. You gotta talk to Cheryl, because her house is brand new, but I think that house is also creepy. When we stayed there a couple of times, Brian said, "Mom, did you hear noise?" "You know, I thought I did, but didn't think nothing of it." He goes, "No, there's something in Aunt Cheryl's house." So even Aunt Cheryl says that now, but you gotta talk to her about that one. I think that's all I can remember.

I mean, at Mom's house there were always so many different things. Before it would always happen at night when you went to sleep, but then it started getting braver I think, because it would happen during the day. You know? When we were getting ready to leave, or just there. It was crazy. Dad always said that there was something there, because it would take his blanket off, or just mess with him all the time while he was sleeping. And for Dad to say something like that—Because he never would say anything. He would tell Mom to bless the house because it was something. And Cheryl said that somebody had died there in Mom's house before we got it.

Jed: How old was that house?

April: That house was a hundred years old. When they tore it down? It was over a hundred years old.

Jed: When did they tear it down?

April: Let me see. Mom passed away in 2006. 2006, right? 1998, something like that? 'Cause she only survived there seven years *[in the rebuilt house]*. Because if she would have survived the eleven years it would have been paid off, but she only survived seven years, so I had to refinance the whole thing, that's how I know, yeah. They didn't want to tear it down because it was historical, but it was too far gone so they had to tear it down.

[Inaudible on the recorder, but she began to describe her current home again.]

I would even see the shadows. When I was hearing all the noises? I would see a shadow sometimes, looked like somebody was walking down the stairs. I'd be doing something, I'd look up, and I see a shadow walk back. I'm like, whoa, I guess I'm seeing things. And I'd see it again. I'd say, "Brian, were you upstairs?" And he goes, "No." Or sometimes he would tell me, "Mom! Did you call me?" I said, "No." He goes, "I swear I heard you." But it would do things like that.

Or when I was up there working, I could feel a shadow, like someone came by me again. I would look and nothing. This would be late. You know how I worked overnight? So, it'd be like one, two o'clock in the morning.

Jed: You'd work the phones at night, yeah?

April: Uh-huh.

Jed: And there wasn't like a TV or anything where there's flashing lights or changing lights? The lighting was all just static.

April: Yeah.

Jed: But you'd see movement in your peripheral vision?

April: Yeah, movement. Or I'd be working, and I look downstairs 'cause I would hear either Chris call, or Evelyn say, "Nana!" So I'd come down here, and I'd look around, and I'd look at Chris, "Did you hear Evelyn?" He'd say, "No, she's asleep." But like I said, after I blessed it and cleaned it and stuff, we haven't had any more. But the neighbor next door, when I was telling her the things we were hearing? She was saying they were hearing things and things were happening in their house, too. So again, I don't know. I think that's the one that told me that there was an old burial ground years ago. I was like, "Yeah, 'cause all these houses are new." She said, "Yeah, we're the only owners." But they were having stuff like that happen to them. So, that said, I don't know if it was because stuff that was here before or what.

Jed: When you mentioned the man in black before, were you able to move when you woke up and saw him, or how long would it stay there?

April: I would turn around. I would just like turn around and I would see him, and I'd be scared to move. Because he was like literally—

Jed: It's not like you couldn't move, you were choosing not to move?

April: Yeah. It wasn't like I couldn't move; I don't think. I think I was just scared to move. Because he wouldn't do anything. He would just be on the bed and it would just be a figure looking down. And I remember, it was just all in black. He was all in black. And his face you couldn't see, 'cause it looked black. But you could see it was... I don't know... black pants and black overcoat. Just all black, and face just black. You couldn't see any features, anything. It was just a figure, a black figure. It was right there. And then when I would move to wake up Mom, it'd be gone. But this happened for a while, every night until she gave me the Rosary. If I started to see him, I'd say the Rosary and I'd look, he'd be gone. Or not the Rosary, the Hail Mary. And I was the only one seeing him, besides Elijah hearing him in the room. I think I saw him, and Elijah heard him and maybe saw him like one time. Because he said a man all in black, and that's when Mom told him, "Well, that's what's standing over April's bed at night."

Jed: That's not something you'd talked about before.

April: No, uh-uh, no. Because Elijah told Mom, "I keep hearing a man's voice or something messin' with me in the room." Do you remember that old room that used to be Mom's after everybody moved out? Got the front room, dining room, then Mom's room? It was that room. Elijah goes, "I keep hearing a man messing with me, but I don't see the face." He goes, "But one time I saw it, and it was all black. Couldn't see a face or nothing." It was weird.

Jed: How old were you?

April: I was young. I was in elementary. Elijah must have been maybe in his late twenties? Late twenties, thirties. Yeah, 'cause I was still in elementary. Or maybe not, I was little. 'Cause I slept with Mom for a while. I don't know if I was in kinder, first? I was like that little, you know what I mean?

That's all I remember from Mom's. There's probably some other stuff that I'm forgetting. I know for a while, though, it got to where I wouldn't stay there by myself. Then Cheryl wouldn't stay there by herself, it would really mess with her. I used to tell her 'cause she was so bad. And I remember, I saw so much and everything happened to me. Mom and them would tell her, "Well, you're so bad, that's why. You're so mean, that's why it messes with you so much *[laughing]*!"

Oh! I think I was in junior high, and actually at this time I was talking to Mia. Which I was really surprised, because you know we didn't always talk. But we had went walking at Highlands High School, and it was me, her, and I think Thomas and Alyssa were small, and we were walking around the track and we heard a cry. And I said, "What is that? You hear that?" And she goes, "Yeah." And then we heard a call. It was crying, real loud? You know?

Jed: Like a person crying?

April: Like a lady cried, real loud. And I was like, "What is it?" And she goes, "I don't know." Then we heard it getting closer, like louder? And she goes, "Come on, let's go. I don't like the way that sounds." And then, all of the sudden we see something white, like a bird or something? It took off. We were running back to the car. I go, "What happened? What was that?" And she said, "That was a Lechuza." It was a lady that used to cry. I forgot what they said happened to her, but she used to scream and cry like that. All of the sudden we heard like the wings go, and—

Jed: Flapping?

April: Something, and I'm like, "Did you hear that? What is it?" And I just remember seeing something white.

Jed: She saw it after the wings were flapping?

April: Flapping.

Jed: You saw the white in the air?

April: Like white, but she was like, "Come on, don't look at that, let's go." So, we went back.

Jed: How big was it in the brief—?

April: It looked big. Because I looked, but all I caught was a glance of the white, and I remember we ran back to the car.

Jed: Was it thin bodied, like a swan? Or heron? Those types of birds? Or like an owl?

April: I just remember hearing the ruffles of the feathers and then just caught a glance as it was coming up. All I know it was white. But it was too fast. Know what I mean? When I looked at it, I think it looked like a bird or something? I don't know, but I just got a quick glance and she turned my head said, "Don't look at it." I was like what the heck? But I remember that ugly sound, it was like a lady crying.

Jed: And it stopped, as the flapping—?

April: Yeah. And we took off running. She was crying like *[mimics a wailing cry]*, because I think she lost her kids crying, you know? She was crying for them like that, real heavily.

202

Jed: And who were you with?

April: Mia, and when we got home, I remember her telling Mom about it, but I said I don't want to hear it and walked off. Yeah. It was an ugly cry, a wicked cry. A hurt cry, but kind of scary crying. I just remember that we never went to walk back around that Highlands track again.

[I followed up with Mia later, but Mia had no recollection of this.]

Jed: What time of day was that?

April: It wasn't in the evening. It was about six.

Jed: So not fully dark yet?

April: No, I think it was when it starts to get dark. It wasn't pitch dark, you know, it was light enough when we took off.

SOPHIA, ISABELLE, AND APRIL

[The following takes place immediately after April's interview, as Sophia happened to be visiting April for an unrelated reason. Sophia's daughter Isabelle, my younger cousin, is with her so I welcome her to sit in as well. Isabelle is adept at keeping her mom on topic, and I end up letting her lead the interview at times. April also takes the opportunity to ask questions. They sometimes talk over and interrupt each other, but the discussion helps the conversation continue to flow easily.]

Sophia: I was in Eagle Pass, 'cause they only took me and Mia, didn't take anybody else. They would show us how to sew, cook, clean. I think we were basically their little maids?

Isabelle: Get to what you saw.

Sophia: We were there and there were neighbors, and the house is still there. My dad's mom and dad's house. And his tia *[aunt]* lived there with 'em. So, we'd go there every summer, or they'd pick us up, and then the people next door sold vegetables and peaches and apples. They had like an orchard.

Isabelle: How old were you?

Sophia: I don't know, I was like eight, maybe eight. Seven, eight maybe. I think eight, because it was Mia and I, and Cheryl.

Isabelle: She was just a baby. She probably wasn't even born at the time you were eight.

Sophia: Well, I'm saying she remembers going. The neighbors were outside, and we were looking out the window because it was already late. When we were looking outside, I said, "Oh look! There's a beautiful horse flying, with wings!" A beautiful white horse with wings. And they called that the... What was that name?

April: Lechuza!

Sophia: Lechuza! It was a witch riding on it, but it was a beautiful white horse with huge wings.

Isabelle: It was in the day?

Sophia: It was in the nighttime. We were getting ready to go to bed. The windows were like that, they were big *[motions the broad shape of the windows by spreading her arms up and out]*.

April: But, I thought the Lechuza, when I saw it, it looked like a bird.

Sophia: This one was a horse and it had wings, and there was a witch on it, or somebody was on it. They said Lechuza, Lechuza! The people next door came running out, too. Because the house was like, you know, on the hill.

Jed: On the hill, one house was above the other.

Sophia: Our house was on the hill, and their house dropped below. And so, we were watching them, they walked out, but we couldn't—

April: You didn't hear it crying?

Sophia: Some whistle or something. It was gorgeous. I just thought it was beautiful. But then they scared me not to look at it.

Jed: Who was with you that saw it?

Sophia: Aunt Mia.

Jed: Mia saw it, too?

Sophia: Aunt Mia saw it because she was with me. It was a lot of us that actually saw it.

Jed: You saw a person on top of a horse.

[As creepy and unnerving as many of the stories in the interviews can be, this was the most surprising by far. I don't believe there was any way I could be prepared for my aunt to tell me she saw a woman riding what I would call a Pegasus.]

Sophia: On the top of a horse. It flew and they said it was the whatever.

Jed: But the neighbors did, who were adults?

Sophia: The neighbors ran out, too, and they said, "Did you see that?!"

Isabelle: They were adults, right?

Sophia: They were adults. Well, they were like Mia. Teenagers, adults. Pretty much adult, because they were already 19, 20's whatever. I was young so, you know, you don't know...

Jed: How old people are.

Sophia: You don't know how old. You think twenty's already halfway dead. And when you're older, you're going God, I thought 20 was old, now I'm 20 and I'm halfway dead.

April: Then what else?

Sophia: And then at Mom's house I used to see—Not Mom's. The one where we were at in Eagle Pass, we used to be under our house because the house was on stilts, because they built a house on a hill. So, part of the hill was in the front, so you would walk in the front door straight, the whole house is straight, but then when you walk out it's down.

April: See, that's what I remember as I got older, Grandma's house in the back, you had to go down some stairs and she had trees and plants. That's my vision of the house.

Sophia: She had a lot of peach trees in the back, and you couldn't touch 'em! You couldn't get the peaches; I have no idea why *[laughter]*! Don't touch that peach or I'll cut your hand off *[still laughing]*! She was mean.

April: What was under the house?

Sophia: Under the house was just rocks and dirt, because it was built on stilts. It's like a little hill, so there's nothing but dirt and rocks and stuff. But in the summer, when it was too hot, we used to sleep under there. On cots and stuff, because it was cooler outside than it was inside.

April: Who slept out there with you?

Sophia: They did. I guess they weren't that old, but they were old.

Isabelle: Who?

April: You're great grandma.

Sophia: Dad's mom and everybody.

Isabelle: So, they would be outside under the house sleeping.

Sophia: Yeah, because it was summertime, so everybody would sleep outside.

April: So, what happened?

Isabelle: That's crazy.

Sophia: So, um, I would see people walking by. I would say like, "Who's that?" I thought somebody was up. But everybody was asleep. I'd see people walking by me.

Isabelle: By the house?

Sophia: No, by me.

Isabelle: While you're under the house.

Sophia: Like if you're walking by me. And how are you going to see a shadow in the dark?

Isabelle: Right, right. But—

Sophia: We're asleep under the house.

Jed: You're under the house, but what she's asking is, when you see people walking, is it the impression of someone right next to you, or at the edge of the house?

Isabelle: How much room is under the house?

Sophia: You could walk under there, that's how tall it was. A whole level. They built an apartment downstairs years later.

April: So, you saw people walking? What did they do when they walked by you?

Sophia: They just stood there, looking down at me, or they walked around like—I mean, you couldn't see them anyway, because they were dark.

April: It was just a dark shadow that you saw.

Sophia: Yeah. But you saw like a person standing. When I was in the light, like in the outer part, it was the dark right here when you would sleep under it *[uses hands to show a center and an edge].* Out here is like the end of the house, they would have lights and stuff. You could see a person, or it was a man. And one time it was a lady with long hair.

April: And they would just walk by you?

Sophia: They were standing over me. One would go *[makes a sound like passing quick and close]* like that, like walk by me. But you know, you close your eyes, 'cause who's going to believe you?

April: You didn't tell Mom?

Sophia: No. Who's going to believe me? I was thinking it was because I was scared, I was asleep. But we slept under there so much, I wasn't really scared. I like to watch scary movies. Why would I be scared? And then I told myself I was half asleep, maybe it was someone checking on us, but I would look up and everybody was asleep.

Jed: You say you're kind of half asleep, were you like—

Sophia: Yeah, I was thinking I was half asleep, but I looked around and everybody was asleep.

Jed: You move your head and look around.

Sophia: Yeah, you're on a cot, and everybody was on a different cot. And the person was standing next to me. Or I thought it was somebody next to me, but they weren't there, 'cause when I looked again, they were gone. See, but I looked around to see if somebody had got up to check on us, but everybody was asleep. The parents, the grandparents. Because like a camp out is what it was. You cook outside, you do whatever, the kids would all play outside. And then when it was time to go to sleep, everybody would just go to sleep on their cot. 'Cause there were so many people, I think she only had like one to three bedrooms in the house. Yeah.

Isabelle: How many people were sleeping outside?

Sophia: I don't know, whoever went with us. There was me, Mom, Dad, because Grandma and Grandpa were inside. And Mom or Dad was outside with us, and it was like Mia and I, I think Donna. I can't remember anyone else. I mean you're little. You don't think any of this is important when you're small. You know what I mean? You're playing and running around.

Isabelle: They never said anything to you, just looked at you?

Sophia: Yeah, they were just standing there.

Jed: You said one was a woman with long hair.

Sophia: Long hair.

Jed: What made you—You could see the hair?

Sophia: 'Cause you could see like this part *[motions to her face]*, and her hair. Swaying.

Isabelle: Was it black?

Sophia: It was black.

Isabelle: But could you see her face?

Sophia: No. It was just—You could see it was like a pink, not black. But the one that was under it was dark *[motions to lower body]*, because you know you can't see in the dark, I guess.

Isabelle: Oh, 'cause you saw her like when you were at the edge.

Sophia: On the edge of the building. Because I remember sleeping next to a pillar, a big square pillar. You know how they build them.

Jed: You said you saw a pink color that was part of her—

Sophia: Her face. Her features.

Jed: It wasn't just shadow, you actually saw some color.

Sophia: I actually saw somebody. See this one, this one was a shadow because in the inside, like further in, it was just dark. But it was a man. I could tell it was a man, it wasn't a woman. You know, when he was just looking like that. So, I thought it was like Grandpa or somebody checking up on us. You know?

Isabelle: But could you see clothes? Or just a shadow?

Sophia: No, it was just dark. Like one time I was walking home towards Mom's house on Telford. Remember Melissa had a friend on Bailey? Well, from her house, and there was somebody walking behind me. I kept hearing them, but every time I heard the footsteps, I turned around and all I saw was a shadow. So, I started running. Then I said, ah, I'm just scaring myself, no one's walking behind me. Right? Because it's just my shadow. So, I stop to hear if somebody was behind me, and I turned around, my whole body, I turned around to look and nobody was there. I said I'm just scaring myself. Let me just walk, I'm not going to scare myself, I watch scary movies all the time. I started walking again, and all I heard was a man's footsteps. Like the hard soles of his shoes?

Jed: Yeah.

Sophia: I said to myself, I just looked, nobody's there, so I kept walking. Then I'm thinking, that was my shadow, but it couldn't have been my shadow, because my shadow was on the side of me from the *[street]* lights. So, I thought, let me go home right now, and I ran home. I think we were in junior high at that time.

April: Not me, I was still a baby.

Sophia: But I don't know how old I was. I think I was in the seventh grade. Yeah, I think I was in the seventh grade. But at Mom's house on Telford, I used to hear everything. They used to call my name.

211

Everybody'd go to the store, I'd stay there and watch movies. Everything would be dark the way my house is now, because I could see the movies better. You know? I could see the pictures better. They'd call me from the back room, "Sophia!" And I would get up to go see if maybe somebody stayed, was still home and I didn't know. I went and nobody was there. I think, maybe I'm just hearing things. Then I sit down and hear it again. I'd lower the TV. Where are they calling me from, outside? Or the back room? And it came from the side bedroom this time, instead of the back bedroom. I opened the door and walked in there and nobody was in there. I went back into the living room and sat down, and then you'd hear a lot of noises, people talking, whispering. More than one person, like two, three, four people whispering, talking *[mimics whispering]*. You know, like whispering or talking to each other? There's a lot of people talking to each other, that's what I used to remember.

Isabelle: At Grandma's house.

Sophia: At my Mom's house on Telford.

Isabelle: Did you ever go back there and see?

Sophia: Yeah, I would go back there to see, but nobody was there. But you would hear a lot of people talking, a lot of people whispering, or—

Isabelle: Only in the back room?

Sophia: Or having a conversation.

Isabelle: Only in the back room?

Sophia: No, it'd be in all—

April: It'd be in different parts at different times.

Sophia: Yeah.

April: It'd mess with you.

Sophia: And when you would get closer to it, to go see, to see how many people were there, it would calm down.

[Talking over each other.]

Isabelle: I think that still happens *[inaudible]*.

April: At Grandma's house *[to Isabelle]*?

Jed: As you got close *[to Sophia]*?

Sophia: As I got closer.

April: Hold on Sophia.

Isabelle: Yeah.

April: You hear that at Grandma's house now? The new house?

[I wasn't aware at the time that Isabelle was staying at the newly built house on Telford.]

Isabelle: Yeah. Um, so, remember when I first moved in? I was washing dishes, and I was by myself. No music, no TV, no nothing, just washing dishes. I had the window open, because I like to look out, makes you feel better, right? So, I'm washing the dishes and I like felt somebody over me, like you know how tall Brian is right? My ex-boyfriend is like 6'6". Grandpa was like 6'1", right? I'm only 5'4", I'm washing the dishes and I feel somebody over me, and I look, and there's nothing there. And then I feel it again, but I feel it like somebody's stand—I can feel their body, right? I could feel, like, their presence. And they're standing there like this *[near]*.

Isabelle and April Together: Like it was Grandpa.

Jed: Looking over your shoulder?

Isabelle: Yeah! Looking over my shoulder, like, what are you doing? And I looked, and I just saw it go shoo *[mimics a quick movement away]*!

April: But it wasn't a scary feeling.

Isabelle: No.

April: It was like a peaceful feeling?

213

Isabelle: But, there was that one time when she was saying people would call her name. It sounded like... You *[April]*, Grandma, my mom. Because y'all all sound the same, right? I'm in the shower at the house. Grandma's new house? I'm in the shower, washing. And they said, "Isabelle, what are you doing?!" Like clear as day. And I'm like, nobody's in the house. It's nine o'clock in the morning. I'm not drunk. Then they said, "Isabelle!" And I was like, I got to hurry up. And I'm like, what the hell? They always tell me these stories, them saying their name. I'm like, I get it. So, I got out the shower and I know nobody's here, but it's just the point. And then sometimes I'll hear stuff in the kitchen.

Jed: Uh-huh.

Isabelle: Like a cabinet *[shutting]*, or something will fall. Or like somebody's hitting, not hitting something, but when you walk into—

Sophia: Banging into the side of the door.

Isabelle: Not slamming. I mean like when you walk into the cabinet or something. I'll hear that.

April: When you're hearing this, though, does it feel like it could be Grandma or Grandpa, or does it feel like an eerie feeling, like it's scary?

Isabelle: When I washed the dishes I felt scared, but I didn't feel like someone was going to hurt me. But sometimes I feel scared. Sometimes I feel like it's probably like you said, like a friendly one.

April: I think that even though because it's a new house, it's still on the same land. The same lot.

Isabelle: I hated sleeping in that back room. Because I remember when we were living with Grandma there was a washer and dryer back there. We slept on the bed, little cot, whatever, in the back and Christopher wasn't even born at this point.

April: Just you and Charlotte?

Isabelle: Just me, Charlotte, and Mom. And I hated it, because it either got so cold back there or so hot. And you would hear things, because the little room was probably smaller than this little area *[uses hands to divide living room]* right?

Sophia: I always saw people standing in that room.

Isabelle: And I hated it. Because y'all used to have curtains to close it, but it would be open and there would be a lady standing there. Just looking at you. I'm like, what the…?

Sophia: And it was a white lady.

Isabelle: I was a kid, I didn't know what she was. Like, I just saw a lady with her hair, and I'm like, "Mom, Mom, Mom, Mom." She's like, "What?" And I'm always scared, and I didn't want to scare Charlotte, because Charlotte was already scared.

Sophia: They'd always wake up scared, and I'd just tell 'em, "Pray, pray, pray."

Isabelle: I remember them telling us stories like when they would pull the blankets off of Grandpa, and his feet—

April: That's what I was telling Jed.

Isabelle: So, one time we're in the back room, and we were tiny and could all sleep in that one area, and I'm like, "Stop pulling the blanket!" I'm at the edge, because Charlotte was the baby and my mom was at the wall, there was nobody there! But I kept saying stop pulling the blanket. They were pulling the blankets off of me. I'm like, what the hell? That's why I was like, Mom, I don't want to go to sleep. Remember when Grandma's—I didn't mean to take your time talking. I was trying to remember, you know how at Grandma and Grandpa's you could see the floor in the restroom?

April: Yeah.

Isabelle: Because it was so old? I used to hate that. I would see like, shadows going under there. That was the scariest thing. I'd hate going to the restroom, I'd hurry up, but you could see the shadows like going under the house.

April: I don't know if you remember, do you remember Jed?

Jed: Vaguely.

April: In Mom's old restroom, there was a little hole Dad had to cover because the floor was getting rotted. You could see through to the ground.

Jed: I didn't remember until she mentioned it, but I do now, yeah.

Sophia: He fixed it each time, but there was a leak—

Isabelle: The house was just so old.

Sophia: In the tub, so...

April: It would rot.

Isabelle: I would get so scared. What I was saying the last time I saw you, my mom was at the hospital having Christopher and we stayed at Grandma's house. When you first walk in, it was Grandpa's living room, and then Grandma's room and Grandma had her bed right there, and the TV was in the corner, and you could still see the dining room from Grandma's room, right? So, we were in the bed. It was Grandma, Charlotte because she was a baby, and it was me. Well, at the end of Grandma's bed, I kept hearing somebody like, "Help me, help me." And I'm like, what the hell is that? There's always a lot of people at Grandma's house, but it was just me, Grandma, Charlotte, and Grandpa. Somebody was maybe sleeping in the back, I don't remember. I was probably like eight. Seven or eight. Right? And this lady kept saying, "Help me, help me. Somebody, help me." And I'm like...

Sophia: That's when I got sick.

Isabelle: Yeah, you were in the hospital. So, I hear it, and I look up. Like I pick my head up, and there's a lady at the edge of the bed dressed all in black. Clear as day. Like, you know how Louisiana, Southern people go to funerals? Old school? With the net *[gestures before her face]*?

April: Yeah. The old black lace?

Isabelle: Lace, yeah. She had a hat, and the lace over her face, a lace dress, old school Southern. And she's like, "Help me, help me." And I'm looking at her, I couldn't see her face because she had that lace over her face. And I'm like, "Grandma, Grandma!" And then Grandma wouldn't wake up, I'm like, please, please wake up. And she kept saying help me. It looked like she was coming closer, she wasn't, but her arms were coming closer and closer which is weird. And I woke Grandma up, and I was like, "Someone's at the edge of the bed!" And Grandma's like, "What? What are you talking about?" And I'm like, "Somebody's right there!" And then, she's gone. Grandma was like, "There's nobody there."

Jed: While you were shaking Grandma, she was still there?

Isabelle: Yes. And that was the craziest thing, and I was like, I'm not going to sleep. I just stayed up and I cried, and I was like, I wanna go! I was scared as hell. But I remember when we lived there for a little bit, we were staying in the back room. In the kitchen you would always hear like, the cabinets closing, or like somebody cooking.

Sophia: The dishes, yeah.

Isabelle: And there was nobody in there. It was just weird, like I hated being... I loved being at Grandma's house, but I hated being there by myself. I hated going to the restroom by myself. I hated going to the back room just because I was scared of hearing or seeing something. Now at the new house that I live in, Grandma's new house, I just hear noises, like something dropping.

April: At the beginning they used to do like a playful thing, like just making noises here and there, but as it kept going on, it got mean.

Sophia: There was giggles. Like some kids.

April: Yeah. But as it kept going on, it's like they started getting ugly. You know, they would pull my hair, or poke Grandpa's—Like, you know, just being ugly.

Jed: Things escalated.

April: Yeah.

Isabelle: Didn't Grandma used to leave like a cup of water, like a candle or something for them? I remember Grandma used to leave something out, as a peace-making, offering thing.

Sophia: I think I remember that, too.

Isabelle: Like water or food or something. She used to leave something out, and I asked her one time—I know there was water, but I didn't know if it was holy water or something, but she was like, "Oh, so the bad spirits won't think that we want them out."

April: Now I remember.

Isabelle: Like we were letting them live there so they won't be ugly.

April: Yeah, it was a glass of water. It was a glass of water and it was something else. Now that you triggered my memory, I do remember that. It was a glass of water and something else, to let them know, hey, you can be here. We don't want to help you, but we don't want to hurt you.

Isabelle: Yeah, I remember every night Grandma would do that, and I had asked, and she said it's so that the bad spirits know that we're friendly.

Sophia: We don't want to push them out, because then they get angry.

Isabelle: Yeah, because I think at that point that's when they were being ugly. And we were like, okay, we can't do anything. Didn't Grandma have somebody come to the house?

April: Cheryl had two priests go in there to bless it. They said it was really haunted, because it wasn't peaceful and they blessed it twice.

Isabelle: Yeah, I remember. I was little and I remember that. I probably should have that done now. Just to see, you know.

April: You can. I mean before you moved in, I blessed it, yeah.

Sophia: But it doesn't last that long apparently, because even when I'm there and I was there taking care of the house, I would hear the door slam or something, BANG, on the wall.

Isabelle: Yeah, there's always—

Sophia: 'Cause she used to tell me, "Well, maybe it's the water heater."

Isabelle: The water heater's right there, so when you turn on the water and get out the shower...

Jed: It's like a pipe moving.

Isabelle: Yeah. I was scared one time and I'd told my friend Brandon. He was like, "You're tripping." I was like, "No, I can hear somebody slamming the door."

Sophia: Yeah, or hitting the wall.

Isabelle: I was like, "Go check outside." He was like, "There's nothing outside, it's the water heater." I realized, okay, that's the water heater. But it's not always the water heater.

April: I know when I was painting Mom's new house, I was there by myself during the day. I was painting it, and I started getting like an eerie, scared feeling. And I'm never scared in the new house 'cause I talk to Mom every time I'm in there. I was scared. I was sitting in the hall, and I was painting, and then I just got this, ugh, like the goosebumps on my skin.

Isabelle: Near the second room?

April: Right there. Exactly. Right there in that second room where the room is built. I was outside in that hallway. And I was painting—

Isabelle: I don't like that room.

Sophia: You know what, that was where the original bedroom was.

April: The old bedroom, Mom's bedroom. You remember where I told you Elijah used to sleep? Where he saw them, where he heard the man that one time? That was where the old and where the new room is. But I was outside that hall and I started getting that eerie feeling. First, I thought maybe I'm scared because I haven't been here in so long. I just started talking to Mom, and said, "Mom, show me something so I know you're here with me, because I'm starting to get scared and I don't know why. Show me something so I know you're with me, take this ugly feeling away because I need to finish your house." And then I heard the chimes moving.

Isabelle: Mom, didn't I tell you? Those Moo Moos *[the cow chimes]*!

April: It wasn't windy, Jed.

Isabelle: I left those Moo Moos in the back for that reason.

April: I had to have the doors open to let the paint dry. I had the screen door locked and the windows open. I got up and looked outside, why are they moving? I said, "Okay, Mama, I got you, you're here with me. I'm better now. Just stay with me until I finish your house." *[Laughing]* So, every day that I'd go over there I would just talk to her, because it made me feel better.

Isabelle: I've heard the chimes. That's why I left them there. The cows, right? One day, I was cleaning the house and doing the outside, cleaning the porch and everything, washing the windows. It was hot, it wasn't windy, and the chimes just kept twinkling. At first I was like, oh, they're making noise. But then I looked, and I was like, there's no wind. That's weird. Then I was like, "Oh hey, Grandma!" *[Laughing]* It was just moving, and I was like, okay, I'm okay. But I hate that room. Sometimes I'll hear it—Grandma's new room, right?

April: Uhm hm.

Isabelle: I can hear everything from that room. Say at nighttime, I'll get scared because I hear everything. Now I sleep with the TV because of the times that I've heard stuff.

Sophia: She's called and told me I'm scared of something, a noise, something's moving.

Isabelle: Scary right? And you know how the lights on the side of the house, they come on when things get near? I used to think it was the dogs. But it's not the dogs. I mean, it could be like whatever, squirrels, or something.

Sophia: It has to walk right under it.

April: It has to be heavy enough to catch the sensor.

Sophia: Right.

Isabelle: Right! The dogs aren't even—And I have to come up close even with my body.

April: Yeah.

Isabelle: They always come on.

Sophia: You have to be like right under it almost.

April: Yeah, you do. I had it set to where if somebody walked close enough, it's gonna go off. It's not going to go off just with every little thing.

Isabelle: Right. And so, I thought about that because I thought it was probably the dogs. But then I realized after a while, I literally have to walk up to this light, right? For it to come on. But those lights always come on.

Sophia: Always.

Isabelle: The ones specifically by my room. Paul's *[Sophia and April's brother]* doesn't hardly ever come on, but the one by my room always comes on.

Sophia: And there's nobody out there. I look out there, too.

Isabelle: When I first moved in, I used to look out like all the time, and I couldn't sleep. Because they stole the lawn mower and all that stuff. I'm like, I'm scared, right?

April: But when Mom lived there and I used to stay with her—You know how me and Wanda used to stay with her, I stayed for four days and Wanda the weekend? That light was always the one to come on. Because I would have to get up, and I would look, there was nothing. It would be the light right there by Mom's room.

Sophia: When I went outside, I had to get right under it.

Isabelle: You do. I don't know why. Like you said, you literally have to be under it.

Sophia: Somebody's going up to it. Something. That's what I think.

Isabelle: Yeah. And remember that cat was crying by my window? But it was Irma's cat. That cat ended up dying, somebody hit it. I picked it up from the street and put it in a bag. I went and knocked on their door. It wasn't a bad cat, though. When I first moved in, it would come and would not leave me alone. When I would come home, it would be at my door. On the carport.

Sophia: It was Irma's Cat.

Isabelle: The cat from, I guess, the next-door house from where they moved out. She took over it. But it would be at my front door, just waiting for me. And I'm like, can you move? And it'd be like *[mimics being pushed, refusing to move]*. And in the morning, it'd be there, too.

April: That's crazy.

Isabelle: Yeah. It was like always there. And then one night—

Sophia: When I got there, I said oh my God, it was right at the door.

Isabelle: Always at my door, waiting for me. And then one night it was crying. You know how they sound like baby's crying? I woke up out of my sleep and it was right there at the window.

Sophia: Was there another cat there?

Isabelle: No.

Sophia: She called me and told me, "Mom, can you here it? It sounds like a baby."

Isabelle: Crying, crying, crying.

April: 'Cause I know when they mate, they scream like that, but there's usually another cat right there.

Isabelle: No, just that one cat.

Sophia: Remember Mom used to say when they cried like that, it was because somebody died or something like that.

Isabelle: I don't know why, but it was crying and crying. I was like, "Go away, go away!" I was talking to the cat, "Please go away, leave me alone!" Because at first, I was like, what the hell? But then I started thinking something bad happened. Right? Because they're crying. And I looked, and it was scratching at my window. I was like, "Please go away, leave me alone." I was like saying a prayer, because I just thought it was evil.

April: I never heard them do that. I mean I heard them crying and looked out because I knew they would mate right there.

Sophia: But she called me crying and crying because it would not stop. And I heard it, it sounded horrible, like somebody was dying.

April: Mom used to say if a cat is crying by itself like that, it's because of something bad. But there's usually another cat, right there. But they don't scratch at the window to get in.

Sophia: This one was scratching and crying, and it was by itself. I was on the phone with her for like an hour or two and it was still there.

Isabelle: It was scary.

Sophia: I felt bad for her, because she was by herself.

April: You should have called me; I was closest to you.

Isabelle: I know, but you were asleep.

Jed: Sophia, you said you saw a woman in the back room, by the washer and dryer, too?

Sophia: Yeah. I was a teenager, I think. Yeah, I was in junior high. She wasn't even born yet.

April: I was born, you were a teenager.

Jed: What you saw, was it like you saw the shadows other times? Or was it something—

Sophia: I would see shadows passing by me all the time. Like when you're passing by somebody, just walking? I would see people passing by me all the time. The women you could tell because of the way they looked, the man was more masculine and the woman with the hair.

Jed: In that back room—

Sophia: In the back room was a lady with long hair.

Jed: Did you see it clearly or was that a shadow as well?

Sophia: No, I saw her clearly. I just couldn't really say like the features. It was a white lady with long hair.

Jed: Could you see what she was wearing?

Sophia: She was wearing like a blue, I don't know, an off-blue shirt or dress. I couldn't tell. I saw the color. One had a red blouse on. The one I saw that I remember was a lighter color, it was a lady with a blue dress on.

Jed: What do you mean, one was—

Sophia: See, one like in the backroom with her back to me had a red shirt on.

Jed: So, it wasn't just a shadow, sometimes when you saw things out of the corner of your eye, it was actual color and people.

Sophia: Yeah, people, yeah. That was weird for us to see that, but then you're like, you're a kid, you just try to forget it. You don't want to remember that. It's not your mama, you know? And it's not your aunts or sisters, because everybody was young. I was in junior high and they were, I think your mom was in high school. No. Yes. She was in high school.

Jed: Did Grandpa or Grandma ever tell you anything about things that they saw?

Sophia: My dad would say he saw something. You know how Grandpa was, "Yeah, yeah, mija *[Spanish for "my daughter"]*, I saw it." Just blow it off, because there's nothing you could do about it. So that's the way I looked at it, and I wouldn't really say anything, because what are they going to do, you know what I mean?

Jed: Yeah.

Sophia: You know, I would keep a lot to myself anyway. I think April's the only one who I talked to a lot, Cheryl, too. And your mom, but I didn't really say much of what happened. Because I would figure, well, they're not going to do anything, what can they do? It's just going to scare them. And I just told myself don't get scared. You know what I mean? You're a kid, it's like okay I saw it, it's gone. Then you go play and do whatever.

Jed: When you said that you woke up Grandma at different times—

Sophia: Scared. You'd actually get scared. Then you're like, what is that? She was packing something or doing something. The one with the red shirt and curly hair. She had curly hair. Wavy hair. The lady with the blue dress had long hair. But the one with the red, the white lady, or Mexican with the red shirt on, was packing a black suitcase or putting— Had something black in her hand and was doing something with it. But I couldn't tell, because she was facing the wall, the windows, facing outward and I was looking at her back. The one with the blue dress was just coming around the corner. Like here was the sink, I don't know if you remember the little sink with the washer and stuff. But she was just coming around the corner where the cabinets were, and she stopped, and I looked. And she just stopped and looked at me, and I looked at her. Like, who are you? And then all of the sudden, it just, kind of like...

Jed: How old were you when you saw the women?

Sophia: I think I was 12. I know they had to be separate times, because they weren't there together. I know we were in junior high when we moved there, so probably seventh or eighth grade. It was a nice big house. I liked it because it was big, but it was just, you know. Nothing you could do about it, though. It was better than the house we had. It was a pretty cool house unless you scared yourself. And there's no way I was going to scare myself more. I said, no one's going to believe me anyway, so why say anything.

Jed: Yeah.

Sophia: I just never really said anything. To me it didn't make any difference, because they had already disappeared and there was nobody there. But she stopped right there at those two doors, like she was coming around as I was walking into the room, and I stopped because I saw her. She stopped because she saw me. And then after that, she was gone.

Isabelle: She was wearing what?

Sophia: A blue dress. A light blue dress. Like a sky-blue dress, not the dark blue. Aqua blue dress, there you go. That color. But I mean, you can't really see their features, you just see... I mean I saw things in color, I don't know about anybody else. But my dreams are in color, much less my ghosts. They have to be in color, too *[laughing]*! I don't know, but some of them, some of the ones that I saw were like shadows. Black, black shadows. Like the ones that I told you about in Eagle Pass and the other one, the other lady. Oh, and that lady that was flying, she had long, beautiful black hair. I thought it was the most beautiful thing I saw, until they told me it wasn't beautiful *[laughing]*. It looked beautiful.

Jed: They told you that you should be scared.

Sophia: Yeah.

Jed: How high up did it seem?

Sophia: It was pretty high; she was in the sky. She was going like this *[gazing down]*. And the wings were flapping, and she was looking down at us and her hair was just flowing. It was like a picture. I thought it was beautiful. The horse was so white and beautiful, and the wings were like you saw it in a cartoon. They said, "Look, look!" And we called everybody to look. They said, "Look at the lady flying the horse! It's got wings!" And I was telling Mia, and Mia said, "Oh my God." And then the people next door ran out and were looking up, too. I know it wasn't something that we thought we saw, it was something everybody saw. I said, "God it's so beautiful, doesn't it look so beautiful?" And they said, "No, don't look at it, don't look at it!" And I'm wondering, why? It was beautiful. But they said don't look at it, because then she'll come back for you. I mean, I don't know about the face, but the hair was like a picture. Everything was flowing, the wind was blowing the hair, and the wings were just like this *[spread arms]*. The horse was beautiful, it was white.

Jed: Could you hear the wings?

Sophia: Somebody was whistling, they said it was her. I don't know how. Whistling or screaming. You should ask Mia, she was the one who saw it with me. Her and the people next door. They said, "Don't look at it, don't look at it, she's going to come back for you." I said, "Come back for me?" Because I wouldn't stop looking. I mean, who sees that? And then I figured, God, it's real, because they're running out to see it, the next-door neighbors were running out to see it. So, yeah, it was a lot of people.

Jed: Any doubts you had—

Sophia: They were gone *[laughs]*. It was real. You know, you hear about it, but you never see it. You think it's something somebody made up so you could be scared and stuff, but it was true. But she didn't come back to take me home *[laughs]*. I mean, she would have had to come back for everybody! Because it was a lot of people that saw her that night, and they were all kids, too. And teenagers. Aunt Mia was a teenager, I'm sure. I was just seven or eight. Eight, maybe? Nine? Yeah. That beautiful hair was so long. You know how long their hair used to be, right? Past their butts and stuff? Well, hers was long. I don't know. With a hat.

Jed: What kind of hat?

Sophia: I don't know, but it was a weird looking hat. But they said anybody sees her she'll come get you. I said why? Let it come get me. But everybody's still alive that saw her, so, you know. Maybe she's still getting all the other people that saw her and is going to come back for us later *[laughing]*! Who knows?

[April was asking Isabelle if she had ever heard crying like she had.]

Isabelle: Oh, the whistle from whatever, the Lechuza right?

April: And the crying, yeah, um-hm.

Isabelle: But I don't, I never heard a cry, but my mom she was at the hospital...

April: February.

Isabelle: Valentine's Day. She was in the hospital Valentine's Day, and she was there from like February to March, like the whole month and a half. And she kept telling me, "I hear a whistle. You don't ever hear the whistle?" And I'm like, "What whistle, Mom?"

Sophia: And then she was in the other room, and I heard it. It was—

Isabelle: Olivia's birthday party wasn't 'til May, right? And I guess it was like that Friday morning. No, Saturday morning we're getting everything ready, blah blah blah, just me and my mom. And shoot, I heard a whistle. I thought it was somebody outside. I didn't know, I just thought I heard a whistle. And then she says, "Isabelle, Isabelle! You hear it, you hear it?" And it goes *[whistles]* like LOUD *[her emphasis]*.

Sophia: Loud.

Isabelle: Like, clear. Like I could hear it in the house. The doors weren't open. Nothing was—

April: It was that loud.

Isabelle: Yes.

Sophia: I said, "See baby, it's not a bird."

Isabelle: And it was like bright as day. There was no crying, but I heard the whistle, like somebody was whistling next to me. And I was like, what the…?

Sophia: We went outside, right?

Isabelle: I went outside. I went outside and I said that has to be a bird on the side of the house. Right there by the kitchen, right? And I looked. Nothing. And I said, "Mom—"

Sophia: I said, "See, I told you."

Isabelle: I told you. And I'm like, what the hell?

Sophia: 'Cause I heard it all week.

Jed: While you're at the house?

Sophia: After I got out of the hospital, I kept hearing it over and over.

Jed: While you were at the Hospital, too?

Sophia: That's when I came out of the hospital. I heard it at the hospital, but I heard it again when I came out the hospital.

Isabelle: I just remembered, because I thought of what happened recently—

Sophia: But I've never heard that whistle before at that house. And then I told her, I was hearing it—

Isabelle: I kept saying, "Mom, I don't know what you're talking about."

Sophia: But she couldn't hear it. The whole week, right?

Isabelle: The whole time you were there from February to May. I just heard it the third week in May.

Sophia: And that was it. After she heard it, that's it.

Isabelle: I haven't heard it.

Sophia: I haven't heard it at all. I guess because I was really pretty sick or something, 'cause I had to stay there.

Isabelle: It was clear as day.

Sophia: It was really high. It was really bad, that was scary. And I couldn't breathe, remember I couldn't breathe or do anything? I was on oxygen, I put it on last night, too. But it was bad.

Isabelle: We haven't heard it since.

Sophia: After you heard it, that was the last time, right?

Isabelle: Um-hm.

Sophia: I was lucky she heard it. Well, not lucky.

Jed: How long would it last?

Sophia: You know how bird's whistle? Like they go *[imitates bird]*, and then they stop. But then you didn't hear no more, and then later on you hear it again.

April: Was it like one time?

Isabelle: When I heard it with her, it was twice. Well, three times. The first time, I was like, "Who's whistling?" And Mom was like, "See, I told you! You hear it?!"

Sophia: I ran to the back to tell her!

Isabelle: I was like, what the hell? So, I'm walking up—

Sophia: And I said, "Let's go outside, and I'll prove to you it's not a bird."

Isabelle: And it did it again.

Sophia: And nobody outside.

Isabelle: Nobody's outside. And then it's silence. And then, I walk back to the back room again, and I heard it again.

Sophia: But it was only inside the house. It's not outside, because we went outside and we didn't hear it.

Isabelle: It sounded like somebody was whistling right next to you. Clear as day. Nobody was arguing, fighting. Everything was good. Like Olivia's party went great, nobody argued, fought, nothing. I just don't know why we heard it.

Sophia: I don't know what it is. I was trying to figure it out the whole time. I was there by myself, she had to work 'til nine, you know what I mean? And it was just horrible.

April: And it's not the water heater.

Sophia: No. This is—

April: Well, you know because sometimes the water heater—

Sophia: This is a whistle, like somebody *[whistles]*.

Jed: *[To April]* I know what you mean, sometimes if I'm in the garage I can hear the—

April: The pressure, the whistle.

Jed: Yeah.

Sophia: Oh, I never heard that.

Isabelle: I know the difference, because I used to scare myself with that.

Sophia: But this is like a whistle if somebody whistled with a little whistle.

April: A high-pitched whistle.

Sophia: Yeah, but it was a different whistle than that. Like if you blow in it, and it's a long whistle, that's how long it was, but it's a different kind of whistle. Like a high pitch whistle. And I couldn't—

Isabelle: Y'all kept saying whistle, so that's what triggered the memory. Like, oh, I remember her complaining, saying she keeps hearing this whistle.

April: That's when you remember, when you hear other people talking. Yeah, I totally forgot about Grandma pouring that water out.

Sophia: 'Cause I was the only one that heard the whistle. I was the only one. And I'd tell her every day.

April: You thought you were going crazy *[laughing]*.

Sophia: I thought I was going crazy.

Jed: While other people were around, you were hearing it and they weren't.

Sophia: Yeah. Nobody's hearing it but me.

Isabelle: But I heard it that time.

Sophia: But she heard it that time. 'Cause I would hear that whistle and ask everyone, "Did you hear that whistle?" Nobody heard a whistle. Yeah, it was only me hearing it and then she finally heard it.

DONNA

[The interview with Donna is conducted by phone, as she lives in another city. Wanda sits in on my end. I explain my goals and what I'm interested in and ask Donna to begin.]

Donna: Well, one of the main ones that I remember is when I was in elementary school, and we lived in the house on Amanda. They only had like three rooms and an add-on bathroom. I remember one morning getting dressed by the wood-burning heater and looking over where there was a water—What do they call those machines, air-conditioned but it wasn't air condition, it was one of those water coolers?

Wanda: Water coolers. They had them back then.

Donna: Yeah, and over that window and I say I saw the devil walk by, over the window. And it was really weird, because the window was closed, I mean, but it was—And that was it.

Jed: What do you mean?

Donna: You know how they always have the picture of the devil, what that looks like on the bingo cards? It just looked like that. But I'd never seen bingo cards until I got older. But I just saw it. I could smell sulfur, it stunk you know, but I just saw it walk past the window. On top, over that water cooler. And that was when I was really young.

Jed: Was that like inside the house or outside?

Donna: You know, I couldn't even tell you. I couldn't even tell you. It looked like probably... I couldn't even tell you. I just saw it there. You know, the windows were solid. They didn't like have window blinds and stuff. So, I couldn't tell you outside, inside. I just saw it going across the water cooler from the window. I never even thought about it. And that was the only thing that happened when I was really young. I think that's probably the first thing that I ever remember of things that happened like that to me. Then Wanda has all the stories from we were in the Yamauchi house, when we lived up there.

Wanda: Yeah, but remember sister—?

Jed: What do you remember?

Donna: Well, I remember that I could hear noises at night. I could hear stuff. I could hear Dad at night saying *[translated from Spanish]*, "Who's walking over there, who is it?" And then the water turning on in the kitchen and him having to go turn it off, and there was nobody there. Or again, the toilet flushing and nobody was there. Just weird things like that.

So, every night I would just be scared. I'd be lying there, hearing noises and stuff. We all slept in twin beds. It was like two or three of us on one twin bed, 'cause there were two twin beds in that one room. The doorway was right there, and then our heads were toward the end of the doorway. All of a sudden, I could hear something, then I felt this hand right on top of my chest. Just right below my neck, right on the chest area, right there. I just thought, oh my God, I'm going to die. I got brave enough to touch it. It was like a man's hand. And you know how men have hair on their hands, on their fingers and stuff?

Jed: Yeah.

Donna: That's what it felt like. And I couldn't move. I was frozen. When I told Mom in the morning about it, she said, "Why didn't you turn on the light?" Hell, I couldn't move, you know?! I mean   , it was the scariest thing in my life. It never happened again, but that night it did.

Jed: When you said you felt it, you touched it with your other hand?

Donna: Yes, yes. I thought—Well, you know when you're scared, you just think you're imagining it. So, I put my hand on the hand, and felt it. And I looked at Dad's hand in the morning?

Jed: Yeah.

Donna: He didn't have any hair on his hand. So, I knew it wasn't Dad's hand. Yeah, and it was like, that was it. And it just scared the hell out of me. I was so scared, I couldn't move. I didn't sleep all night long. At that same house, we always used to see a fire behind the garage. It was a separate garage, further back. I think the fire we used to see was the garage at the Yamauchi house. We'd go out there, but there'd be no fire. It wouldn't be just me, it would be Wanda and Leelani *[a neighbor]* and Mia *[their sister]*. We'd all go out there, nothing there.

Jed: Why were you sure it was a fire?

Donna: Because you could see it so bright and red, and just like when a fire is behind something, you see like a flickering type thing?

Jed: Yeah.

Donna: That's why we thought it was a fire, but there was nothing there. It was weird. At Mom's house on Telford, there used to be a man that would just stand in the corner, watching. Couldn't tell what he looked like, couldn't tell anything, but I knew it was a man, standing right there.

Wanda: Sister, that was in that room next to the dining room. By the bathroom, in the front.

Donna: No, that was—Elijah saw him, too, in his room, which was the front room next to the dining room. I used to sleep in the back room where Mom's room was?

Wanda: Yeah.

Donna: Remember we used to have a bed in the dining room?

Wanda: Yeah, we had beds everywhere.

Donna: Everywhere, right. So, there was a bed in the dining room, that's where Mom slept. The rest of us had more beds in the back room, and that's where I slept. By that back door in the back. And that's where I saw it. Afterwards, Elijah used to say he saw him in the corner.

Jed: Where—?

Donna: I'd get up and go lay down with Mom and say, "Mom, I'm scared", and she'd say, "Alright," and I'd get in bed with her.

Jed: That was the end of it.

Donna: It was weird. He never—I never saw him walking, I never saw him move. But, he was there. And then when Elijah said he saw him, I thought, oh my God, at least I wasn't imagining it. It was quite a while later, but I thought, okay, it wasn't just me.

One other thing that always used to freak me out. My grandparents used to live on Yorkshire, right there by Page Junior School, or whatever? In San Antonio. And I stayed with them most of the time. Elijah and I stayed with them because we were just too much for Mom to handle. So, we'd stay with Grandma and Granddad a lot of the time. And when they lived there, Grandma used to have epileptic seizures. They lived in a house that had two bedrooms an open living room, dining room, then a small kitchen. Well, we used to sleep on the floor in the living room and they had a rocker in the corner. Their bedroom was right there, about 10 feet from where we're sleeping. And they'd always sleep with the door open. But that damn rocker would rock every frickin' night. It would just rock. Nobody was up, nobody was close to it. It would rock back and forth all night. Like, oh my God. After a while, we just got used to it.

Jed: When would it start each night?

Donna: It would just start in the middle of the night. I don't know what time or nothing. It's dark, we're kids. We weren't even in junior high school yet. We were in elementary school.

Jed: Yeah, it's not like you could check your phone and see what time it was.

Donna: I wouldn't move either. That was really weird. I mean, that was just like, what? You know, but that would always rock. And we used to tell Grandma, and she'd get up. Sometimes I'd wake her up and she'd check, and yup, it'd be rocking. It was crazy.

Though, you know, as far as like sensing things? You know how you have those feelings of something's going to happen type of thing? We were scheduled to come up to Dallas and there were four of us from Travelers that were going to come up here. It was Angie and Lisa *[her friends]*, and Sophia and myself. We were all going to come up here to the Dallas Cowboys game. But I couldn't do it. I kept thinking, no, if I go, I'm gonna die. I can't do this. And my girlfriend finally said, "If you really have that feeling, you shouldn't do it." "I'm not going." So, they left without me, and sure enough, they had a car wreck.

Jed: Wow.

Donna: It wasn't really bad, but they had a car wreck. So, it's like, okay, I need to listen to my senses. A different time—It was really weird, because usually in my dreams I can't see faces and stuff. But I had this dream, and it was flooding. I mean, it wasn't even raining here in this area, but it was flooding, and it was raining, and I saw this car. I could feel all their feelings about how they're drowning. This lady and this young boy were in the car, and I could see him in the car. You know, when the car went over and flipped into the water. I was really worried like, God, what happened? What am I dreaming? I mean, I saw these people, I felt they're feelings. The next morning, they had it on the news that this lady and her son had gone over the bridge and drowned. I thought, oh my God, this is just too weird for me. Stuff like that I just sort of, I sense things. And I think, well, I've always been like this, so I don't really think anything of it.

Jed: Anything like what happened down here ever happen in Dallas?

Donna: Ah, no. No. You know, that's the weird part. I've lived in the apartment, and I lived in *[inaudible]* house, and I lived here *[her current home]*, and I haven't had anything happen here. Except for that dream. You know?

Jed: Yeah.

Donna: That's it. So that's sort of strange, but yeah, no. All that other stuff was down there. Really strange now that you mention it. It's like, yeah, what happened? Did I lose my power *[laughing]*?

Jed: Do you remember how old you were the last time you saw something, or had something like what happened down here at the houses?

Donna: Well, the last time... Let's see here. We moved to Telford my senior year. So, I'd say that would have been probably the last time that I felt anything like that. Because after I graduated from high school, I left and went up North for a year or two, then came back and got my own apartment. So, I'd say when I was 17 was probably the last time. Well, no, no. It wasn't. That was at Mom's house. The last episode was when I knew something was going to happen. I was already working at Travelers then, and that was—I started working at Travelers in '77, so, maybe a couple, two, three years after that. So, I was probably 22, 23.

Jed: Yeah.

Donna: Something like that, because I think I got married when I was 25.

Jed: Do you remember anything—Mom, do you remember Donna being there when April was a baby?

Wanda: Yeah, that's what I was going to ask you, Donna. Don't you remember when we were at the house on Amanda, and Mom and Dad used to go with Yamauchi to pick up the boys that worked at Earl Abel's at night? They'd leave at 2:30 in the morning, or midnight? We were taking care of April, and we were arguing, and I went back to the other room by the kitchen. Then you told me, "Wanda, better stop playing with matches. I'm going to tell Mom." And I said, "I'm not playing with matches, you are, I can smell 'em." And I went back into the living room with you, and the crib was in the corner window, on the opposite side by the door? And we heard wings fluttering in the crib where April was at. The curtains, the window was closed.

Donna: That explains why she's a demon child *[laughing]*. I remember we always smelled sulfur. We always smelled the matches and stuff. But you know what? I recall that, but I don't recall all of it. I mean, 'cause we always did smell it didn't we, sulfur around that house?

Wanda: Dad said anytime somebody was fighting it was because the devil was around. And I remember that night because I was in the back room on the other side of the kitchen, and we were mad at each other and you were in the living room. I was in the back and you tell me, "Quit lighting matches, I'm going to tell mom," and I go, "I'm not lighting matches." So, I come real quietly into the room and April was in the crib sleeping, and we hear wings like a bird.

Donna: Fluttering, yeah.

Wanda: Yeah. And the curtains by the crib started moving. And that's when we got April out of the crib, because it's like, oh my God. And we started saying our prayers because it scared the heck out of us.

Donna: Yeah, I don't even remember. I remember always thinking somebody was lighting matches.

Wanda: Yeah.

Jed: Is there anything in the houses that smells like sulfur?

Donna: It smelled like sulfur quite often. You know? It was really weird, because it was just all of a sudden, and then it'd just go away. It's not like it happened every day, but it happened quite often that I remember. That's how I learned what sulfur smelled like, living at that house.

Jed: There're no factories nearby?

Wanda: No, not on Amanda.

Donna: Nope, nothing.

Wanda: Nothing by us.

Jed: There was no gas or anything like that there was there?

Wanda: We had gas. No, you know what we had? We had propane. That don't smell like sulfur.

Donna: Yeah, that was propane. I mean we could be outside smelling it, it could be anytime.

[Apparently propane is combined with a rotten egg smell like sulfur to help detect leaks, but when they refer to sulfur, they are referring specifically to the smell of matches.]

Wanda: Remember the other time we were at Yamauchi's house, and we thought the Lechuzas were out on the on the power lines across the street?

Donna: Yeah, yeah!

Wanda: And that time, too, Paul and Elijah were fighting with each other, ran down the street to the old house, they came back running and said they smelled sulfur. And Elijah was mad at Paul because he popped him in the ear. And that's when we saw those giant birds.

Donna: Yeah, what'd we always call them, Lechuzas?

Wanda: Yeah, yeah, I mean they were—

Donna: And we all ran in the house, because we were scared to death.

Wanda: Yeah, and we're looking out, and they were just sitting there. And they were big! And it's like, are those the Lechuzas they tell us about?

Donna: You know the thing with those? It's like people say, they're not real, Lechuzas. But you know what, we used to hear them fly around. You don't hear birds fly around at night. Big birds.

Wanda: They were big. They looked big.

Jed: The thing you saw, Donna, did it look like an owl? Or what did it look like to you? What do you remember?

Donna: Oh no, honey, you couldn't really see 'em close up. You just saw that they were big birds. It wasn't like you could say, oh, I know the shape, the color or what. They were just like big birds that we saw up there on the lines. But when we were outside, you could hear like something big flying around. And to this day, how many birds do you hear flying around at night. Bats maybe sometimes.

Jed: All I can think of is an owl.

Wanda: No, but these you could see them, the outlines on the line. It looked like a giant bird, and it was two of 'em, sitting there.

Jed: I think what Mom was telling me, I was imagining an owl, but you're not saying it was an owl. It was just a really big bird.

Donna: Yeah, a big bird is what it looked like. A big something sitting up there.

Wanda: Just a big outline.

Donna: Like, oh Hell no. And we knew Lechuzas, so we moved.

Jed: Did Grandma or Grandpa ever tell you anything about things they saw?

Donna: I think Mom said something when she was younger. I don't remember.

Wanda: I don't remember Mom. The only thing I remember is Dad, when Mom said that—

Donna: Oh yeah, that one when he couldn't talk.

Wanda: Yeah. I don't remember why he got mad. With his sister, right?

Donna: I don't know why. He was walking home from a death, but he was mad or something. And then something was either whistling at him or yelling at him, and he started to run. And it was chasing him, and it scared him so bad, whatever that thing was, that he lost—He couldn't talk. He lost his voice for I don't know how long.

[This is an example where I have left in multiple retellings of the same story in order to show the slightly different variations.]

Wanda: What I remember is that, he said he was walking down the street and—Yeah, somebody whistled at him or something. And, threw a brick at him. And he turned around and he was going to go reach a brick, pick it up, and throw it back. But as he had it in his hand and was getting ready to throw it, it disappeared.

Donna: That's exactly what he said. Yeah. Just nothing there, and that's what's scared him.

Wanda: And the eyes were just red, and he couldn't see anything. He just saw this man throwing stuff and he couldn't—And he did it a couple of times, so it scared the hell out of him.

Donna: Yeah.

Wanda: I remember that one. That's why he was very, don't do this.

Donna: Yeah. And he was young, that was in his young days.

Wanda: Very young. Because I thought he said he was like 13 or something, or Grandma said or something.

Donna: Because he was out roaming the streets when he shouldn't have been roaming.

Wanda: Yeah.

Donna: That was the only thing I remember from Dad.

Wanda: Yeah, I don't ever remember anything of Mom. Except when we were in that house on Telford, because she'd always say she felt, she saw that man in that room. Where she slept. He'd always be in there. She'd wake up and—

Donna: Yeah, I think we found out afterward that somebody had passed away there, though. People that lived there or something? Somebody passed away there.

Wanda: We didn't know that when we moved in.

Donna: So, those are all my experiences.

Wanda: Yeah, I couldn't remember any more.

Jed: Did your grandparents or great grandparents ever tell you stories? Like you said, Mom. Which one was it—?

Donna: Grandma Cortez and Tia Delia used to have stories, but I have to say, I don't remember them.

Jed: It was a long time ago.

Donna: I don't remember, but I remember they used to tell us. And they're the ones that told us about Lechuzas stuff.

Wanda: Yeah, those are the ones from Eagle Pass.

Donna: They used to have stories about stuff like that, but I don't remember them.

Jed: Yeah, I wish I would have thought to ask everyone's stories 20 years ago.

Donna: Yeah, yeah. I mean, like, I remember those things that affected me and stuff, but I couldn't tell you every detail. I accepted years ago that, hey, I'm going to sense things and feel things, but it's not like I'm a medium, you know *[laughing]*? But you know, at times it's a lot stronger than others. Used to be anyway.

Wanda: And in the house on Amanda, we always used to hear a baby cry in the kitchen. We thought it was outside. As you went through the doorway where the stove was in the door, in the kitchen—In the living room? There was always a baby crying, and you could sit there and go check and stuff like that. And it wasn't Nathalie, because they didn't have any kids.

Donna: Uh-uh. And Annette and them were our age.

Wanda: Yeah, yeah.

Donna: Yeah, I don't remember the baby crying. I just remember that house being sort of scary.

MIA

[I contact Mia by phone. It's very convenient for the Cortez family and their schedules. I ask my mother to sit in on the call after I felt the conversation with Sophia, April, and Isabelle was successful. I let Mia know Wanda is in attendance and ask her to begin after describing the types of experiences I'm interested in.]

Mia: Okay. Let me think. The only one that I can really remember, and it's like stayed with me forever, was I guess back in 1968. I was living with my grandparents and my aunt in Eagle Pass.

Jed: Yeah.

Mia: My aunt and my grandma would always have this… I don't know if you'd call it a ritual, just that it was a time to say their Rosary every night. They'd pick like 9:30 or 10 when everything was really quiet, and we'd go sit on the front porch. There was like the little walkway and they walked back and forth and said the Rosary. I'd sit there and just watch them. One particular night it was a real clear sky, beautiful sky. All you could see was the stars, no clouds.

Jed: Yeah.

Mia: And it was real quiet. So, they got done with the Rosary after a few minutes, and they went and sat down. We had chairs there on the porch. My cousin left for the night; he'd gone out of the house somewhere. Anyway, I happened to look across the street, there was like rural houses, telephone poles. There was this one telephone pole where I saw this like, dark object. It didn't look like a bird, because it was too big, and we really couldn't make it out.

I told my aunt, "Look," and she said, "What is that?" I said, "I don't know." And we kept looking at it, and just watching it, and it was just there. It was big enough to be almost the size of a person, but it couldn't be a person. It was humongous, right, it was huge. So, after watching it for a few minutes, we saw it just like, levitate from the telephone wires, or whatever the wires are. It just rose up, and then came from across the street. And we were watching it. It was just coming toward us.

As it got closer, it was the weirdest part, because my aunt, my grandma, and me, we're all sitting there, looking up at the form coming towards us. But the thing is, the form was invisible. I mean, you could make the form out, but you could see through it. It was kind of almost like a fog thing? And it wasn't a cloud, because there were no clouds in the sky. It was the way it came right above us. I mean, it was just climbing. The wings were extended. It was just this, it was... I'll never forget that. I didn't sleep for a few nights. But anyway, you could see through it. It was transparent, yet it had a form, if that makes sense.

Jed: It does. But you couldn't get any details about, what—?

Mia: We couldn't make details whether it was a bird—I mean, it was like beyond our imagination that it'd be a person, you know? But it was big enough to be a person, the size of a person, but we couldn't make out exactly what it was. We were sitting there looking above us, and it glided over us until it went over past the roof of the house and disappeared. We were stunned. My aunt and my grandma, of course, started praying because they didn't know what it was.

Then about two days later our neighbor who lived three houses down came over and she was sitting there with my grandma and my aunt. She was saying Angelica, which was her daughter, my friend, had come in scared to death, and our neighbor said Angelica was white as a ghost. She said she came in swearing up and down that she saw a woman floating over her. Anyway, they compared the time. Because when they went, it was about, I guess, 9:30 to 10 o'clock at night. And in Eagle Pass during those years, people's home was fenced off all the way around. And during those years, people would actually take a cot outside and sleep outside because nobody bothered them. You know, it's not like today.

Jed: Right.

Mia: But anyway, she was out there, and she said she told her, "Angelica, you were dreaming." She says, "No, I wasn't, I hadn't even gone to sleep yet. It was a woman. I saw her, you could see through her, but it was a woman." And she says, "No, she was just dreaming." And my grandma said, "No, we saw the same thing, but we couldn't tell what it was." It was scary. I mean, you don't know what to think.

Was it real or what? But three people saw it. If it had been just me, I would say, "Oh man, you're losing it or something." But it was me, my grandma and my aunt. And then my cousin had just gotten there, so it was actually four of us, because he was standing there looking up at the same thing we were watching. And we were like, "What is that?" We didn't know, it was just scary.

Jed: Yeah.

Mia: But yeah. That's one I remember the most.

Jed: You said it definitely seemed like it had wings, even though you couldn't quite see details?

Mia: Yeah. It looked like it was like, gliding. Like, you could see the form, but it wasn't solid.

Jed: Right.

Mia: I guess you would say like a ghost or something, where you could— Well, you've never seen a ghost, I'm sure, but I *[inaudible]*. But whatever it was, you could make out the form, but you couldn't physically see it. Like if we had reached out to touch it, we couldn't touch it. Our hands probably would've gone right through it. But you could see that form. It wasn't, it couldn't have been a gigantic bird, because it was just too huge. It looked like the size of an adult, but we couldn't make out what it was. But when Angelica saw it, she said it was a woman. She could see through her, but it was a woman. She never got over it either.

Jed: Do you remember ever being in Eagle Pass with Sophia?

Mia: Umm, yeah.

Jed: Because she had also mentioned seeing something one time, not with Grandma or any of the adults. She said it was outside with the neighbor's kids, the teenagers. And she said she had just remembered it was her and you and them, like she thought the other kids were grown up because they were teenagers.

Mia: Yeah.

Jed: She said that she saw something in the sky. I don't know if you remembered anything, but she had said that it was a woman on a horse, and it was I think an evening or afternoon or sunset, something like that.

Mia: I don't remember that one. But I do remember the one that we saw, all four of us, my cousin and my aunt, grandma. I mean, it was right above our heads and then disappeared over the roof of the house.

Jed: But you could see it at night.

Mia: Uh-huh, at night. I mean, I don't know what that was, I don't. Up to now I can't tell you what it was. I know it actually happened because there were too many of us that saw it. I know Cheryl and Donna had things happen to them.

Jed: Yeah. Well, I mean that's just interesting that you even saw something flying, even though it wasn't the same thing that Sophia saw.

Mia: Yeah.

Jed: Did the family in Eagle Pass ever tell you about any of the things that they saw or experienced?

Mia: No. The only thing—I don't know if they had anything to do with, or what people believe in—I have no idea. Sometimes I wonder about that. Because I know that next door to us where my friends had moved to, every once in a while I'd go outside and I'd see this flame just above the house. Just a flame, burning there. It wasn't on the house, the house was never on fire or anything, but yet it was there. It would just appear like, you know, the one big flame. I don't know if it has to do with maybe what some people practice there? Or, there's some things that you just can't explain.

Jed: Yeah.

Mia: You know, what is it and why does it happen?

[I had previously discussed with my mother the need to let people tell what they remember and trying not to lead them with questioning, but I can see she has something to say.]

Jed: My mom has a question, Mia. What were you going to ask, Mom?

Wanda: Hey sis.

Mia: Hey Wanda.

Wanda: Hey, on that fire, was that at Yamauchi's house? Or in Eagle Pass?

Mia: No, that was in Eagle Pass. That was our neighbors' in Eagle Pass. It was the other side neighbors next to Grandma's house in Eagle Pass.

Wanda: Yeah. But see, we saw it when we had moved to Yamauchi's house. We had seen a flame behind one of the garages, too. And there was nothing burning.

Mia: It's weird right?

Wanda: Yeah. It was a quiet fire, like somebody lit up a fire, and there was nothing there. No ashes, no nothing.

Mia: And there was nothing there. But what they've always said, and this goes back to the folklore thing, that whenever you see a flame burning somewhere it's because there's money that's been buried or hidden or something in that location. If you see a flame burning where there's no fire, and there's nothing burning, there's something buried there. But who knows?

Jed: What do you mean when you say that there was a flame above it? Was it day or night? What were you seeing?

Mia: It was at night. Both at night.

Wanda: Yeah.

Mia: I mean, it's always at night when you see stuff like that. Very rare, I think, that you experience the paranormal or whatever you want to call it during the day.

Jed: Yeah.

Mia: It's rare. I mean you can, but most of the time stuff like that usually happens at night. I don't know why.

Jed: Yeah. Well, did Grandma ever talk to you about anything like that?

Mia: Cortez? Grandma, your grandma?

Jed: Yeah, or even stories from her parents, because I don't think anybody else really spoke to them as much as you.

Mia: No, not really. I mean, yeah, you have the stories about La Llorona and stuff like that. But those have been carried over from way back when, you know.

Jed: Sure.

Mia: But other than that, no. And then when my friend saw it, she couldn't sleep either for days. It scared the heck out of her, because, you know, you don't know what to think.

Jed: Yeah. How high above you do you think it was when it flew over you?

Mia: What did I think it was?

Jed: How high above you do you think it was?

Mia: It was pretty high, high enough. Basically, if you imagine the roof of a house, and it went over the roof of the house. So about the height of the roof of Grandma's house, a little bit higher than that. And after that it went over the roof and we didn't see it.

Jed: Got you.

Mia: But we didn't follow it either.

Jed: Right.

Mia: We were kind of like frozen, stunned. Because we didn't know what to believe or what we saw or what it was.

Jed: Yeah.

Mia: So, it was pretty close to *[be able to]* see.

Jed: Yeah. Okay.

Wanda: Hey, Sis, did Grandma ever talk, or did Mom and Dad ever talk about when he saw the devil following him, that he was scared to death?

Mia: Oh yeah, Daddy, yeah.

Wanda: Yeah.

Mia: I forgot about that.

Wanda: Because I wasn't sure. Go ahead and tell Jed, because I don't know if I remembered everything. I told him what I remembered, but maybe you remember more.

[I believe the above statement is a great example of persons without training being able to pick up useful interviewing skills. Where previously she shared her own experience to see if her sister recalled the event, here Wanda asks for her sister's experience specifically.]

Mia: Yeah. Yeah, I remember that. When he was brought up, he said he was about 13 when he'd seen it, because it was him and his cousins. He left home about that age. You know how Grandpa was always swearing up and down a storm, that was his thing. So, he said that when he was about 13 or 14, that he always used to cross this cemetery right where his cousin used to live on South New Braunfels. I don't know if you're familiar with that area. There's an old cemetery there. He used to cross the cemetery, go across the tombstones to take a shortcut to get to his cousins', to go home.

Jed: Right.

Mia: And one night, he said that he thinks somebody's following him. He was feisty, I guess he started swearing. He went to pick up some rocks to throw at whatever he thought was following him, and as he picked them up, he said that they would literally just turn into dust. And he said it scared him so much, that he lost his voice for a year. He couldn't talk for a year.

Jed: Wow.

Mia: He said that he thought it was the Devil, because he was in the cemetery. He could see eyes, but he couldn't see anything else. You know, that is scary. I mean, what we saw was one thing, but what he saw, that was scary.

Jed: Yeah.

Mia: I forgot about that Wanda.

Wanda: Yep. But what about Amanda, where we lived? Did you ever hear a baby crying, any noise there?

Mia: I didn't. I don't know about Cheryl or Donna. I don't know who else experienced stuff like that. I didn't in that house, or even in the one on Telford. I know they said that they experienced stuff there, but I never did.

Wanda: On Amanda, I used to hear a baby cry, but that was between the kitchen and stuff. But I always thought it was something from outside or a cat or something. I always tried to explain it.

Mia: Yeah. Wasn't it at Yamauchi's, and Cheryl said that they'd seen a hand on her chest or something?

Wanda: No, that was Donna at Yamauchi's house.

Mia: Was it Donna?

Wanda: Yeah. But the one where we lived, the little house, that's where I used to hear a baby cry.

Mia: Really?

Wanda: Yeah.

Mia: The weird thing about that little house is every once in a while, and I don't know why, but every once in a while, I dream about that little house. I dream about walking through each and every room. It's such a weird dream. It doesn't scare me, but it's like, why am I dreaming about that little house?

Jed: Yeah.

Wanda: Yeah, because it was only three rooms.

Jed: That's a short dream.

Mia: Couldn't get lost in that house.

Wanda: Yeah, exactly.

Mia: Even if we tried. We couldn't get away from each other, we were stuck.

Wanda: We were stuck, yeah.

[We were wrapping up and discussing the book generally, but I was glad I had kept my recorder on.]

Mia: We were into shows where there were other dimensions and stuff.

Jed: Yeah.

Wanda: Did you ever see a flying saucer? Hey Sis, did you ever see a flying saucer?

[Mia is silent for a moment.]

Mia: ...Ah, yes. But you know... Alright, Wanda. You know, Alyssa *[her daughter]* was making fun of me, but I have been justified.

Wanda: No, because...

Jed: No, because a lot of the family has.

Mia: This isn't paranormal.

Wanda: No, no, no. Some of the family has, that's why *[he's asking]*.

Jed: Both sides of my family, Mom and Dad's, have experienced stuff that people would consider paranormal, but they've also seen UFOs.

Wanda: Yeah.

Mia: Well, let me tell you about—This is like, really true. First of all, let me set the background here.

Wanda: Yeah.

Mia: It was me, your dad *[James]*, Elijah, and Donna, okay? We were driving two cars, and this is in 1977, I can tell you that for sure. In 1977, we were driving from Texas to St. Paul, Minnesota, because Donna had this—I think she was going to move back to Texas.

Wanda: Yep.

Mia: So, we were going to go up there and help her load her stuff and bring it back. It was my little red bug and Donna's car. Let's see, we were about two hours from St Paul. That night Elijah was driving. I was with Elijah, and Donna was driving with your dad. Elijah said, "Look." And he's looking at the window, and I said, "What?" And your Uncle Elijah was like your grandpa, he swore a lot. He looked and said, "It's a UFO." And I said, "What?!"

He pulls over to the side of the road. There was no traffic. It was dark and it was about three o'clock in the morning. We get out the car, and we're standing there, and your Uncle Elijah was really into it. He goes, "Come on, you so-and-so, F-you so-and-so's! Come on and get me! I want to go where you're coming from." I mean, thinking back it's funny, because I can remember telling Elijah, "Elijah, stop calling them because I don't want to go anywhere!" And it was funny, now it's funny, but then it was scary because there's this bright, bright light. I mean up in the sky, right?

Jed: Yeah.

Mia: And then it's just there. It's not moving, it's not a plane, not a helicopter. It's just a light. Then out of the clear blue, you see these little other lights coming, full speed ahead, just in a split second from different directions. It was the weirdest thing, because they're shooting from right, left, every direction, coming and meeting up with this bright light. I mean, it was that quick, just "zing, zing, zing," really fast. And they all connected to that bright light we were watching.

Elijah said, "It's a UFO, I know it is." Sure enough, when all these lights came together, to that one light, all of a sudden that bright light just zipped off. It was like gone. I told Alyssa this story and she's like, "Oh yeah, Mom. Hippy that you are, you're probably—" I said, "No, it was true." So now she's watching all this stuff on that Area 51 place in Nevada. I said, "See, I told you." I said, "They exist. I don't care what you say, they exist." But yeah, we did see them.

Jed: When you stopped, how far away was the light from where you were?

Mia: We're talking like up, way up in the thousands and thousands of feet up in the sky. It was like way up in the sky. It was just there. That was the craziest part, it was just there. Normally you see an aircraft, you see a plane, it's going to move.

You know, you see it moving, and it wasn't. It was too high for a helicopter, way too high for the helicopter, and it was high enough for a plane, but it wasn't moving. It was just stationary, and it only moved after all of the other lights came and flashed and went into it. But the thing is, we were listening to the radio on the way to St Paul, and people were calling in and saying, what were those lights we saw? So, it happened. Whatever it was, UFO or whatever, but yeah, we saw it.

Jed: Right.

Mia: I believe in UFOs and aliens.

Jed: When you see them, it's hard not to. The lights that came and met them, how far away could you see that they were coming from? It's not that you saw lights that were already near?

Mia: No, they looked like little stars. It's weird because you didn't realize that they weren't stars until you saw them zip right to the main light from different directions. It was like all of a sudden, it's a little light and then zip, there they go. And then here comes another one, and then another one. And then once they connected to that big light, that big light just zoomed off. The weird part is that when it zoomed off, it left like a haze where it had been. Crazy, huh?

Jed: Yeah.

Mia: And I wasn't on drugs, Jed.

Jed: Donna and my dad were in another car…

Mia: But they pulled over. Yeah. We all pulled over. Your dad would probably remember. I mean, it left an impression on me, and Donna still remembers.

Jed: I'll have to ask my dad.

Mia: We all got out the car and we were watching it. Yeah, ask your dad, he should remember.

Wanda: I knew that somebody had said they had seen it.

Mia: It was '77. I remember the year.

Jed: I talked to Donna, but she forgot, I think.

Wanda: She forgot, yeah.

Jed: Because, I mean, I understand why. If you don't think about something for years, it's like I'm essentially telling you, "Hey, try to remember this one thing that was really out of the ordinary that happened 50 years ago."

Mia: Yeah.

Jed: And I'm not telling you specifically what it is.

Mia: Yeah. You got to admit it's been a long, long time.

Jed: Sure.

Mia: I have a brain that remembers things that I think are important, they're like put away in my computer and I'll remember it.

Jed: Yeah.

Mia: But like that incident in Eagle Pass, and that UFO thing. I don't know, it just stuck in my head. Donna remembered it the other day, because I said, "Hey Donna, do you remember that trip when Elijah, I, and you went to Minnesota?" And she says, "Oh yeah, I remember it now." I'll never forget that. Elijah was so funny, and I was like, "Elijah, don't call them because they're going to hear you and I don't want to go nowhere." I think that's why I never forgot it, because I was like, "Elijah!" Like they were really going to hear us, right? I mean, if they were really UFOs, were they really going to hear us? Probably if they could get that far *[Laughing]*.

[I followed up with James about the UFO that Mia described. Note that he remembers the event itself, but the details are vastly different in some respects.]

James: You want me to tell you exactly what happened?

Jed: Yeah.

James: Okay.

Jed: Was this on the way to or from?

James: On the way to, and it was late evening. It was twilight. And Elijah was driving, I was in the front seat. The girls were in the backseat, Mia and uh... What's her name?

Jed: Donna?

James: Donna. Yeah. Okay. And I looked up ahead and I saw a flicker and light, and I said, "Look at that! Look at that flickering light!" And Elijah said, "Well, that's probably just an airplane." And I said, "No, it's not acting like an airplane." He says, "Ah, you're just tired."

So, we get closer and it's still over the highway. We pull over to this rest area and people are out of their cars, they're looking up at this flickering light. Because it's zigzagging all over the place, you know? And we're watching it and it's getting darker, and then it moves over, it comes closer to us. So, we get in the car and we actually go off the road; we were following it. Me and Elijah are really curious about what this thing is. It finally stops, and we're underneath it, and there's three lights. In like, in a triangle? And you can't see anything—You can see stars around the triangle, but you couldn't see anything through the triangle. And then we watched it, because it kept strobing. All of a sudden, it started moving, and then it just kind of disappeared at an angle into the sky. We finally got to St Paul, Minneapolis, to their friends', and we were telling them about it and they say, ah, you guys are probably just smoking dope. We said no, so they even called to see if anybody had reported anything, and nobody had. They teased us about it, that we were tired. It wasn't until about a week later that I think they sent Donna a newspaper clipping of a UFO sighting in the St. Paul area.

Jed: How high do you think it was?

James: The thing was probably... When we were close to it, I'd say it was probably about one, two, three hundred feet off the ground. You know a telephone pole is 60 feet, so just imagine about three hundred feet. That's how close it was.

Jed: Were you close enough that you had some idea of relative size, or how big it might be?

James: Relative size? I would say that it was probably about the size of this whole property with the house and the yard.

Jed: From point to point to point?

James: I would say about, I would say about sixty, seventy... Probably 80 by 80 by 80 feet.

Jed: Yeah.

James: It was pretty big.

Jed: Did it always have three lights with it?

James: When we got closer to it, we could see three lights. I saw three lights; I saw a triangle shape. I saw that I couldn't see the stars through it. It kind of stood out like a triangle in the dark. You could see stars behind it, but you couldn't see through it.

Jed: Before it left, did you see any other lights approach it or join it?

James: No, before it left, the lights started to flash faster and faster, then it went up at an angle and disappeared. We didn't see anybody looking at us.

Jed: As vivid as that is, I'm surprised you didn't remember it when we talked before.

James: I didn't think we were talking about—You know, I think it just never came up. I didn't go back far enough and forgot all about it until you brought it up.

Jed: Because we talked about the ball of flame and some of the stuff while you were driving.

James: Oh yeah, while I was driving in West Texas and stuff. I guess I was fixated on that area. Yeah, but that's about as detailed as I can get. As a matter of fact, bringing it up I can see it clear as hell.

[An additional note:

Wanda stated she clearly remembers James and her family members saying they saw something in the sky after returning from the trip, although she does not remember the details.]

CHERYL

[Cheryl often works nights, so I contact her by phone for her convenience. My mother is again present, and Cheryl begins after I describe the breadth of types of experiences others have described previously.]

Cheryl: My first experience of haunting, I don't know if your mom was there, but we lived on Amanda. I don't know where Mom and Dad were, but I remember your mom was there. There was something at the window, and it like flew in. It seemed like something flew into the window, into the house literally. But there was a curtain there, and I think it was a bed or something next to the window, and we all just freaked out. Wanda, I don't know if you were there, but I was like going into third grade, I remember that. We moved the curtain with a broomstick and there was nothing there. We all freaked out.

Jed: The window was open or closed?

Cheryl: It was closed. Yeah, it was closed.

Jed: Why did you think that something flew in?

Cheryl: Because it like hit. Like it hit, and the curtain moved. You know like the wind blows, and the curtain blows in the wind? The curtain was literally moving, so it's like, "A bird just flew in!" And we were like, no, the window's closed. There's only like one window there by the door. It was a real tiny house. I was little, but I remember it was Sophia, Melissa *[one of the twins]*, and I could swear your mom was there, but I could be wrong. But I knew it was my older sisters. They stayed with us when Dad and Mom went somewhere. It was late at night, so while somebody got a stick, a broomstick, it just stopped.

They moved the curtain and there was nothing there, the window was closed. It scared the shit out of us. To this day I will not watch any sort of horror movies. We moved, we got our house on Telford, and Mom said it was a big, beautiful house. I remember very clearly it was third grade. I came home *[to Telford]*, that window in that second bedroom was broken, so I got in that way. When I got in there, I closed the door and everything, nobody was home. I was looking in all the rooms because I thought Mom would be home, but I didn't know Mom was in the hospital. I remember them saying your Uncle Paul was coming home because Mom was sick. I remember seeing Paul's duffle bag there.

Anyway, I sit down and grab a banana. All of a sudden, something said, "Cheryl, come here!" I thought, that's weird, and went to the back room. I said, "Joseph, stop playing! Where are you?" I'm looking, couldn't find Joseph. I think whoever it was, whatever it was, kept calling out my name. I said, okay, I blew it off. I went back into Mom's bedroom, then I heard somebody walking! In the kitchen. So then, I was sure Joseph was playing with me, because it was like a man's voice.

I went into the kitchen, and I don't know if you remember Grandma's old house, the cabinets were glass. The dishes, and I swear to God it scares me to even talk about it, the dishes in there started rattling. Moving. And I freaked out. That table that your mom gave me the other day, that Grandma had, it was that old table where you could get under there. I went and I got underneath it. Then the phone rang. Whatever it was, I swear to God—Oh, Wanda! Were you with us when we played with that Ouija board?

Wanda: I don't remember. You'd have to fill in all the other parts, before I remember whether or not I was there.

Cheryl: Okay, I think it was you. It was Donna, it was all of us. Okay, this is where I think it started Jed, and I didn't put it together until I started reading up on the Ouija board. Somebody found a Ouija board in that backroom in the closet.

Jed: Really?

Cheryl: They were playing with it. The older girls were playing with it. Wanda goes, "How many babies am I going to have?" And everybody you know—It was you Wanda, I remember, it was you. We had a candle lit, and you were playing with someone else, and somebody says, "Well, how many kids am I gonna have?" and "Am I going to get married?" And that thing was like zoom, zoom, zoom. It was like going crazy. It was just all over the table and I sat there like, "Oh God!" So, Dad walks in, and Dad says *[inaudible]*. You know, he was telling us don't play with that, it's evil. Well, the candle split in two. I hope you remember that, Wanda. That's really when it started. *[The candle]* split in two and he took *[the Ouija board]* away from us and somebody flipped on the light. We were playing in the dark. Well, I didn't play it, but I was watching the older sisters play it. Dad turned on the light, took it from us, and supposedly ripped it up and threw it away. After that, that's when that incident happened with me.

Jed: That was in the Telford house?

Cheryl: That was the Telford house.

Jed: How old were you?

Cheryl: I was in third grade, so what does that make me?

Wanda: I think you were...

Cheryl: Eleven, twelve?

Wanda: No, not third grade.

Jed: Ten maybe?

Wanda: Nine or ten, Cheryl, 'cause April was—

Cheryl: She's six years younger than me.

Wanda: Yeah, yeah, and when you said the curtain had moved—

Cheryl: We were on Amanda Street.

Wanda: Yeah, and she was a baby.

Cheryl: I was young.

Wanda: She was in the crib at that time.

Cheryl: That's right, it was the crib! There was a crib by the window, I remember that now! I did say crib right, the bed or crib.

Wanda: Yeah, and that's when Dad and Mom had gone to pick up Paul and Elijah at the Argyle when they were working at midnight.

Cheryl: That's right. That's right! That is right. That's the first time that I, I don't know who was there, but that's the first time we encountered it. April was a baby.

Wanda: Yeah. But at the old house we used to, I don't know if you remember, we used to hear a baby cry in the corner of the kitchen door.

Cheryl: That's right! Oh, I forgot about that, too!

Wanda: Yeah, 'cause it was always—Somebody said there must have been a baby, because the neighbor never had any kids.

Cheryl: That's right!

Jed: You remember hearing the baby now, Cheryl?

Cheryl: Yes. Hoo! I get chills guys, I'm serious.

Jed: I believe it. I've talked to other people, and they get chills, too. Because it's not stories, it's memories. I don't think people realize the difference when they're reading the descriptions.

Cheryl: It's so horrible. I ain't going to lie to you, it makes me want to cry, that last incident at Telford, because it was sooo real. It happened. I heard somebody walking in that house. The phone rang; I ran to it and I'm like, "Hello, hello," and they wouldn't answer. I got up, and that front door, you know that big thick one?

Wanda: Yeah, the one in the living room.

Cheryl: Yes, that big thick one. The TV came on *[voice starts to waver]*, and it went off. Came on. The front door opened, and I was going toward it, and it closed. It closed on me. I went to the other door in Mama's room, where the glass was broken? I tried to get out that door, I couldn't get out. It started calling my name again, "Come here, come here." The dishes were rattling, the TV was going off and on.

Jed: The TV kept going off and on and the dishes were rattling the whole time?

Cheryl: Yes.

Jed: Oh wow.

Cheryl: I was a little girl; I was so scared. I thought, this isn't real, this isn't real, this isn't real. I kept telling myself that. Anyway, I went back underneath the table and just let it do whatever. Something in the back kept calling out my name. I wouldn't get up anymore, because I checked and there was nobody there. When the phone rang a second time, I ran to the phone again and they didn't answer. I went back underneath the table, and all this is still going on. I was crying, "God help me, God help me, God help me," and the phone rang a third time. I ran to the phone again and it happened to be Uncle Elijah. I was like "Hello, hello!" He goes, "What are you doing?" And I was like, "There's something in the house, and it won't let me out the house!" He goes, "What do you mean? Get the f—- out the house!" And I said, "I can't! It won't let me out the house!" And he goes "What do you mean?!" I said, "The door opened by itself, and then it closed, and I can't get out. It won't let me out." He goes, "Well, you haven't seen anything, just get out the f—- house!" And I ran, and I went out Mama's bedroom door. He told me to go to Miss Hammen. You know, Miss Hammen?

Wanda: Yeah. Miss Hannek.

Cheryl: Hannek. I ran over there, and I pounded on the door. She opened it and she said, "Honey, are you alright? You're pale. What happened?" And I could not, I could not answer her. I tried and I could not speak. So, she says come in and she pulled me inside. She gave me a spoon of sugar. I didn't know what that meant. She says, "What did you see?" And I still couldn't talk. Well, Uncle Elijah came home, he was on a motorcycle. I guess he went through the house. He came over to Miss Hannek and she told him, "Your little sister is so frightened, she can't even speak to me and tell me what happened." So, he says, "Come on, let's go home." I didn't want to go, but he was there with me, so I went home with him.

He asked me what happened, and I told him. Mom came home that night and I told her, but nobody believed me. I said, "Mama, I'm telling you it happened." Later on, a few months down, she says to me "You said you heard a man calling you?" And I said, "Yes, Mom, it was a man calling me. I thought it was Joseph." I don't know why I thought it was Joseph, but I guess it sounded like Joseph.

Then she says, "Well, I've been seeing a man all in black." And I was like, "Oh, Mama..." She said, "But there's also a woman that I see. Whatever it was, I saw it, but then your daddy got the blankets pulled off of him." And she started telling me things that happened. I was like, "Oh my God, Mom, I gotta get a priest in here." As I got older, they were seeing things. She told me that something pulled, grabbed Dad by his toes.

[The timeline and how much time passed regarding the above and below is unclear.]

And whatever it was, was becoming violent. I can't remember who it was, somebody felt like they were suffocating, somebody put something over their face. When Mom told me, I said, "Okay, Mom." I went to St. Margaret Mary's and I told the Father about Mom and them. She says, "I'm sorry I didn't believe you." I said, "It's okay, Mom." Elijah said that room where he used to sleep, something did the same thing to him and pulled him out of bed. But Mom said something kept touching her in the back room. I had the priest go over there like three times, each time they prayed, and they brought the holy water. I guess it took four times that I went and got a priest, and you know, you pay them a little something. It slowed down, whatever it was, it stopped for a while. Then I was working at Fort Sam. This is all makes sense now. Dad used to meet me at that bus stop right there on, what is it? Piedmont, right there by our house?

Wanda: Yeah, yeah. Piedmont and Rigsby, where you take the bus.

Cheryl: Right, because I used to work at Fort Sam in high school. Dad used to meet me at the bus stop; I'd get there at 8:30. He met me at the bus stop, and there was this little old white lady. I don't remember seeing her on the bus. She says, "Is that your dad?" And I said, "Yes, ma'am." She goes, "He's very kind, he meets you every night." I said, "Yes, ma'am, I come home late. He meets me and takes me home." She says, "Do you live in that second house?" And I said, "Yes, ma'am." She says, "You've been there long?" "Yes, ma'am, since third grade."

And daddy's walking beside us, right? She goes, "I live right down the street from you." I said, "Oh, you do?" *[Inaudible]* white lady, real tiny. She says, "You don't mind that I walk with you?" And I said, "No, ma'am." I don't know why she was out that late on the bus, but check this out. As we're walking, she's asking these questions and Daddy says, *[inaudible]*. I told him that she was asking if we live in that house. He's walking with his hands behind his back. She says, "Do you know those two people that got murdered in that house?"

I was like, excuse me? I don't know if it's true, but this is so weird and to this day, this freaks me out. I hate to even think about it, but she says two people got bludgeoned to death in that house, a man and a woman. I was like, oh. Then Daddy turned around and looked at her, and he asked me again, "What did she say?" I told him, "She says two people, man and a woman, got killed in our house." He says, "Sí," then he looks, and he goes, "Donde esta la Senora?" Don't know where she went. That is the honest to God truth, and he told Mom that we were talking to some lady, and we don't know where she went.

Jed: That little old lady smaller than you, suddenly disappeared from beside you.

Cheryl: Disappeared. But she was real. She got off the bus with me, she walked with us. Then Daddy says where did the lady go, and I was like I don't know. I turned around 'cause I was looking at him. She was old, she couldn't go nowhere. She just disappeared in front of us, and that was the last thing she said. That was the last one. I got the house blessed after that, and then we had the house rebuilt. That scared the shit out of me, because we all like *[inaudible]*. I remember Daddy said don't play with that Ouija board, because it opens the doors to darkness or to evil, I think that's what he said. And then everything started falling into place, you know, the house being haunted. Because when we lived there, nothing like that ever happened. Wasn't until we played with that damn Ouija board.

Jed: How long had y'all been living there?

Cheryl: We had just moved in when I was in third grade and I was going to Highland Park, so not very long, maybe about a year.

Jed: When you said the candles split, do you mean like vertically down the middle?

Cheryl: Yeah. Okay, you have the flare, the fire. Right before Daddy came in, the flare literally split in half. Like the top portion was like no flame, and then there was flame, so it like split in half. That's when daddy walked in, and I don't know if you remember him doing that Wanda, but I know you were there.

[It's unclear, to me at least, what she was describing.]

Wanda: I remember playing with it. I don't remember, it's weird. I don't remember.

Cheryl: It was weird right?

Wanda: Yeah.

Jed: You remember it happened, but nothing specifically from it?

Wanda: No, no. I don't remember the candle or anything like that. I think that was probably another time. I played it once or twice and said I ain't into this, so I don't think I was there when y'all played it again with a candle.

Cheryl: Yup, we played it with a candle, I'll never forget it, it scares me. There are things in my life that I do not forget. I mean, I've always worked at night. For 22 years I have worked the graveyard shift, and the hauntings come out at a certain time. There was this job that I had at a university. There was upper campus, and then you had lower campus. I was the only female at night, and so we used to split up and do our shift work. We had two patrol cars, but only the Sergeants used to ride. Well, they gave me upper campus.

So, we used to have to walk through the buildings. And always between two and three o'clock they come out. Don't know why, but they always come out between two and three. So, they said, "You're going to be up in the upper campus," and I said, "Oh my God." I hated it, because lower campus was where you had all the dorms. It was okay because you always had somebody in the dorms, but in these buildings is where you had your classes, and you had your admin offices.

So, I was going into this one building they called the gold room. It was like five floors, and in the center was a planetarium. It was all glass, and it was like a square. So, it's glass on the inside where you can look down to each floor from the top to the bottom. I'm on the fourth floor and I'm looking down, and I said, oh my God, there's a professor in here. He's sitting in the gold room with his legs crossed, little old man just sitting there. He just looks up at me, and I look at him, and I wave at him, he didn't wave back. So, I go down to the first floor where he is. As I'm walking in, I say, "Good morning, Sir," and I'm just talking to him from the glass, because I can see him looking at me. "I'm sorry, Sir, but I'm going to have to ask you to leave. It's after hours and I need to lock down the building." I'm going to the door. It's like you walk down the end of the hall, take a left, you're facing another wall, then you take a quick left, and you walk into that office where the gold office is. Where there's a couch.

I see him and I tell him that he has to leave. I see him get up, like I see him rise. I'm like, that looks weird. He's real smooth-like, just gets up like he's coming toward the door. I think I'm going to meet him at the door, right? I get there, and it's clear, I can see him, he sees me. I go in there, he's nowhere to be found. There's only one way in and one way out, and that's the door that I entered through. I walked through there to check if there were any other offices, maybe he went back into an office somewhere in that one gold room. There were no other offices, there was just one room, one square room and one door.

It freaked me out so bad. I went back to the office and sat down. I was trying to get myself together, thinking, I didn't see that. So, I called in Brother Thomas, this officer. He said, "Hey girl, you okay? You look like you're scared." And I said, "Brother Thomas, stop playing around." He goes, "What did you see?" I said, "Brother Thomas, I didn't see nothing." I don't want to tell him, because I was the only female. I didn't want them to start playing tricks on me, you know? He was becoming a, what do you call it, a minister?

He sits down with me, he says, "Okay, what did you see and where did you see it?" And I say, "Brother Thomas, I ain't saying nothing." He says, "I'm a minister, you know that, right?" I say yes. "I know when I see fear, and I see fear in you right now." I said, "Brother Thomas, I saw in the gold room—" He said, "A man? An older gentleman?" I looked at him and I said, "Brother Thomas, you seen him too?" He says, "I think we all have." I said, "Brother Thomas, let me ask you, what have you experienced in the auditorium?" He said, "Probably the same thing you have. Just tell me what you've experienced." So, I said, "When I go in there, the lights could be on, but the lights will go off. And I just thought, okay, well, maybe it's on a sensor—"

[Lost connection]

Wanda: Hello?

Cheryl: I go, "I always hear like somebody's crying." He goes, "A woman?" I said, "Yeah, Brother Thomas, what's that about?" He says, "Well, there's a rumor that there was a girl on the catwalk that was pushed down, because her boyfriend thought she was cheating." I thought, that's why you'll hear her crying. I said, "How do you experience it, when you're a minister? You believe in God, your strength is powerful." He says, "Yes, because I'm a minister, though, they try just as hard on me, because I believe, I have my faith. And I said, "Brother Thomas, I can't stand to go in there." He goes, "They pretty much attack you when you go in, huh?" I said, "Yes, I can feel somebody's pulling on my hair." And he says, "Yeah. From now on, you and I'll do this together." I said, "Really?" He goes, "Yeah." And so, he would sneak up from his lower campus to come do that with me. I said "Every night that I come to work, I hate it because I see something." He goes, "Where else have you seen the ghosts?" And I said, "In the chapel."

And they have a chapel there, it's beautiful. Again, it was between two and three. So, he says, "Is it a woman?" I said, "Brother Thomas, you see them all, too?" "I tell you, they test my faith." So, I go in there and there are beautiful huge doors, probably about 10 feet tall, maybe three or four-inch-thick doors. I'm trying to pull these doors closed, and I turn around and at the end of the pews, at the front of the altar, there's somebody sitting there. The lights were dim in there, they weren't bright, but I could see her because it was just slightly dim. I said, "Good morning, Ma'am. I'm sorry, but it's late. I'm going to have to ask you to leave."

She didn't say anything, so I went on my way, and I went to lock up the other four doors. I was trying to get everything done quick, because I know the hours they come out. So, I lock up those doors, I'm starting to walk down the aisle. Wanda, do you remember those, I don't know if they call them Chantilly lace? Or the Spanish used to. Mama used to wear them to church. Lace over their head, long...

Wanda: Yeah, like lace scarves or something like that.

Cheryl: Yeah, real long and pretty, the Hispanics used to wear them to church. I know Grandma used to wear them. So, she was wearing all black. I could see the pretty lace on her. Her dress was lace, and her scarf was lace. But I couldn't see her face, 'cause her back was turned to me. As I'm getting closer, it was a long walkway down the aisle, so soon as I get close to her, I said "Ma'am, I'm sorry, but I have to ask you to leave.

It's late. I got to lock down the building." She rises. I'm like, oh shit, oh Jesus, oh my God. She rises. She turns sideways to come out of the pew. She starts floating. I'm like, oh my Jesus. And I'm in a church. Who would've ever thought you'd see a ghost in a church?

Wanda: Not me.

Cheryl: Not me either. At first it didn't scare me. I don't think it scared me. I think it pretty much surprised me. But then it did, I think, afterwards, because Brother Thomas came to the rescue again, and I was shaking. And she just floated toward the altar in front of me, and just vanished.

Jed: Was it gradual, or was she just all of a sudden gone?

Cheryl: At first it was gradual. She just kind of floated up, then just kind of floated real slow, gradual, toward the altar and vanished. Just like that. I got the hell out of there. Brother Thomas found me, and he said, "Are you okay?" And I said, "Brother Thomas…" He said, "You saw the woman in the chapel?" I was like, "Oh my God, I can't take this, I can't do this." He says, "Yes, you can. You need to pray out loud." I said, "Well, I think I get so scared, that nothing will come out, but Jesus help me." And he goes, "Well, that's good, that's a prayer." So, I was like, "I never thought I'd see a ghost in a church." He says, "They're everywhere."

Every night from that day forward we started working together, because I don't know what it is, but I always see hauntings. I don't know if they follow me, I don't know why they follow me, I don't know why I see them, but I see them, and it scares me.

Then I went to my other job. These guys said, "Cheryl, I need you to come open this building." This is at another school, it's a big old house where they have all kinds of weddings, I forgot the name of it. Anyway, I had to work there at night. Now, this house had a basement, a first floor, a second floor, and then a third floor. On the third floor they supposedly used to bring prostitutes in. There's a hidden door in the center of the house you wouldn't even know it's there. When you open that door, there's a spiraling stairwell that goes up. They even used it as a morgue back then in the basement, and they also had a bowling alley in it. Anyway, I was working there and those old houses have hidden stairwells. There's one main one, but on the side their maids used to go up and down. I was coming down the stairwell, and it felt like somebody pushed me. I said, okay, that was me, I tripped. That's what I'm telling myself. Then when I went upstairs, somebody pulled my hair.

I asked one of the staff, "Do any hauntings bother you here?" A wedding is what it was, I was working a wedding. She said, "Please don't say anything to any of our customers." And I was like, "Okay, well, there's something in here, because I've been here by myself and I hear footsteps, and I've had somebody pull my hair." I also got an alarm in there. That was on a different day. There was an alarm, so I went to go check it out and oh my goodness, somebody else is in here. A basement door was open, so I had to go in there and check out the building by myself, and so I heard somebody on the upper floor. I checked the whole place, there was nobody.

The following weekend I had to work a wedding again. She found me and said, "Officer, can I talk to you?" I said yeah. She says, "Look," and pulls open her blouse to me. I said, "What happened to you?" She starts crying. I said, "What happened to you, who put their hands on you? Are you okay? Is it your husband?" I was guessing, because she couldn't even tell me. "Let me get my thoughts together." I said "Okay, okay, take your time." She said she was going down the back stairwell, the one that I felt like they pulled my hair and somebody pushed me. She said that something grabbed her and shoved her so hard into the wall she had bruises on her chest where it was pinning her down. She couldn't breathe. I said, "Oh my God." "You're right," she goes, "I stayed late at night." Because I told her, don't be staying late at night in this place by yourself. She'd said, "No, I do it all the time." And I said, "Okay, be careful and if you need an escort, call us and we'll escort you." She says, "I won't do it again."

Another time, these other officers said, "We need you to meet us over here *[at the same building]*." They went in by themselves and called me, "Are you already here?" I said, "No, I'm not there yet." "We hear you upstairs, stop messing around." I said, "No, I'm not there yet." They heard the same thing, the footsteps, so they swept the whole building. When I got there, and this is scary, we went up to the third level 'cause whenever you get stuff like that, you have to sweep the whole building. So, there was three of us, two guys, they said, "Let's do a sweep." Okay, so we did a sweep. Well, when we were up there, something said, "Get out."

And I said, "Okay guys, it's time to go." And they said, "Why?" "You didn't hear that?" And then it said it again. They said, "Oh shit, uh-uh, somebody's messing with us." I said, "No guys, it's time to get out."

Jed: What did it say?

Cheryl: It said get out.

Jed: Oh wow.

Cheryl: And then *[the other officer]* says, "Stop f—- around." I said, "Dude, I'm not playing with you. I told you this place is not a place to be in at night. We need to go." But we still had to check it. They said, "We heard somebody here." And I said, "Dude, I'm telling you, I'll talk about this later, let's get the f—- out." He goes, "Nah dude, it was you, you said it." And it said it again. This time we're talking to each other and it's like, "Get out." So we got the f—- out. And then they said, "Cheryl, what is it you got to tell us?" I said, "Dude, that place is haunted."

[Inaudible]

Cheryl: —Had no legs. And you can see her some places, we've seen her at the windows. This just always happens at night, graveyard shift. At first, they thought it was a guy doing it. Like, "I thought you did it when I turned away from you!" *[His partner]* goes, "Nah man, I didn't say nothing." When it did it again, we were looking at each other face to face, so they realized it wasn't us.

We left and those guys were shaken. I said, "I told you, I never want to go in there again." But I had to go, because I had to help them sweep it. I was like, okay, relax. Let's just get on with it. I never went in there again unless I had somebody with me. That was enough for me, but I've always experienced stuff like that, and I always pray out loud when I have to work nights. I hate it. I hate it. And I will not watch horror movies, because I've experienced so much in my. I can't do it. I freak out.

[Lost Connection]

Oh, on another occasion when I went with Dad and Mom—Mom used to take us on the weekend to Eagle Pass. Grandma told me, "Go outside." They had like a, do you remember Wanda, they had an orchard where they'd grow pears, fruit? But the house—

[Lost Connection]

Wanda: It was a slant. Their backyard slanted.

Cheryl: Yes, you had to go down steps to the backyard.

Wanda: So underneath the house to make it level they had like a garage in the back, but it wasn't a garage, it was like an outdoor room.

Cheryl: Yeah, and I don't know what fruit it was she had out there, but Mom says, "Go outside, stay on the porch. I don't know what's down there, so don't go down there." I said okay. It was in the evening, but it wasn't dark yet. I went out there on the little patio on the porch they had. I stood at the house looking, trying to see what they had down there, and nothing.

I went back inside, came back out. Then it kind of got dark. It wasn't really dark, but I heard a *[tries to whistle]*, something whistling. Mom is doing dishes, and I heard a whistle again. I said, "Mom, I hear somebody whistling." She says, "Get in." I said okay. I turned around, like as I walk in—And Grandma's house is little. I looked up, and Mom goes, "What are you looking at?" She could see me *[from inside the house]*, right? And I said, "I don't know, Mom, it's a big bird. It's ugly with like a woman's face." And she's, "Get in, get in!" And it whistled at me. And I'm still looking at it, like, I can't believe what I'm seeing. She's yelling, "Get in!" And it started opening its wings, right? She opened the screen *[door]* and pulled me in. My grandma says, "What's wrong?" It didn't scare me, because I didn't know what I was looking at. She and Mom said that I saw at a Lechuza. I said, "What's a Lechuza?"

I didn't know what a Lechuza was. Mom started to explain to me, but then Grandma and Tia *[Aunt]* started praying the Rosary. Mom says, "What did it look like?" I said, "Mom, it looked like a big black—It looked taller than me." It looked like a woman's face, but you know how you see the hard, hard faces like they make for the witches on Halloween? You know, the black face, hard—

Wanda: Almost like plastic?

Cheryl: Yeah, almost like plastic. Yeah, yeah, like plastic. And a nose, a long nose. And the whistle like coming up, and it was like—I can't whistle like it did. It just said *[whistling]*, and then it started opening its wings. That's when she opened the screen and pulled me in. That's what they asked me, and that's what I told them, like big, taller than me, and the wings were starting to open, and the face like black and hard. Then Grandma said it was the Lechuza, and someone had evil thoughts about them or something. They were praying. I said, "Mom, what's a Lechuza, what is that?" She says, "They're like human beings, somebody has witchcraft." I don't know, I think she said they usually take people. I was like, "Why would they want to take me? I didn't do anything bad." But I never knew that people have seen them. But that was the first time, and that was so clear as day. But you know how it gets dim, when it's about 6 o'clock and it just starts getting dim? It wasn't even dark.

Jed: How far away was it above you?

Cheryl: Just—Okay. The house, how tall is a house? Eight feet tall?

Jed: The house was probably eight feet to the ceiling so maybe another eight feet to the roof.

Cheryl: Well, their house was little though, remember Wanda? So right down on that patio, what would you say, about ten feet?

Wanda: Yeah, the reason it looked higher, or lower, in the back was because it's sloped, and that's why she had all those plants back there.

Cheryl: Yeah, so what would you say it was about?

Wanda: It was about ten feet. Eight, ten feet. Because you had to walk up the stairs from the back, because the way the slope was, yeah.

Cheryl: But see, I didn't go down the stairs, I stayed on the little porch. So, it wasn't very far from the ceiling. I was trying to figure from the little porch they had back there, because remember you had to walk down the steps.

Wanda: Yeah, but all your houses are still about the same sizes, height-wise. But how far away was it from you? Was it on the house or the trees?

Cheryl: No, it was on top of Grandma's roof. Like, I would say—You know how Grandma's back door was, right? Okay. Take it like if you walk, there was a patio instead of steps, say five feet away from me. By the time I looked up, he was like at the corner of the house, but it was almost like—

Wanda: Oh, that was close, that's why you could see the face.

Cheryl: Yes, it was that close. I didn't know what I was looking at.

Jed: That's how you could tell it was bigger than you. How tall do you think you were at the time?

Wanda: Cheryl's not very tall now.

Cheryl: Me? I'm 5'4". I don't think I've ever grown any. I think I'm still the same height I was when I was in high school, so I think it must have been taller than me. It was the biggest thing I've ever seen in my life.

Wanda: Probably about 4 feet. Yeah, because in high school she wasn't too tall.

Cheryl: I'm 5'4", so it had to be taller than me, and it looked humungous. It looked like—Okay. Imagine me now, I'm a big girl, so I think if you rounded off, like on the sides of me? It was humongous. Like obese humongous. You know you have fat, obese women, like let's just say something like 400 pounds? Imagine that, but all in feathers. Because it just looked like it was oval at first, until it started opening its wings. It didn't open it all the way, but it was just slowly opening them up.

Now, the second time I saw it, I was on duty. But I was with a partner. We were walking in the back of where we were working, on the northeast side of town. I told him, "I've got to do phone checks, but you know I hate going out in the back because it's wilderness." And he said, "Well, I'll go with you, because I'm working with you tonight." I said, "Really?" So, I had a partner and I was relieved. He said, "Yeah, we're going to work tonight." Okay, cool.

We had to walk through the wilderness, and we came back, and they were just building this building, right? We're talking away, just talking and talking. I said, "Dude, listen. I think somebody broke into that building." I mean, there were no windows on it yet, but the frame was up. "I don't hear nothing." Then you hear stuff being thrown around. He looks at me and says, "Hey, I got high, you got low." I said, "Okay, I got you." Which meant he was going up the stairs first, and I was going to have his back. I had to be facing backwards up the stairs and go up behind him.

So, he gets up to the top of the stairs. He gives me the hand signal to stop. I'm still looking down to make sure that nobody comes up behind us. When I stopped, something up there starts throwing things. He's Hispanic, he's like, "I don't know what that is." He goes, "Hey!" He turns on his flashlight, right? And he has his pistol in his hand. He turns on his flashlight, "Hey, come out! Come out now!" He starts yelling at it. Nothing. They're still throwing stuff around. So, we start moving in again to clear it.

Before we could ever take the second step, it was a Lechuza. The wings were at least ten feet wide. When it came at him, he dodged and dropped his flashlight. I turned around; I got a fire off, but I didn't hit it. He goes, "Holy f——!" He said, "That was a f—- Lechuza!" Another one came at us out of nowhere. There were two of them in there, they flew out the window. I would never have imagined that it would be that big, but then I remembered back to when I was younger, how big it was. But I didn't see the wings fully spread until I saw this one.

He said, "Girl, I would never have imagined I'd be facing a Lechuza this close." We were shook up because it dove at us. If he hadn't fallen on his ass, or ducked when it came at him, I think it would have grabbed him. I think that was the intention. And when the second one came around, it dove at us again. I was still at the lower part of the steps, and he was at the top part of the steps, and it just flew out the window.

Jed: How big were the windows?

Cheryl: The windows are humongous. Okay, you know, imagine a gym. It was like they were building a gym. Okay? The windows are like big ass picture windows. If you ever went by there, you could see how big those windows are. It was wide open. There were no windows up yet, nothing. They hadn't even finished all the walls yet.

Jed: Did you just see the wings? Did you see features like last time, or anything?

Cheryl: Yeah, we saw the features. It was the same kind of face that I remember from the first time, but the only thing that I noticed different were the wings. Okay, imagine this. You've seen those black crows, right? Okay, the black crow, imagine that kind of wings, but real thick, wide wings. They were just flapping. All you heard was—You know like, when wings are flapping, but real big. When I fired the first time, I didn't expect the second one to come out, and neither did he. So, I think we froze out of fear. The first time, it was like, "Whoa, did you get it?" "I don't think I got it," because it was so quick. Because at first we didn't know what it was. We didn't tell anybody.

Now, the other deal I experienced happened in front of Mom's house. Lisa *[Cheryl's friend who lived down the street]* came over, you could ask her to this day, and for some reason we started talking about UFOs. She goes, "Oh my God, Cheryl, I forgot about that. I never told a soul, because I didn't want anybody to think I was crazy. I didn't think they'd believe me."

So, Lisa came over and it was late. We had no business being out late, because we were sitting out in the front yard in the grass. Just talking girl talk. We were high school kids, you know. Daddy was outside, but it was late. It must have been about one in the morning. Daddy says, "It's time to come in!" Okay, Daddy, we're going to come in. She stayed the night. We're sitting in the little grass, we're just talking, and all of the sudden I say, "Look at that bright light! Oh my God, that's a star." So, I start singing that song, starlight star bright, first star I see tonight, you know? Then she says, "My God, yeah, let's make a wish!"

All of a sudden, this bright star from a distance zoomed in! Not like right over us, we're still miles, like, I couldn't even express—It was in the sky. It wasn't like right in our face, it was still a distance, and it zigzagged. I said, "Oh shit, Lisa, it's zigzagging. Is that a UFO?" "I don't know what it is." All you heard was *[makes something like a zipping sound]*. And I don't know if it was playing with us, but then it hovered for a while, it just kind of stayed in one place. It was just one big bright light. You heard this—You know that electricity sound, like electricity—

Jed: Like the hum?

Cheryl: At my house if I sit in the backyard, I have these electricity poles where you can hear bzzt, bzzt. Like electricity going to the lines? I said, "Are you hearing that, or is that my imagination?" She said, "No, I'm hearing what you're hearing. Those are UFOs." It must have been like two or three of them, because they were like all over the sky.

Jed: Just zigzagging?

Cheryl: Zigzagging. They would stop and hover for a while, and you could see the light was like, shaking, but you could hear the *[buzzing sound]*. Then move like, in seconds. I can't explain how quick it would zoom, zoom, zoom. It was so weird. I said, "Lisa, I don't know about you, but are you hearing anything other than that *[buzz sound]*?" She said, "It's almost like *[repeating noises]*. Something like that, right?" I said, "No, we aren't hearing that. It's time to go in." We got up and we were watching it as we're walking towards the steps, and then they just, zoom, were gone. She said she never told a soul.

Jed: How old were you?

Cheryl: Probably senior year in high school, 'cause she was staying the night at our house. Yep, that is the honest to God, truth.

Everything that has happened to me in my life, that I have experienced, I hate it. I hate it. They come out at night. They haunt you at night. They like to scare the shit out of you at night. Those are the hours that they come out, two and three. There's just so many things that I don't even like to talk about. Even if I see the beginning of a scary movie, I'll have nightmares.

[Cheryl and Wanda were speaking of the house on Amanda while I changed the batteries in the voice recorder.]

Cheryl: Yes! That's right. That's right. Because remember for a while there we had, we had a dirt floor in the living room, because Daddy was fixing the floor. Wow. And see the other time, Jed, was... What was the other time I had...? Oh. Oh, oh, oh. We went to Austin. We stayed— I'll never forget the hotel. It was that very famous hotel down there, Driskill or something like that.

I'm on the treadmill in the gym, and I'm the only one in the gym, right? I turn and look, this guy's there. He startled me, and he says, "Hi." I said, "Hi. You work here?" He says, "Yeah, sometimes." I'm like, oh okay. "You work part time?" You know, making conversation because he's standing like three feet away from me, kind of leaning on a piece of equipment. I kind of slow down my walk on the treadmill and said, "So, how're you doing tonight?" "Good. Is this your first time here?" I said, "Yeah, yeah." He goes, "Yeah, I've never seen you before." And he's a short little white guy, and I said, "You look young. Yeah, it's our first time here, we're celebrating our anniversary." He says, "Oh, well, you enjoy your anniversary." I said, "You been working here a long time?" And he goes, "Oh, longer than you could imagine." I thought, okay, that's a weird statement. You're young, why would you say that? You know what I mean? I thought, okay, I don't want to go into that, because that's just like, odd.

This lady walks in. There was a little table where they had towels laid out, rolled up nice and pretty. I'd looked down to my treadmill, because it scared me when he said that, longer than you can imagine? I'd turned around and looked at the treadmill because I was getting ready to turn it off, and then I heard a door slam. The guy was right there, but when that lady came in, I thought, did he go out the door?

I said, "Hey, did you see where that guy went?" She goes, "What guy?" I said, "There was a guy standing right here. He's young, says he works here." And she says, "There's nobody in here, but you." And I said, "No, I was just talking to this young guy. He said he works here part time." She goes, "We don't have anybody working here part time. I run the gym."

I was like, "You're messing with me, right? He was just right here, I heard a door slam. Is there another door?" She says, "No, I came in the only way in and out." I'm like, "Okay, is this place haunted?" She says, "Yeah." "So, I was talking to a ghost?" "You could've been." I'm like, oh my God, I have to get the hell out of there. She said, "I'm sorry, we do have guests who tell us they were talking to somebody, and we know who works here." I'm thinking, they can actually come that way, like as a human, real.

Jed: What time of the day was that?

Cheryl: It was about ten o'clock at night. I had already been on the treadmill already an hour. I usually walk on the treadmill for an hour or two, but that scared me, so I only did an hour. It was like nine o'clock when I went in there, when I left there it must have been about ten.

Jed: What were the guy's clothes like compared to the person—

Cheryl: He had—I remember, and this is weird, he had like a red polo shirt on and something like grey pants. He had like light brown hair, not brown, brown. But sandy brown, I guess? He looked so real, that I really thought he was human until she told me there was nobody there. He had a uniform on, so I assumed he worked there. Because she had something similar, a little polo shirt on, but it wasn't red. I'm like, holy crap, I just can't believe how these ghosts come like they're real.

I don't know about you, Wanda, but I have not seen Mom, and I didn't see Daddy until I was in surgery. I never dreamed of Daddy. Mama I have. I've dreamed of Mama and you Wanda. But I've never dreamed of Daddy. Not until I had that cancer surgery and my blood pressure dropped. I remember I heard voices saying her blood pressure is dropping, call the doctor, and stuff like that. I don't know if it was a dream or not, but at the foot of the bed, there was Daddy. He was sitting sideways at the foot of the bed with a smile. He turned and looked at me, and I remember telling him, "Daddy! I haven't seen you. Are you here for me?" He looked at me and he smiled. And he just—I didn't see him after that. So, I don't know if that was my conscience or he was really coming to me, but that was the first time that I ever dreamed of Daddy ever.

Now here at this house *[her current home]*? I don't know if it's me or what, because there's a door in my kitchen—You know my house,

Wanda, the door that goes into the washroom? It would be closed *[by something]*. And I was like, okay, it's time to bless my house. Romero *[her husband]* said, "Ah, it's just the air." I was like, okay. But before Diamond *[her dog]* passed, Diamond was—You know dogs see things.

Wanda: Oh, yeah.

Cheryl: Well, Diamond started seeing things. I don't know what it is, but I keep seeing a shadow right here by the door. I took a picture of it outside. And I have it! I still have that picture matter of fact, I have it somewhere. You can see a shadow of a—I'm not sure, I can't say it's a person. I don't know what it is, but it's holding a lantern. Now right here, I fell three times from my steps, and each time it feels like somebody's pushing me. Donna even fell here; Donna broke her ankle.

Wanda: I thought she broke it—I guess she did break it at your house didn't she.

Cheryl: Huh?

Wanda: I thought she broke it on the curb or something, but I guess she did break it at your house.

Cheryl: No, she broke it here at my house. You should have seen it. Like I said, my steps right here, I was walking down the steps with all three kids. First one was Arianna, the second time I fell was with Isaiah, and the third time I fell with Destiny in my arms. At different times, different months, days, whatever. The first time I fell, it felt like somebody pushed me from behind. I went down, and I was like, oh my God, because I had the baby in my arms. I felt like somebody literally pushed me, but I somehow twisted my body so my back hit the door. I didn't want to fall on her. Then the second time was Isaiah, same thing. I think it's like the third step up. I don't know what it is. The third time was with Destiny. Okay, I keep seeing a shadow here, so I need to bless the house, it's time. Then the fourth time, Donna stayed here. She's like, "Cheryl!" She's screaming for me. I think it's probably about one o'clock in the morning. She was coming down to get water and she said, "I don't know how I fell, I felt like something pushed me." I'm thinking, oh my God. She broke her ankle in four places.

Wanda: Yeah, I still have the picture of the pins in her ankle.

Cheryl: Yes, yes. So, I started realizing when Diamond was alive. 'Cause she'd walk toward this door like she sees something. You know how they put their ears up, like look at you? She started walking toward whatever it was, and she'd back up like it was coming at her, and she'd go at it again. And I said, "Okay, Diamond, it's nothing." And I started praying. So, she backed up to me, but she's backing up looking at it. Then when I started praying out loud, she calmed down. I don't know what it was, but I had to bless the house again.

Then the back door, where it goes into the laundry room, her and I were sitting up here. I was working swing shift. So, you know when you get off swing shift, you're not exactly ready to go to bed, because your adrenaline's going. Her bedroom was in the washroom, she had a little bed in there and everything. I said, "Come on, mama, let's go watch TV." So, she comes and watches TV with me. All of a sudden, the door starts the *[she makes an "eeeee" sound]*, like squeaking? Like somebody's opening it. I don't see anything, but I can feel there's something there. She jumps off the couch, and she goes at it barking crazy. Diamond never barks unless she doesn't like something, or something startled her. So, she's barking and barking. I get up, I say, "Mama, there's nothing there." And I said, "This is God's home. Don't worry about it, Diamond. Come on."

But no, she keeps backing up and going at it. I start saying my prayers out loud, and then I guess it left her alone. But anytime that back door did that, she would run to it. And I'm thinking, okay, she sees something. And then when I came home, she just recently passed away like a few months ago, I came home and I went upstairs, "Come on mama, let's go to bed." Normally when she waits for me, I'll yell I'm home and she'll know I'm going to bed and come with me. She looked at me like, uh-uh, I ain't going. I said, "Come on, mama, let's go to bed," and I went upstairs. She took real slow steps. Usually, she runs upstairs and beats me. This time she was like, uh-uh. She took a few steps and stopped. She looked at me like, let me see what you're going to do. When I got up the stairs, all my pictures were on the floor. I said, "Okay, Diamond, I see." And that night she would not go upstairs with me.

I got my holy water and my sage out, and I started praying. It's calmed down, but it's time to re-pray. I have come to a point where it scares even me, because I don't know if it has a lot to do with my faith or that I pray as much as I do. But, if I sense evil in somebody, I'm like, uh-uh. I think it was with Diamond, too. I think she felt something. She let me know. And I said, "Okay, mama, I know, I know. We're going to repel this evil, this whatever it is lingering." Because they say when you go to the graveyard you can bring something back. Whatever it was, I might have picked something up and brought it home.

But I only bless the homes of family. So, this happened to me, this is the honest to God truth. I drove to DC to go see Mia and them and I took the kids with me. I was on vacation for three weeks for the summer, so I drove there. I said Mia, I need to bless your home. I got into her home, and it just felt like, ugh. It was weary, you know? I said, "You know what Mia? I even brought my sage." Alyssa had a beautiful home. She had a basement, a first floor, then a second floor, and her bedroom was on the third floor. So, I blessed her entire house. I went through it a couple of times, because as soon as I got in that house, I just felt tense, I don't like it. It just feels too dark. They said they'd been talking about that lately.

I prayed the Rosary on each floor, basement first. I prayed the entire Rosary, and I had this prayer that I read off my phone that I use when I walk through the house and pray. I have my Rosary on me, and I have St. Benedict on me. So, I went to the second floor, opened up all the windows. I said, "You have to open up all the windows." She said, "All of them?" I said, "All of them. Even in the basement, open that thing down there." I said, "'Cause when you pray, you bless the home, you got to wash out the evil spirit." You know, because I can remember asking Grandma how you bless the house. So, I used to do that to my home, and I did hers all the way up to her bedroom. Then when we were leaving, I blessed the first floor. I bless myself and clean myself up and everything, right? The door was like about four steps away from me; we were going to go out Alyssa's patio, because that's where my truck was parked. I'm near the storm door, I said, "Come on, Alyssa, let's go!" Or whatever. She's, "I'm coming, I'm coming!" We got the kids and everything.

Like I said, I'm getting ready to take a step toward the patio door. Something shoved me out. There was nothing on the floor. The floor was hardwood, I didn't slip. There was no rug on the floor. But whatever it was got pissed off at me, and as it was going out, it took me out. Thank God I knocked off the screen. The patio screen door was closed, so I went through the screen door and fell on the patio. Mia says, "Oh my God! Something pushed you!" And I was like, "I felt it." And she says, "Cheryl, you were just standing there." And I said, "I know." It shoved me out the house, and that's why I carry my St. Benedict. Whatever it was, I pissed it off and it was not happy with me. I said, "Mia, it felt like you pushed me." She said, "No, I was standing over here. Are you okay?" "I'm okay. I'm all right." But it pushed me out, so I won't bless anybody else's house unless it's family. I won't, that's stuff you don't want to play with. But it's stuff like that that has scared the crap out of me.

Wanda: That's a lot.

Cheryl: That's a lot, right? April told me to bless her home, I did it for her once. And I was like, oh God, I can feel the darkness in Brian's room. I blessed the girls' house *[referring to her daughter and grandchildren]*. The girls told me "Grandma, we hear footsteps in the hallway. We get up and check and nobody's there." And, "I think it's a lady, we keep seeing a lady." I said, "A lady?" "Yeah, Grandma, we hear her footsteps." Because their room's at the front of the house, and Stephanie's *[her daughter]* room is in the back. Stephanie says, "Yeah, Mom, I hear the same thing." I said, "Yeah, Stephanie, your house is too dark for one, and I have seen shadows." So, I blessed their house and asked, "Do y'all hear footsteps anymore?" "No, Grandma." But recently they told me I've gotta come back and bless the house. Because I've seen shadows, Stephen's *[her son]* seen shadows, Stephanie says she has, too.

It's usually on my night shift when I see 'em all. There's something else that slipped my mind I wanted to tell you... Oh! Sometimes at night you work graveyard at these schools, you want to get off the streets, right? So, we go into these buildings. My partner says, "Hey, let's get off the street for a while, let me work on the East side *[of the campus]*." I'm like, "Where do you want me to go, man? I don't know where to go. I don't like going in these buildings by myself." "Nah, you don't got to go in by yourself, we're going into the school together." So, we go into a building on the East side, I don't even remember which one. We go in and there's a couch in there.

I said, "Dude, I got to go to the bathroom. You're going to be right here, right? You're not going anywhere?" "Nah, I'll be right here." I said, "Dude, I don't like to be in these buildings by myself, so don't leave." "No, I'm not going to leave you. I'll be here." He's very religious, he used to pray and this and that. So, I went to the bathroom and came back. He's like, "Okay, let's get out of here." I was like, "We just got here like 10 minutes ago." He's like, "Yeah, but let's get out of here." And I said, "Dude, are you okay? What happened?" He says, "I'll tell you later, let's go." So, we go and get in the car. He says, "We're staying together all night." And I was like, "What did you see?" He said he dozed off when I went to the bathroom, and that he woke up and a person was sitting next to him.

He woke up, he jumped up, and said, "Who are you?!" And they didn't say anything to him. He goes, "Who are you?" Same thing. So, he goes, "You need to leave the building." Well, whatever it was disappeared in front of him, but we get outside, and his keys were gone. The car keys. And I was like, "Dude, where's the car keys?" "They were right next to me." I said, "Ah man, we got to go back in there." But he was still, "You got your keys?" And I was like, "Yeah, but I saw the keys. They were on the arm of the chair when I left you. You could have picked them up. Did you drop them when you freaked out?" He's, "No, no, no." We go back in the building, look for his keys, but his keys weren't on the couch. I was like, "Could you have moved them?" "I walked out with you. I didn't move from where I was." He was freaked out, I was freaked out.

We found his keys, but not where he put them, not where he sat. Whatever it was, I didn't know they could move stuff, but apparently they can. We had to look, we had to hunt for them, and we found them, on top of the desk, behind the desk. Like, you have a high desk and sit down below. That's where we found it. He says, "I'm not doing this anymore. I'm not going into these buildings anymore." I said, "I told you, this isn't the first time this stuff has happened to me. That's why I don't go in these buildings. I don't care if they fire me, I'm just going to check exterior doors. When I get alarms, I'm asking for backup."

He was so scared after that, he quit. He said, "I can't work nights." But again, he was studying to be a minister. But that night, when I left him by himself, that's what I was scared of, but it happened to him. So, I was like, yeah, they test the faith.

Your mom knows I have a lot of crosses in my dining area. In every room I have a cross, I have a Rosary. And I'm trying to do that for Stephanie, and I got to do that for Stephen. I have to, 'cause it's too much for me. I'm trying to remember what else happened on Amanda Street; what happened in my old house? Let me think. There's something else I wanted to tell you, too. I hate it because there's so many stories, I got to get them right. I know there's more, but I can't think offhand what they are right now.

[Spends some time trying to remember.]

Cheryl: Am I the only one who's seen hauntings in the family?

Jed: In your family, or in either?

Cheryl: No, I just mean my family, my sisters, my brothers.

[It seems that the Cortez family either hasn't shared any of their experiences with each other, or Cheryl just doesn't remember if anyone else has done so.]

Jed: I think you're the only one that's had the physical things happen. Do you ever remember being in Eagle Pass with Mia and Sophia?

Cheryl: Not with Mia and Sophia, I used to just go with Mom and Dad. I don't remember seeing stuff in Eagle pass. Oh, I remember when we used to live off of Southcross, when Michael *[her ex-husband]* and I got married and lived in his mother's house. I had to call the cops, and I guess my neighbors called the cops, too. I was home by myself, I heard a lady screaming. There was a small yard behind his mother's house that was already deteriorating. It was kind of sunk down, like going into a creek. Which I think was also connected to the Pecan Valley Creek. So, it's connected to that. Anyway, I was by myself, and all of a sudden, I hear this lady screaming *[mimics wailing]*. It sounded like she was so, so close, right? I thought somebody was raping somebody in the back of that creek.

So, I called City *[referring to the city police]*. City comes out, they say what you got? I say, "I hear a woman screaming and hollering, crying like somebody's torturing her." "We got units on the way; we've received several calls." They came in through my house, went out the back door. They went to the creek area, they had 'em looking. And they heard the woman crying! "We hear her *[mimicking an officer talking into their radio]*, it's coming from the creek." They went looking and looking. They had lights and everything, they could not find her. Finally, it stopped, and they're like, okay, that's weird. "We had the whole area that goes into San Antonio Creek covered, we can't find this woman screaming or crying." So, this one guy says—He was a Mexican cop. That was probably the, uh, how do you say that?

Wanda: La Llorona?

Cheryl: The Llorona. And I said, "Oh, I heard that story. Because that's what it sounded like to me." And that cop's like, "Yeah, I think that's what it was." I go, "But you guys heard her, too!" "Yeah, we heard her." But it sounded like somebody was pouring their guts out. I don't know, I honestly think that was La Llorona. Because you should have heard the scream and cry. It was horrible. It was too real. Several of the neighbors called, so they came with a whole lot of cops and still couldn't find nothing. They all went down there. That was what she was called right Wanda, La Llorona?

Wanda: Yeah.

Cheryl: I don't know, but they like to attack me. I mean, I've actually had the physical things. And you know that movie that came out, "The Poltergeist"? The first time that came out, I just saw bits and pieces and I just freaked out. I can't do it. I start shaking all over and I'll have horrible nightmares, and I just can't do it. It was the worst thing I experienced in my entire life, that situation where I was trapped in my own home and couldn't get out. I pulled and pulled on the door, and I went to the other door that was unlocked, and I couldn't get out. My name was being called, dishes were rattling, the cabinets were opening and closing. It was horrible.

When we tore Mama's house down, she said to me, "Well, I guess the ghosts will be gone now, right?" I said, "We're starting with a new house, Mom." She said, "Yeah, ghosts should be gone." I said, "They'll be gone." That house was over 100 years old. You know that, right?

Wanda: Yeah, the first one that we moved into?

Cheryl: Yeah, it was over 100 years old. That's why they wanted to preserve it, but it would have been too much to preserve it. I don't know, but I have those kinds of things that happened to me, and If I'm the only one, it makes me wonder.

Jed: No, you're not.

[I shared some of the other stories already recounted.]

Cheryl: Well, I have to tell you, every night and every day, I say my Rosary and I ask God to please protect all my siblings, their children, and their children's children. There's so many of us I can't name everybody, but I pray for everybody. I do. There's nobody I leave out. I pray for everybody, and sometimes when I get scared, when I get a feeling sometimes when I walk into my house, especially when I walk upstairs, I say it out loud, this is God's home, this is where he lives with me. He takes care of us. You are not welcome here. Spirit, you are to leave us. I pray out loud here in my own home, I pray out loud in my truck. And I do, I pray for everybody, because there's so many things going on, the world is so evil. People are so evil. I deal with so much evil at work, you know?

We have to go to training classes, right? And we had to go to this PTSD one, and they say, "Oh, you know, all military have it." And then it dawned on me, I said to the instructor, "I have a question for you." He says, "Sure, ask me." I said, "Is it possible for officers to have PTSD, even if you've never been in law enforcement?" He goes, "Do you see faces blown off?" I said, "I've seen it. I've seen guts hanging out." I've seen this and this and this. He says, "Yes. Firemen, law enforcement officers, and EMT guys. Yes, you guys could have it." And Stephanie says I'm real protective, but I tell her, "Yes, I am very protective, but I'm also cautious. If you knew half the stuff that I've gone through and having to deal with those cases. Then when you have nephews and nieces who are so little, I kind of like, I worry. I get scared. I catch myself saying, I guess I am kind of paranoid *[laughs]*. I hope I'm not crazy, but...

Jed: Well, most people have the luxury of not realizing all the bad things that are happening.

Cheryl: Yeah, yeah. But it says so much. I don't wish anything that I've experienced on anybody. I don't. I've seen ghosts that look like real people and they're not. That's what freaks me out. That a ghost can look so real, and not be real. You know? I heard that's possible, but I guess

I've experienced it and talking to ministers, yes, they can do that. There's some that are very violent.

And that's what the ghost at Mom's house was becoming, I think. It was becoming violent. But I'm glad it slowed down at the end. I think. She didn't tell me anything else about it after that. Until her house was getting knocked down, and she says, "You think the ghosts will be gone now?" I said, "Yep, starting new."

CORTEZ FAMILY ANALYSIS

There were 66 total events described in interviews with the Cortez family. Of the people who reported events, the average and median numbers of events by individuals were 9.42 and 8 Figure 12), with Cheryl having the most total experiences at 19. This is less than the Santiago family (Figure 1) even when Elena is removed from consideration (Figure 3). There was one more person reporting for the Santiago family than the Cortez family, so the fact that the average and medians held higher would seem to indicate the Santiago family experienced more events. However, when we delve deeper into sleep paralysis later, we may want to reconsider this idea.

The average numbers of events experienced as a child or adult were nearer than the Santiago family at 5.29 and 4.14 respectively (Figure 12). The proportion of experiences by the Cortez family were fairly even overall between childhood and adulthood, at roughly 56 and 44 percent respectively. Nearly all of the Cortez family had more experiences as children than as adults, i.e., in the Amanda and Telford homes (Figure 12). Cheryl's experiences as an adult are an outlier and are in large part responsible for the similarity in proportion of experiences as children and adults. If Cheryl is removed, the results become 72 percent of events experienced as children, 28 percent as adults.

	Total Events	TE as Child	TE as Adult
Cheryl	19	3	16
April	12	7	5
Sophia	9	7	2
Isabelle	8	4	4
Donna	8	8	0
Wanda	7	6	1
Mia	3	2	1
Average	9.42	5.29	4.14
Median	8	6	2

Figure 12

Finally, averages and medians by individual for events reported by time of day were more similar (Figure 13). Cheryl had the most experiences at night by far with 17 (next most was 6). She also has had multiple jobs where she patrolled large buildings and properties overnight while remaining on high alert, perhaps putting her in the position to have these experiences in the first place.

	AVG by Person	Median by Person
Day	1.86	2
Night	6.86	6
Unknown	1.86	2

Figure 13

The Cortez family reported events at two different residences on Amanda, and it was difficult to discern which was which. As a result, they were combined together simply as "Amanda". This in itself is a variable that complicates analysis by location. The most events occurred at the home on Telford with 24, followed by publicly accessible areas (universities, parks, roads) at 15 (36 percent and 22 percent of all events respectively).

Tactile experiences were the next fewest types of experiences reported at 14 in total. These could include a change in temperature, a door not budging, or being pushed, touched, etc. The average and median numbers of experiences by those interviewed were 2 and 1 respectively (Figure 14). Cheryl had the most of these types of experiences, and the most violent. Of her experiences, 2 were of her being pulled, 6 of being pushed (including being pushed down while carrying children). The number of tactile experiences reported by Cheryl effectively doubled the average reported tactile experiences compared to anyone else in her family.

	Tactile
Cheryl	9
April	2
Sophia	0
Donna	1
Wanda	1
Isabelle	1
Mia	0
Average	2
Median	1

Figure 14

There were 37 experiences that were auditory in nature, such as footsteps, noise (rattling of objects, etc.), and vocalizations (speech, whistling). The average and median numbers of reported experiences were 5.23 and 4 respectively (Figure 15), with Cheryl and April reporting the most of such experiences.

	Auditory
Cheryl	12
April	11
Sophia	7
Donna	2
Wanda	1
Isabelle	4
Mia	0
Average	5.23
Median	4

Figure 15

Vocalizations were the dominant auditory experience (Figure 16), cited 21 times. 12 of these 21 vocalizations were split evenly between mimicry (a voice recognizable as a family member beckoning from another room) or talking (whispering or unrecognizable speech from another room). Additionally, 5 of the 6 reports of mimicry by the Cortez family were in the Telford house. While there were 6 experiences where individuals reported hearing talking in other rooms, it was less likely to be referred to as a specific event. They were more likely to use language like "you would hear". Cheryl and April reported 13 of the 21 experiences that were categorized as vocalizations. Cheryl was notable in that she described an experience in the exercise area of a hotel, where she had a conversation with a man who seemed to disappear into thin air when an employee of the establishment entered the room.

Noises consisting of experiences such as dishes rattling, water from the faucet, and literal bumps in the night were the next most sizable portion of auditory experiences (Figure 16). Notably, 7 of these 10 were in the Telford house. Many of these were centered around the kitchen area, and the china cabinet specifically. Additionally, you will notice that there is overlap among individuals with reports of footsteps and generalized noise, and that those who reported both reported the most vocalizations. However, you can see that there were reports of vocalizations from individuals who did not report footsteps or noise.

	Auditory	Footsteps	Noise	Vocalizations
Cheryl	12	3	3	6
April	11	1	3	7
Sophia	7	1	1	5
Donna	2	1	1	0
Wanda	1	0	0	1
Isabelle	4	0	2	2
Mia	0	0	0	0
Average	37	6	10	21

Figure 16

There were 40 experiences that were observed. The average number of experiences was 5.71, the median 4. Cheryl reported the most with 12, while Sophia and Wanda reported 7 each. Cheryl and Wanda drove the subset where items were seen moving or the environment changed at 5 and 4, with most of the remaining interviewees not experiencing anything in that category (Figure 17). Cheryl and Sophia led the subset where human figures were seen with 4. Sophia's daughter Isabelle seemed to corroborate similar sightings as her mother in the same room of the Telford house. April was the only other individual to report seeing a person, albeit a shadow person near sleep. There was April's additional report of a face on a monitor, but it could be explained as pareidolia, or the propensity for us to see meaning in patterns.

	Observed	Object Changed or Moved	Human
Cheryl	12	5	4
April	4	0	1
Sophia	7	0	4
Donna	4	1	0
Wanda	7	4	0
Isabelle	3	0	2
Mia	3	0	0
Average	5.71		
Median	4		

Figure 17

Donna, Wanda, and Mia each reported seeing a flickering flame behind or above buildings. Donna and Wanda observed a flame behind the detached garage on Amanda that left behind no indication of heat or ash when their father investigated. Mia recalled a flame above, not on, the home of one her friends in Eagle Pass. These were recalled unprompted, and while not numerous, the fact that they were recalled by two individuals at the same residence, and by another at a different residence altogether are interesting at least.

Cheryl, April, and Sophia each reported at least 2 experiences seeing a shadow, but Wanda and Mia did not report seeing any shadows (Figure 18). April described two different types of shadows, or shadow figures. There were figures "all in black" that would be watching her when she was waking from sleep, and on another occasion, she reported seeing from the corner of her eye and at full wakefulness a passing shadow descending the stairs in her home (she also reported her mother seeing the latter at Telford). Cheryl reported seeing 2 shadows like the latter described by April, and it was generally hard to differentiate from Sophia if the figures she saw were apparitions of clothed people heavily in shadow or a shadow person.

	Shadow
Cheryl	2
April	3
Sophia	2
Donna	1
Wanda	0
Isabelle	1
Mia	0
Average	1.29
Median	1

Figure 18

Experiences near sleep were only cited by four individuals, with the most by April at 4 (Figure 19). While April had the most by any individual overall, there were far fewer total reports near sleep by the Cortez family. As seen below, there were individuals in the Cortez that did not report any experiences near sleep. However, as all of these are based on memory, it's possible that events of sleep paralysis were just not memorable in and of themselves to those interviewed.

	Near Sleep
Cheryl	0
April	4
Sophia	2
Donna	1
Wanda	0
Isabelle	1
Mia	0
Average	1.14
Median	1

Figure 19

Like with the Santiago family, UFOs eventually worked their way into the interviews. I considered Sophia's sighting of a woman on a Pegasus-like horse in Eagle Pass an unidentified flying object as there is obviously no explanation for the image, and it occurred during the light, with other witnesses. It was so wholly unexpected I didn't know what to ask, except for whatever details she could remember. She stated her sister Mia was there with her, but after following up with her later, Mia did not recall the event. It would have been interesting to speak to another person there at the time, who did remember the event.

In a different report, Cheryl saw the stereotypical "light" in the sky behaving erratically, with movement occurring in multiple right angles. Interestingly, while Mia did not remember ever seeing anything in the sky like what Sophia described, she had reported seeing the floating ball of flame above her friend's home while visiting her grandparents in Eagle Pass on another occasion. I am not insinuating they were the same event, or even related, but it's at least two events where these sisters reported seeing objects or figures in the skies above Eagle Pass.

Additionally, Mia reported an experience where while traveling with her sister Donna, her brother Elijah, and James to Minnesota, they saw a large light moving slowly across the sky that they followed in their car. The details are in the interview and James confirmed a similar event occurring on that trip. However, while he is absolutely certain that they saw a UFO, the details James related are materially different. My initial thoughts were that the variation in accounts is due to the fallibility of memory, and the passage of time. As I was completing this project, I was able to speak to Donna and follow up on this event. She confirmed the trip, taken in two cars with the men and women separated in each, and the presence of lights moving quickly across the sky. In short, her description generally matched her sister's more closely than James's. It is possible they discussed it over the years, thus creating a similar memory, but it did not appear to be something she had discussed any time recently. As a result, details were scarce, but again, her description was nearest her sister's, and she was able to corroborate the event generally described by both James and Mia.

The Lechuza is a piece of Mexican folklore that is rapidly gaining attention among paranormal circles. Derived from the Spanish word for a barn owl, the legend of the Lechuza I'm most familiar with described a witch that would shapeshift into a giant bird and would appear whistling at night to take away bad children. This is not dissimilar from other monster tales told to keep children in line common in many cultures. I am sure I was made aware of the Lechuza from my mother's family, but I was never told that she or anyone else in her family believed they had seen or heard a Lechuza, let alone believed in it.

Wanda ascribed the name Lechuza to a pair of birds she saw on a telephone line watching her family's home as a child. While Donna corroborated seeing the birds to an extent, they could be explained away as large birds, more particularly owls. And while several of the events could be dismissed as misrecognizing an animal, namely a bird, what caught my attention more was the thematic presence of experiences related to birds, or flight, i.e., seeing birds, flying women, hearing wings flap, or whistling. These items, although admittedly vaguely associated, are interesting in that they were noticed as out of the ordinary by all of the sisters. Or put another away, these sisters, and Sophia's daughter, reported an experience that was associated with this theme.

The existence of a theme at all could, however, purely be a result of internal bias by myself and/or the persons sharing the stories. By having the Lechuza named in the first interview, perhaps I was primed to ascribe more importance to certain events, to relate them to the folklore of the Lechuza. I can't deny that as a possibility, that my preconceived notions and ideas would inevitably influence what and how I chose to look at the information provided to me.

Be that as it may, Cheryl's experiences especially are interesting. She must have been at least 12 or 13 years old when she encountered the bird she described as tall as and wider than her, sitting on her grandmother's roof. To my knowledge, it's not anything she'd ever told anyone before. And like Wanda, the large bird seemed to reappear later in life, albeit more aggressively in Cheryl's case.

I do not point this out to argue there was a witch from folklore stalking the Cortez family. Frankly, I don't know what it means if all of these memories are accurate as described. One of the goals of this project was to try and find similarities between experiences, the types of things that might be overlooked when these stories were examined by themselves. To have items reminiscent of a creature from folklore come up repeatedly was not something that was expected. As mentioned before, the interview questions were almost too specifically focused on experiences with ghosts and the like, so mention of folklore or a supernatural creature in general came as a surprise. It is interesting that though the Santiago family was aware of the Lechuza folklore as well, only Elena mentioned the Lechuza.

And then, it was only in passing as she shared the folklore her mother was told.

COMPARATIVE ANALYSIS

COMPARING THE FAMILIES

The Santiago family outreported the Cortez family in each of the categories of total auditory, observed, and tactile experiences (Figure 20). However, a significant number of reports are by Elena (Figure 21), and when her reports are removed the ratio is flipped in favor of the Cortez family. The number of her experienced events, 30 of which were at Sheffield, were exceptional compared to the others in both hers and the Cortez family. Considering she only reported 5 experiences away from Sheffield, it begs the question, is the variable herself? The Sheffield location? A combination of both? It was noted earlier that she had a significant number of experiences that were classified as noise, as well as noticing shadows seen from the corners of her eyes. The difference in numbers of reports could also be a result of how she personally categorizes these experiences herself, or simply a result of her remembering more of them.

	Cortez	Santiago
Auditory	37	44
Observed	40	61
Tactile	14	20

Figure 20

	Cortez	Santiago Family - No Elena
Auditory	37	27
Observed	40	37
Tactile	14	13

Figure 21

Tactile experiences were reported slightly more often by the Santiago family (Figure 22). There was one more respondent in the Santiago family, but even if you were to add a person to the Cortez family using the average or median numbers of their reports, it would not make up the difference.

Tactile Reports by Family, by Individual			
Elena S.	7	9	Cheryl
Lilly S.	1	2	April
Andrew S.	3	0	Sophia
Carl S.	4	1	Donna
Tina S.	1	1	Wanda
Matthew S.	4	1	Isabelle
Rose S.	0	0	Mia
James S.	0	---	---
Average	2.5	2	Average
Median	2	1	Median
Total	20	14	Total

Figure 22

The average number of reports per person by the Santiago family is double that of the Cortez family when you remove the persons from each family with the most reports of tactile experiences, Cheryl and Elena. Cheryl had 3 separate reports of being pushed on the steps of her home under similar circumstances, and another report of being pushed out of someone else's home. The majority of Elena's tactile events happened in Sheffield. While Cheryl experienced perhaps the most frightening event at Telford, she experienced tactile events in at least 3 different locations. Cheryl's violent experiences in particular are in stark contrast to the most common type of tactile experience the Santiago family experienced while fully awake, the sensation of being touched. These were often likened to the touch of a fingertip, or a cobweb.

Tactile Reports by Family, by Individuals Top Reporters Removed			
Lilly S.	1	2	April
Andrew S.	3	0	Sophia
Carl S.	4	1	Donna
Tina S.	1	1	Wanda
Matthew S.	4	1	Isabelle
Rose S.	0	0	Mia
James S.	0	---	---
Average	1.86	0.83	Average
Median	1	1.5	Median
Total	13	5	Total

Figure 23

The Santiago family reported more experiences of noise than the Cortez family, while the Cortez family outreported the Santiago family in the category of vocalizations (Figure 24). It is important to note that the

311

category is, like the categories of shadows and noise, reported by individuals in specific instances, but also in the more general "You'd always hear" type of statement. We should consider if individuals are generalizing one category of report because the events were too numerous to single out. Reports of the sounds of talking and mimicry were similar between the families. The overall difference in experiences categorized as vocalizations was largely due to the reports of crying and whistling the Cortez family ascribed to the Lechuza.

	Santiago	Cortez
Noise	21	10
Vocalizations	16	21
Talking	8	6
Mimicry	8	7

Figure 24

Assuming the events involving mimicry happened as described, there appears to be a trickster element where individuals are taunted and made to search for the caller. However, there is a difference in what might be the tone, or intent, of the mimicry between the two families. When the Cortez family would hear mimicry, the intent often seemed simply to lure the person into an empty room where, of course, nothing would happen. These are the types of games a child might play. Only in Cheryl's account did the mimicry escalate beyond taunting or inconvenience. However, the Santiago family reported accounts of both innocuous mimicry while an individual was alone, and mimicry experienced by two individuals simultaneously. In these latter situations, there almost appears an attempt to pit two individuals against each other. I'm specifically referring to Andrew, Elena, and Carl's experiences. Carl's experience can stand as the example, as the experiences of all three occurred while one person was in the shower. In Carl's account, he heard his wife yelling at him from downstairs to exit the shower. She in turn was downstairs and heard him yelling for her to come upstairs to him in the shower. The demanding and insistent tone experienced by both created tension as they attempted to make sense of the experience. While the conflict this created was minor, it was certainly strange to hear such a similar situation repeatedly described.

Let's briefly return to Cheryl, who stands out not just from the Santiago family, but also the Cortez family in the types of interactions she has during her experiences. She is the only one of either family to report having had a conversation with what she believes to be a ghost. Additionally, and it may seem a small thing, she shared at least three occasions where she saw the faces of what she believes to be apparitions, the professor, hotel staff, and Lechuza. Keep in mind how often the face is obscured by fabric or shadow, or simply out of focus, in the reports by others.

Both families saw humanoid, or anthropomorphic, figures. However, the ages, appearance, and even humanity varied by family. The Santiago family saw children in simple white dresses, and aside from the hag and the Native American woman in the alley, mostly a faceless adult male who was often physically incomplete. The latter perhaps in flannel or a white shirt. The individuals in the Cortez family did not report seeing children, but there were many different styles and colors of dress on the apparitions they saw. And while there were reports of more fantastical creatures from folklore by the Cortez family, like with the reports of human men and women these figures were described as if they had more depth or presence versus the fleeting experiences of the Santiago family. In other words, it could be said the Cortez family described these figures as more full-figured and solid, more real, more difficult to tell apart from a living person. However, this could also be a result of the communication styles of the families and the way each would describe their experiences.

While there is certainly room for human error in memory, or even the ascription of the paranormal to the mundane, two themes appear to be present in the experiences reported by the families. For the Cortez family it was the Lechuza, the witch from folklore. For the Santiago family it was the Flannel Man, even if it was not itself a well-known myth yet. An explanation for both may be that an initial belief in the apparition by the family members could result in subsequent experiences being associated with that belief. In effect, the initial experience and relation of the story to other family members could cause that experience to become part of the culture of the family. We do see very similar experiences repeated by multiple individuals within the families, i.e., a man with a blurry face on the one hand and over-sized birds on the other. Interestingly, the only reports of the Flannel Man occurred at Sheffield. Conversely, events believed to be related to the Lechuza were reported near at least two residences and three publicly accessible areas.

Orbs and lights presenting themselves before individuals in unusual ways, not to be confused with UFOs, were reported by four individuals in the Santiago family. Orbs and lights were not present in the Cortez family, however, three individuals reported flames that did not appear to burn anything around them. One of these, the report by Mia, is best described as a flame floating above a neighbor's house. James was the only individual in the Santiago family to report seeing a ball of fire, also in the sky. And frankly, it is only now as I present the information in this manner that I wonder about the similarity between James's and Mia's experience. From her description it did not appear to be something that would be visible far up in the sky as in James's recollection, but that may have been my own assumption having already heard about the fire in the backyard of the Cortez family.

The Santiago family were more prone to experiences near sleep across categories (Figure 25). While the Cortez family reported even numbers of experiences while falling into or waking from sleep, the Santiago family reported double the experiences while waking from sleep. Near sleep reports of shadows were again reported more often by the Santiago family (Figure 25). The Cortez reports that might be described as fleeting shadows were reported from several different locations, while all the fleeting shadows reported by the Santiago family were at the Sheffield house.

	Santiago	Cortez
Total Reports Near Sleep	16	6
While Falling to Sleep	5	3
While Waking from Sleep	11	3
Shadows Reported Near Sleep	5	3

Figure 25

Experiences reported with shadows were roughly categorized as near sleep, fleeting shadows, figures with faces draped in shadows, and fully awake reported shadow man. If you remove the "fleeting shadow from the corner of the eye" types of reports, which were the most numerous, you lose half of all reported types of experiences with shadows (Figure 26). This may ultimately be less meaningful as there are statements like "you'd always see" which implies the experience was more numerous than reported, but then this may also be the most easily explained away type of report. Shadow types of experience near sleep were categorized separately as we have already discussed the problems with such reports due to the very real physical condition of sleep paralysis that can be associated with hypnagogic or hypnopompic hallucinations.

	Shadow Man	Shadow Near Sleep	Fleeting Shadow	Shadowed Figures
Santiago	1	5	6	1
Cortez	0	3	6	2
Total	1	8	12	3

Figure 26

If we then remove reports of shadows near sleep, we are left with 2 each by the Santiago and Cortez families. Of these two, Elena's simple aside, "I see shadows peeking around the corner," is the report closest to descriptions of Shadow Man behavior that was not experienced near the act of sleeping. Although this is a generalized description that hints at more of such experiences, she seems to let it serve as an example and focuses more on the more traditional physical figures she's seen. Sophia did have two reports where the figures she described seemed not to be shadows themselves, but heavily shadowed. This could be a mischaracterization on my part between shadow persons and humanoids. She also described women in these shadows, which to my limited knowledge does not fit into the Shadow Man mythos.

	Shadow Man	Shadowed Figures
Santiago	1	1
Cortez	0	2
Total	1	3

Figure 27

Next, I examined the effect of removing experiences that occurred while falling or waking from sleep on total reported experiences by the families by comparing the change in number of reports by category when those experiences near sleep were removed. In other words, if the initial number of reports in a category was 10, and after removing experiences reported near sleep the number became 7, the resulting change is 3. The idea being that the larger the change between experiences before and after those near sleep are removed, the more likely the described experience is to be associated with sleep, and perhaps hypnagogic or hypnopompic hallucinations. Note again that multiple categories of experiences could be reported corresponding to a single event.

The change in total number of reported experiences after removing those near sleep was more than three times greater for the Santiago family for observed and tactile experiences (Figure 28), while the change for auditory experiences was the same. The Santiago family appeared more likely to have a reportable experience in the observed and tactile categories while near sleep than the Cortez family.

	Auditory		Observed		Tactile		All
	Total	Change After Sleep Removed	Total	Change After Sleep Removed	Total	Change After Sleep Removed	Total Change
Cortez	35	3	40	3	14	2	8
Santiago	43	3	62	11	21	7	21

Figure 28

Based on their descriptions, the Cortez family did not appear to have any near sleep events as adults, meaning such events only occurred at Telford and on Amanda (Figure 29).

	Amanda		Telford		Other Own Residence		All Locations
	Total	Change After Sleep Removed	Total	Change After Sleep Removed	Total	Change After Sleep Removed	Total Change
Cortez	11	1	24	5	9	0	6

Figure 29

The Santiago family had an 8 event change at Sheffield when removing events near sleep, and a 9 event change in their homes as adults other than Sheffield when those near sleep were removed (Figure 30). This is consistent with the above where the Santiago family was more likely to have observed and tactile experiences near sleep generally. Furthermore, this is evidence that the Santiago family has actually had more near sleep events as adults than they did as children, according to their reported memory at least. There was no change for either family for the locations described as visiting another residence or publicly accessible locations. This could be partly due to the fact that individuals are less likely to find themselves sleeping in such areas, or that they were already counted in the cases of Sheffield and Telford.

	Sheffield		Other Own Residence		All Locations
	Total	Change After Sleep Removed	Total	Change After Sleep Removed	Total Change
Santiago	58	8	40	9	17

Figure 30

GENERALIZATIONS AND SIMILARITIES

Based on the proportion of women to men (11 to 4 total), it is easy to come to the conclusion that women are more likely to have these experiences. However, these results are more likely happenstance due to the limited sample size and the individuals who were available to be interviewed being women. If continued research resulted in greater numbers of female respondents reporting paranormal experiences despite an equal number of males being interviewed, it would bear further investigation. In short, there is simply not enough data to indicate if sex has any effect until these factors can be addressed.

Approximately 62 percent of events were specifically said to have occurred at night, 19 percent were reported during the day, with a remainder of 19 percent of events where the time of day is unknown (Figure 31). At all locations, the most reports occurred at night. Additionally, at any given location the number of events reported at night was at least double the number of reports during the day or where the time was unclear. Only at Sheffield were there enough events at unknown times where they and the number of daytime reports together neared the total number of night reports (28 to 29 respectively). However, if we are conservative and say that of the 13 events at Sheffield whose time of occurrence is unknown, that there is a 2:1 ratio of night versus day (there is a 3 to 1 ratio of night versus day where time of day is explicitly stated), then the total number of events at Sheffield during night compared to day would be approximately 38 and 19. If we do the same across locations, the total estimated proportion of events reported at night becomes 72 percent, with approximately 28 percent occurring during the day.

	Amanda	Telford	Sheffield	Other Own Residences	Visiting a Residence	Publicly Accessible Locations	Total	Percents
Day	1	5	15	5	4	3	33	19
Night	8	12	29		10	20	110	62
Unknown	2	7	13	12	0	0	34	19

Figure 31

We previously discussed the subtle differences in the types of mimicry experienced by the two families, but ultimately both families did experience simple mimicry where one would hear a recognizable voice from an empty room. In general, mimicry was a shared type of experience reported by both families. This is important because as we look for significance in the differences between the families, it's just as important to look for the commonalities across families. For instance, another common experience was that of hearing indecipherable speech in another room, or in the room that one was entering. In the latter instance, or if one were to go and investigate the room where the sounds appeared to be originating from, the voices would immediately cease once the person entered the room. The experience of mimicry will be by its nature different for everyone, but the description of these whispers, these indecipherable voices speaking to each other, were similar regardless of who reported them.

"…You could hear whispering voices *[April]*."

"…It just sounded like there was a group of people talking in the den, just having a conversation *[Carl]*."

"And I heard voices. As soon as I walked in the living room I heard like a lot of voices, like a lot of whispering *[Elena]*."

"And when you would get closer to it, to go see, to see how many people were there, it would calm down *[Sophia]*."

Although this is one of those instances where a person would say "you'd hear" at locations like Telford and Sheffield, implying it was a frequent occurrence, it's difficult to say just how frequently since these individuals lived in these homes for years, sometimes decades in the case of Sheffield.

Several accounts of events were shared and remembered by multiple individuals, some experiences sharing similarities across decades, and some experiences corroborated by multiple individuals. An example of the former was the sound of a person running across the roof reported by Elena, Carl, and later Elena's son Andrew. The experience of a UFO sighting was corroborated by Mia, Donna, and James, although each remembered the event slightly differently. This isn't unexpected, as memory is known to be fallible in a relatively short time. However, the major facts as related are fairly consistent, perhaps indicating that while the details of the event might be in question, the existence of the event that created the memory is not.

Both Telford and Sheffield have experiences reported by my generation, and secondhand reports of stories by my grandparents' generation. The Cortez matriarch and 2 other individuals not interviewed lived in Telford during a similar timeframe as Carl and Elena did in Sheffield as adults. This could add to the discrepancy in adult experiences between the two locations and the total number of experiences overall (especially for Elena). The person currently living in Telford did not recall ever having any paranormal experiences as a child or adult, there or anywhere. If another high-experience-reporting person like April were living in Telford for the same timeframe, would there have been additional events reported?

Some of the events experienced by the Santiago family as adults are from visiting Elena at the Sheffield house. The fact they are still experiencing events in Sheffield despite a considerably shorter amount of time spent there may indicate events are more likely to occur there. The family members who had experiences while visiting Sheffield as adults also admitted to spending less time there because of those experiences. However, these same individuals were still experiencing events in their own homes over this time period as well.

As mentioned before, when individuals reported seeing an adult male or female, they usually reported they could not see the face. Or, that it was blurry if they were oriented from a perspective where a face could ordinarily be seen. Women were often depicted as wearing some kind of face covering, typically lace. It was a common theme among the families that the figures are unidentifiable when not turned away or in some other position that would obscure the face. There were exceptions of course, but "I couldn't see the face" was often repeated. There were so few reports of children being observed, it can't be determined if it's significant that in these cases the children's faces were visible, and what's more, that they would lock eyes with the person who saw them.

Those events led me to ask the following question: In observed reports focusing mainly on humanoid figures, how often do these apparitions show awareness (cognizance) of the observer (the person interviewed)? This includes people, creatures, and shadows, but I also included two specific instances of three-dimensional orbs visible to the naked eye. The latter are included because there are two instances reported where a ball of fire or light appears to show awareness, intent, and interest in a person according to the person interviewed. I reviewed these reports among both families, between families, and finally while removing those reports that were described while falling into or waking from sleep.

We will use the change in number of reports again, and we see in this case that for each family removing reports near sleep resulted in a change of a single report per family. When removing near sleep experiences, there was little change in number of reports for figures that did not show cognizance of the observer (Figure 32). So, it would seem with this limited sample size that figures that do not appear to be cognizant of the observer also do not appear to be associated with experiences near sleep, and so possibly hypnagogic or hypnopompic hallucinations.

	Cognizant Figures	Not Cognizant
Total	30	31
After Removing Reports Near Sleep	17	29
Change	13	2
% Difference	43%	6%

Figure 32

There was, however, a large change in total number of reports of figures who were cognizant of the observer when controlled for experiences that occurred near sleep (Figure 33). The Santiago and Cortez families had changes of 7 and 6 respectively after near sleep reports were removed. The total numbers, and changes after the removal of events near sleep, were similar between the families in this respect. From this, events where a figure is observed near sleep appear to be associated with that figure showing cognizance of the observer. My aim is not to paint all these experiences with the broad swath of hallucinations and sleep paralysis, although some do fit that definition better than others. However, due to the high incidence of these types of experiences occurring at the same time as a known biological phenomenon, I believe the responsible approach is to require more and better information to clear that hurdle of possibility. After all, we have to be willing to seriously consider ordinary explanations if we expect others to consider the extraordinary. I find it interesting that while the total reports and changes in reports where apparitions were cognizant of the observer were similar between the families, the Santiago family had 38% more reports of experiences than the Cortez family when the apparitions did not appear cognizant of the observer.

	Santiago Family		Cortez Family	
	Cognizant Figures	Not Cognizant	Cognizant Figures	Not Cognizant
Total	16	19	14	12
After Removing Reports Near Sleep	9	18	8	11
Change	7	1	6	1
% Difference	44%	5%	43%	8%

Figure 33

Although I spent time discussing the appearance of UFOs in these reports, in part because of what I felt was an interesting association between categories of experience, I considered whether to acknowledge them at all. The experiences described by the observers are there to read for yourself after all. Would readers question their credibility? It is an odd truth that while people might be certain in their own beliefs regarding Bigfoot, ghosts, UFOs, etc, they can be aggressively opposed to those other categories when they are not their own.

Conversely, while I initially began counting and categorizing events where children or pets appeared to see or interact with something unseen to adults, I realized a couple of problems in doing so. For instance, who would I code as the experiencer? I felt it was unreasonable to label a child as reporting an experience when the story was being retold by an adult from their memory of decades past. In these instances, whether child or pet, it certainly wasn't the adult watching them who had the experience. Now, if I had spoken to any of these children as adults who could report seeing something, or if I myself remembered any of these events as described, I believe it would be absolutely appropriate to count their experiences among the others. But based on these interviews alone, I deemed it best to leave them out.

Perhaps unsurprisingly, most childhood events were reported wherever the interviewee happened to live. This makes sense anecdotally since the data appears to show these types of events happen more often at night, and home is where children spend most of their time. Of course, the fact that other family members of similar ages had no such experiences while living in the same environment at the same time would indicate these reports are unusual on their face. However, consistent with events reported as children, most experiences reported as adults also occurred in their homes, wherever those may have been. Again, this is where an individual is most likely to spend their non-working, non-recreational time. We do see an uptick in events reported in publicly accessible areas as adults, but these are mostly associated with locations visited while working, traveling, or during recreation. It appears that wherever a person is spending the most of their evening hours is where they are most likely to have a paranormal experience (Figure 31). Even categorically (experiences that were observed, heard, etc.), the total number of experiences reported was predictably associated with the total time spent by all individuals at a location, with the most at Sheffield, their other own residences, and then Telford (figure 34). It stands to reason that Sheffield leads in reports because it covers the lives of several of the interviewees as both children and adults, allowing the time for reports to accumulate more than in any other single location.

Put in numbers, the Cortez family reported a total of 29 events between Amanda and Telford, where they spent most of their youth, while the Santiago family had similar numbers of 21 events at Sheffield as children (Figure 35). The Cortez family did not spend significant time at the Telford home as adults, at least no one interviewed had permanently resided there, and only had 6 reports there as adults. However, the Santiago family had 34 reports as adults at Sheffield, the majority of these attributable to Elena who resided there.

	Amanda	Telford	Sheffield	Other Own Residences	Visiting a Residence	Publicly Accessible
Child	11	18	21	6	8	3
Adult	0	6	34	40	4	20

Figure 34

There may be some relation to having an experience as a child and then as an adult. Not causal, but that likelihood of an experience as a child increases the likelihood of having an experience as an adult. Or put another way, a person who reports an experience as an adult is likely to have had a previous experience as a child based on this sample. Again, there are family members on both sides, and of multiple generations, that have never had these experiences while living in any of these locations. However, of the interviewees, only James reported experiences he couldn't explain as an adult, while reporting no memory of any such experiences as a child. Conversely, only Donna reported such experiences as a child, but none as an adult.

I'd like to return to the experiences organized by location as children and adults, and what this could mean about the notion of hauntings generally. If we remove incidences near sleep and further limit our data only to clearly seen and heard phenomena, we are still left with several unexplainable experiences that are often corroborated by others or are otherwise supported. If we consider hauntings of locations rare, then the odds of nearly all the homes of both families being haunted as both children and adults would likely be astronomical. And, as I keep repeating, there were individuals from both families who reported no recollection of any paranormal events or experiences whatsoever. So, if we take for granted the common wisdom that locations are haunted, the fact that individuals from the same family can have no or numerous experiences in the same location would appear to indicate that the individuals themselves are a variable.

To be clear, I'm not saying these families themselves are haunted. The types of experiences and the specific ways they were expressed at one location were not repeated as individuals moved from one residence to another. The Cortez family did appear to attribute several events to the Lechuza, or something like it. However, while the Lechuza events themselves were thematically similar, the individual's experiences themselves were only consistent within their own experiences, not between each other's experiences within the Cortez family. While I am not implying there is some spirit following the individuals of these families from home to home, perhaps this data indicates there are some people who are more likely to experience a paranormal event than others, and perhaps being in the right place at the right time can increase that likelihood.

After reading the interviews, you may notice there were some who related stories of what I can only call extrasensory experiences, i.e., communication with the dead, telepathy, precognition, an out of body experience. I chose to include (code) UFO experiences and not extrasensory experiences as data due to the ability to tie the UFO experiences to one of the physical senses, namely sight. Additionally, these events definitively occurred while conscious, and were frequently shared by other individuals. Conversely, the extrasensory experiences could be associated with altered states such as being sleep-deprived, while dreaming, or near sleep. The idea of two family members thinking about each other at roughly the same time is not out of the realm of probable coincidence after all. So, these stories were left in for the consideration of the reader, but are beyond the scope of analysis.

While society is dismissive of paranormal experiences, the experiences themselves generally had a negative emotional impact on the people who experienced them. Of the positive reports, nearly all of them involved what the individual thought might be a connection to a loved one who had passed. Only Sophia, who stated she was never afraid and had an affinity for horror movies, reported more positive experiences than negative experiences. Of the remaining 14 individuals, only 5 reported a single positive experience. This could indicate that the negative emotional effect is self-induced due to fear and anxiety of the unknown. If this is the case, using strategies to overcome the fear (i.e., face the fear, be aware of physiological effects to fear and your capacity to control them, discuss your fears with others) may ameliorate these negative effects. However, these are only coping strategies, not solutions to make the experiences stop as many would likely prefer.

CHALLENGES

One of the most persistent challenges that arose was defining the vocabulary of the research. This would begin with the choice of words used when conducting interviews that would unintentionally limit the scope of the interviewees' answers, would extend to the codification of categories and experiences of those being interviewed, and is present still in the expression of my analysis. For instance, it may seem a trivial matter whether to use the word ghost or apparition when describing a sighting, but there are connotations that make one better suited than the other in context. Apparition was chosen due to its generally visual meaning, as it can refer to an unusual or unexpected sight. Likewise, while codifying the hierarchies of categories of experiences an attempt was made to use categories and terms that could generally be tied back to the five senses.

An additional challenge I identified while reviewing the interviews is the complication created by these experiences existing as stories within the families and being retold over and over, and often changing over time in the retelling. As a result, there is the possibility that portions of the stories as told were in part recombined, without intent, into individual's memories of their own experiences. Or put another way, it's the possibility of contamination of details between one's own and their family members' memories. This might particularly be a problem for the Santiago family where I intentionally left examples of family members incorrectly recalling the experiences of others as they remembered them being told. There was at least one occasion where someone from the Cortez family wondered whether their family member was too young to remember the experience they corroborated. However, this problem may simply be the nature of memory and forcing individuals to try and recall experiences that had occurred decades before.

I'd like to briefly recall Lilly's statement, "I lived like a couple houses from Mom's house," where the house she and Carl lived "a couple houses" down from was the Sheffield house. There may be an inconsistency in the resulting data in part due to how the Sheffield house is treated versus the two homes on Amanda. However, Lilly explicitly differentiated the house she and Carl shared from the Sheffield house and so I coded that location generally as other own residence rather than as Sheffield. It can be argued all experiences on this street should have been coded as Sheffield, or the homes on Amanda should have been differentiated as other own residences with an additional regional identifier to notate the experiences in multiple homes in the same geographical area. However, the point is there were experiences that occurred in the same geographic area of Sheffield in two different homes, similar to Amanda. Additionally, Rose and April related stories during and after the interviews where their neighbors explicitly stated they were having unnerving, ghostlike experiences themselves. If we take the argument that these hauntings are real as true, maybe the questions we've asked are too limited in scope. Is it the person? Is it the home? Is it both? Much like the reported sighting of Civil War soldiers at Gettysburg, is it an entire geographic region?

My relation to those I interviewed was also a challenge. While it allowed them to trust me implicitly and inspired a degree of confidence that I wasn't being intentionally misled, it created other problems. I was likely more reticent to question certain statements and subjects than if I were speaking to strangers. They also shared more than they would have with a stranger and required additional editing to protect personal information. There was also the valid criticism I received that I had not asked the necessary questions to acknowledge and eliminate the possible influence of alcohol or other substances.

I also didn't know what to do with the events others described where I apparently had experiences of my own. While these were interesting to hear, I couldn't code them for myself since I had no memory of the events. I could not code an experience for the person sharing the account because it did not happen to them. This isn't a problem I will have in the future, but it's still worth acknowledging. Ultimately, I decided the value of these accounts would be up to the reader to decide, whether they were the easily dismissed words of a child or puzzle pieces to other events.

Looked at more broadly, there are other aspects of the interviews and research methods that could be addressed to provide better data. Interviewing individuals while in the presence of others, for instance. This did have some positive benefits, see Isabelle's corroboration that she was still hearing chattering voices from other rooms at the Telford house. However, this often resulted in the individuals who were "sitting in" on the interview seeking validation from the interviewee for their own experiences. This challenge may be ameliorated by providing instruction to participants beforehand as to what leading questions are and how to broach topics without planting ideas. However, welcoming others into any interview would need to be done with the consent of the principal party, as not all relationships will be conducive to totally honest responses. Additionally, those sitting in on interviews may take any denial of a specific memory personally and would need to be coached ahead of time regarding that fact and the nature of memory generally.

The age ranges for the reported experiences were broad. This was unavoidable since I rarely asked anyone to attempt to narrow down the age of an experience. However, even if someone were unable to provide a specific age, it's very likely they could have estimated a decade as an adult, narrowed down their age as a child by estimating what school they were in at the time, or used some other personally important milestone. Ultimately, I still believe there was interesting information derived from separating the experiences generally as children and adults.

In order to look at the totality of experiences, asking questions about UFO sightings and other events that are out of the normal should become part of the normal course of the interview. As such, it would be important to communicate to the interviewee that there is no judgment or implication in their answers, it's simply information acquisition to more completely round out statistical data and provide better opportunity to find correlations between disparate experiences. Extrasensory experiences should likewise be part of the interview in order to further gather more information to identify any and all associations.

When specifically examining family circumstances in the future, I would like to interview family members who reported no paranormal experiences as well. It would be worth it to corroborate a family member reporting an experience as a child or a different perspective of events. As we get closer to actual research level data, it would be valuable to recognize the numbers of these individuals to gain a better understanding of the prevalence of paranormal experiences within families.

Finally, self-doubt and lack of planning led the interviews to be wide ranging and unstructured. This allowed the interviewee to discuss things they felt were important, but also resulted in missed opportunities to pull at threads of information and eliminated the possibility of any demographic information. Additionally, without some sort of script, each interview became a web of information with new items to question and confirm that might not have occurred to individuals during the initial interview, or that they did not believe was pertinent. And as I mentioned before, there were questions I began asking only in the final interviews because it hadn't occurred to me to ask at the start.

CONCLUSION

While I don't believe the data I gathered answered any burning questions, I do believe there were some interesting associations made between experiences, and the identification of potential avenues for future research. And not necessarily just for myself. Perhaps most importantly to me, I believe this works as a proof of concept that commonly accepted qualitative and quantitative research methods can be used to make the study of paranormal events accessible to the scientific method.

For instance, anyone can take this text and choose their own method of coding, expanding, or ignoring, aspects that I chose to focus on. And again, they can use traditional research methods to perform their own analysis. Scientific literature reviews, critical accounts of what has been published on a topic by past researchers, are common among traditional academia and can provide greater insight as it increases the size of the dataset studied. I think it would be difficult considering the different formats and prevalence of first-person narratives that are likely to leave out a lot of information, but ghost stories are so ubiquitous on YouTube and podcasts now that there are likely hundreds of hours of personal accounts that could be studied and compared.

The next step would be to take what I've learned and continue interviewing other families in addition to individuals, while improving the interviews themselves and creating better datasets with more consistent coding. I believe the strength in examining the experiences of families is that you have individuals who may have had similar experiences at different times, unbeknownst to the other occupants. After all, it was repeated over and over that those I had interviewed had not shared their experiences as they did not feel they would be believed. Additionally, family members without experiences would almost function as controls. Much like the use of twins in medical and psychological studies, this might help enlighten us as to why some individuals report experiences while others don't.

I didn't realize I was doing so at the time, but I created a retrospective study of sorts. Basically, a researcher conducting a retrospective study will select a sample of individuals and look back at the history of those individuals. In this case, I did not create a sample of individuals to act as a control, there was no opposing cohort of individuals without any reported experiences. It would be interesting to conduct a series of interviews and research with similar families, and then follow up with them again after a given period of time. For instance, I have been contacted by several of those I interviewed and told the experiences have continued.

Additionally, I believe persons who are interested in researching the paranormal should spread the idea that individuals should regularly document their experiences as detailed as possible rather than relying on memory. Date, time, room, what could be seen, the texture, sounds, smells, you name it. At the very least, you may be able to find an explanation for the experience. If a person could point to specific repeated documented examples of an event, the event becomes difficult to ignore both personally and academically.

This project has also led me to believe the scientific, and especially Psychology, community has a responsibility to study these phenomena more seriously. There are two reasons why I believe this is a valid research path for the social sciences: honest research into the nature of these experiences, and the psychological effects of the experience.

I will use statements directly from the American Psychological Association to support my reasoning. First, "Psychologists examine the relationships between brain function and behavior, and the environment and behavior, applying what they learn to illuminate our understanding and improve the world around us" (Science of Psychology, 2013). There is a prevalence of reports of phenomena typically categorized as ghost related. And then summarily dismissed. The scientific stigma of "ghost hunting" has prevented research into a wealth of behavioral, cognitive, neurological and developmental research. If we consider the reasoning with which these accounts are so easily dismissed, we are confronted with a host of additional problems. For example, let us consider the following common reasoning: the reporting person is lying, the reporting person is delusional, or the reporting person was mistaken. A 2009 Pew Research Center study indicated that almost 20% of Americans surveyed believed they had seen or been in the presence of the spiritual (Liu, 2009). The former two reasons would require us to accept that nearly 60 million people (Bureau, 2021) are in some respect mentally ill, in which case we should be more aggressively asserting access to mental health treatment to confront this problem. The latter reasoning, mistaken identification, is more reasonable. This still gives rise to a multitude of questions, however. Why are some people more likely to report these experiences? Why the prevalence of shadow figures, archetypes, and commonly recurring auditory and visual figures?

To my knowledge there is no history of schizophrenia or delusions in my family, although sleep paralysis appears to be common. However, one thing the analysis demonstrated was an overwhelmingly negative reaction to these reported experiences. This leads to the more significant reason to research the paranormal, whatever the origin of the experience. "Practicing psychologists have the professional training and clinical skills to help people learn to cope more effectively with life issues and mental health problems" (What do practicing psychologists do?, 2019).

Repeated experiences especially were associated with individuals reporting feeling afraid or expressing continued anxiety. Those with the most exposure described experiences and coping behaviors consistent with trauma, with one person suspecting she might have a form of post-traumatic stress disorder relating to the events she experienced. This stress can have real effects on the body, including loss of sleep, fatigue, anxiety, irritability, anger, and a decrease in productivity (Mayo Clinic Staff, 2019). For those that would argue none of these events and experiences are real, I further argue that Psychology itself is fundamentally concerned with the subjective experience of the world by individuals, and how those individuals interact and cope with the world. Let us return to the Pew Research study (Liu, 2009). If even a portion of those individuals surveyed are experiencing stress from similar experiences, that could mean millions of Americans are going without the help they need because their experiences are summarily dismissed rather than validated and treated.

So, whether the origin of the experience is internal or environmental, perhaps practicing psychologists and professional counselors should begin considering what are the best ways to validate the experiences of their clients while providing the cognitive and behavioral tools to examine and treat the emotional effects. Of course, I wonder how many individuals would feel comfortable sharing such an experience with their counselor, psychologist, psychiatrist, etc., in the first place.

This is an unorthodox approach to paranormal research, and if there is enough interest by others in sharing their experiences I have hope that the more risk tolerant among academia will seriously consider paranormal experiences as substantive research material, and that those practicing therapy consider the effects these experiences have on individual's lives and what they as clinicians can do to help these individuals cope.

BIBLIOGRAPHY

Barber, B. A. (2011). Lifetime Prevalence Rates of Sleep
    Paralysis: A Systematic Review. *Sleep Medicine
    Reviews*, 313.

Bureau, U. S. (2021, March 29).
    https://www.census.gov/popclock/. Retrieved from
    Population Clock: https://www.census.gov/popclock/

Gregory, D. D. (2015). A twin and molecular genetics study of
    sleep paralysis and associated factors. *Journal of Sleep
    Research*, 438.

Liu, J. (2009, December 9). *Many Americans Mix Multiple
    Faiths*. Retrieved from Pew Research Center:
    https://www.pewforum.org/2009/12/09/many-
    americans-mix-multiple-faiths/#ghosts-fortunetellers-
    and-communicating-with-the-dead

Mayo Clinic Staff. (2019, April 4). *Stress Management*.
    Retrieved from mayoclinic.org:
    https://www.mayoclinic.org/healthy-lifestyle/stress-
    management/in-depth/stress-symptoms/art-20050987

Renner, T. (2018, February 15). Episode 26: Encounters with
    the Flannel Man.

Science of Psychology. (2013). Retrieved from American
    Psychological Association:
    https://www.apa.org/action/science

What do practicing psychologists do? (2019, December 11).
    Retrieved from American Psychological Association:
    What do practicing psychologists do?